Ethics of Writing

SUNY Series in Contemporary Italian Philosophy

Silvia Benso and Brian Schroeder, editors

Ethics of Writing

Carlo Sini

Translated by Silvia Benso
with Brian Schroeder

Published by
State University of New York Press
Albany

Printed in the United States of America

For information, contact State University of New York Press, Albany, NY
www.sunypress.edu

Production by Eileen Meehan
Marketing by Fran Keneston

Library of Congress Cataloging-in-Publication Data

Sini, Carlo, 1933-
[Etica della scrittura. English]
Ethics of writing / Carlo Sini ; translated by Silvia Benso with Brian Schroeder.
p. cm.—(SUNY series in contemporary Italian philosophy)
Includes bibliographical references and index.
ISBN 978-1-4384-2851-2 (hardcover : alk. paper)
ISBN 978-1-4384-2852-9 (paperback : alk. paper)
1. Ethics. 2. Writing—Moral and ethical aspects. 3. Thought and thinking. I. Title.
BJ1134.S5613 2009
175—dc22

2009003933

10 9 8 7 6 5 4 3 2 1

Contents

Introduction

Among the most recognized contemporary Italian philosophers, Carlo Sini (1933–) has been Professor of Theoretical Philosophy at Milan State University since 1976. After studying Plato, Aristotle, and Hegel, Sini began his philosophical career under the guidance of Enzo Paci, arguably the most prominent Italian scholar of Husserl's phenomenology. It is to Husserl that Sini first devoted his research and work, moving later to a study of American pragmatism, especially Peirce's thought, but also Whitehead and George Herbert Mead, in particular with reference to the (Husserlian) theme of self-consciousness. This very same topic later lead Sini to a confrontation with Nietzsche and with French structuralism and post-structuralism, most remarkably Lévi-Strauss and Foucault, whereas his concern for the philosophy of language resulted in a deep philosophical involvement with Wittgenstein. His major interest in the linguistic concepts of sign and interpretation brought Sini to the interesting project of building a bridge between hermeneutics and semiotics in the figures of Heidegger and Peirce respectively. It is along the lines of a semiological hermeneutics or of a hermeneutic pragmatism that Sini's thought in fact unfolds in its own original manner, and provides its most creative contribution.

The theme that has arguably interested Sini the most, or at least most constantly in the course of his philosophical career, is that of interpretation, which in the 1980s he recognizes, in agreement with other contemporary Italian philosophers such as Vattimo, as the central issue in contemporary thinking. Whereas Vattimo's philosophy elaborates the Nietzschean concept of interpretation in terms of its ultimately ungrounding and nihilistic aspects, Sini concentrates instead on the notion of sign, as already suggested in the name of the journal he has directed for many years, *L'uomo, un segno* [*Human Being, a Sign*]. In his thought Sini brings thus together in a highly original and innovative theoretical project various philosophical perspectives, spanning hermeneutics (Nietzsche, Heidegger, and Gadamer) and phenomenology (Husserl, but also Merleau-Ponty) pragmatism, semiology (Peirce, Saussure, and various contemporary writers on semiotics), and language analysis of various kinds.

Sini's peculiar understanding of hermeneutics does not rely on an ultimately relativistic notion of interpretation for which, in a Nietzschean–Heideggerian move, there are no facts outside their interpretations, and all interpretations are constantly changing, dependent on their context, and therefore ungrounded. Rather, for Sini, hermeneutics concerns the problematic relation of the horizontal and vertical dimensions of truth; that is, the various interpretations of truth (the horizontal dimension) occur because of the self-eventuation of truth (vertical dimension), of its incision or incidence in the ways of living and knowing. Interpretations of truth, which are transient, and the event of truth remain for Sini separate concepts, albeit linked through the concept of event as eventuation of (vertical) truth in specific (horizontal) ways of inhabiting it. The event becomes thus sign—sign of truth.

Sini is particularly interested in the specific signs that characterize Western civilization—namely, technological signs that develop in parallel with and even shape Western historical–scientific rationality. Heidegger's influence can be easily recognized in the need, manifested also by Sini, to enact a step-back toward the thinking of the origins in order to understand our own times. Sini's originality, however, brings him to focus on a topic left unthought by Heidegger (and taken up instead by Derrida, with whom Sini in fact often converses, albeit to distance himself from the French thinker): not the oblivion of the truth, but rather the activity of writing as the technical mode in which the content of the form of truth presents itself.

Sini's philosophical inquiry does not stop with a descriptive or interpretative analysis of technology and the technical world as it has delineated itself in Western culture. Rather, his philosophical project that brings him to unfold a genealogy (and not simply a reconstruction unable to explain, for example, the passage of truth from *aletheia* to *veritas*, as in Heidegger) of Western technological thought seeks behind its modes of development the possibility of a different experience of the world, language, and even truth. Within the context of his highly fruitful contamination of phenomenology, pragmatism, and hermeneutics, Sini develops the theoretical proposal of an ethics of writing (to which the present book is devoted) as a way of thinking the finite character of truth, that is, of thinking truth as practice. This is in fact the real core of a work such as *Ethics of Writing*, which in many senses gathers in one single volume the entirety of Sini's philosophy: that is, the recognition that truth should certainly not be flattened on the notion of *veritas*, as Heidegger has already warned us. But neither should truth be equated with *aletheia*, with the disclosure or coming to presence of the hidden truth of Being, with the "voice of silence" through which Being reveals itself as *Lichtung*, as Heidegger himself advances. Rather, and this is Sini's original proposal, truth should be understood on the basis of the content of the logical form as defining linearization of the voice. In other words, the ultrasensible vision of truth has as its ground the emergence of the "logical" meaning of *logos* that in turn is the result of a concrete practice that translates previous ancient vocal and gestural meanings into a new universe of sense. Such is the universe of logic with its specific signs.

Signs are not things, Sini argues at several points in his works, but rather relations qualified by a double reference—on the one side to objects, on the other to interpreters. Objects in turn never subsist in themselves but only as indicated by a sign. Analogously, against a well-established philosophical tradition and in agreement with the most recent positions in continental philosophy concerning the statute of subjectivity, interpreters are for Sini neither metaphysical subjects nor empirical figures. They are instead hermeneutically formed by virtue of and within interpretations that are themselves situated within a process of unlimited semiosis understood as event (as Heidegger teaches) and not as fact. An originary form of the eventuation of signs is writing, which for Sini is more than a purely mechanical activity. Writing is in fact a practice that, in the mode of it that is known to us, is characterized by the alphabet. This specific alphabetic practice, itself inserted in various other practices based on bodies, voices, writing tools and material supports such as stone, paper, computer screens, and so on, defines the specific way of being of Western civilization with its values, concepts, and logic.

According to Sini, the sign, particularly the sign constituted by alphabetic writing, becomes the place where the real turning point in philosophical questioning lies. Like other forms of culture, for Sini philosophy is in fact above all a practice and not a theory, because all theories are themselves already a form of practice, a form of inhabiting the world and one's own experience. Philosophical rules are the specific rules of a specific practice, precisely the rules of the practice of alphabetic writing. Therefore, the principles of logic as well as the epistemological and metaphysical topics that interest Western philosophy should all be brought back to the practice of the alphabet and alphabetic writing. This is the form that has directed our civilization toward the notions, norms, and values that specifically characterize it.

The consequence of Sini's analysis is that, as already indicated, the question of the truth is located in a different place than the one assigned to it by the tradition. Now the truth is situated in fact inside a universe of practices. Husserl's model of phenomenology, which certainly inspires Sini, also uses descriptive procedures. Yet its main goal is the establishment of a *strenge Wissenschaft*, that is, some form of hard knowledge. In contrast, the phenomenological encyclopedia that Sini develops out of his own phenomenology of experience consists in procedures that retrace practices again and again. These practices are certainly imbued with meaning. Such meanings, however, cannot establish any ground for the claim that the practices themselves provide or constitute some form of truth as absoluteness. In this sense, Sini claims to go beyond nihilism (that of Nietzsche and Heidegger, with whom he however still converses) and the theories of deconstruction (especially Derrida's). He does this without resorting to absolute principles and without even resorting to hard principles. His is a simple invitation *to dream more truly*, as he puts it. What one could term Sini's "post-phenomenology" is something that proceeds in parallel with our civilization while at the same time criticizing it. Unlike Heidegger, Husserl had already somehow intuited that writing is somewhat involved with both the powerfulness and the decadence of Western rationality. But he did not realize what Sini brings to light, namely, that alphabetic writing (which is only one of the possible modes of writing) does more than simply preserve knowledge; rather, it is at the origin of psychological idealism and the *krisis* of European sciences Husserl laments.

In the end, Sini takes phenomenology further and transforms it into a *phenomeno-graphy*, an exercise in writing, a great effort to translate signs into truth, this being a commitment, or an *ethos*, that each subject takes on him- or herself. The self-comprehension of human beings is in fact achieved only through the signs that orient their "commerce" with the world. Human beings are themselves signs, insofar as they only exist within the system of references constituting the environment upon which they project their actions. This holds true for alphabetized human beings as well as for those of a pre-alphabetic, pre-Platonic, oralist situation. In this sense, human beings have always written in the specific sense of leaving signs behind themselves. Each individual is then the figure and not the foundation of a continuously different practice. In doing so, each person does not set up the rules of the game, but rather becomes a piece in a game that is already being played and is nevertheless very serious. In this manner, truth emerges as inserted in a universe of practices that themselves conform to other social practices while founding new ones. All practices, therefore, including the specific practice of writing constituting philosophy, are linked to ethics, that is, to a specific way of being in the world, to an *ethos*. Once again following Husserl, Sini reveals here his conviction that all theories are in fact the practices through which we inhabit (our) time.

Precisely with respect to the topic of time, the difference separating Sini from Heidegger could not be greater. In Heidegger, temporality constitutes the condition of possibility for the unveiling of beings, and thus for the possibility of various practices. For Sini, however, time does not constitute the truth of Being but rather one of its meanings, since time itself does not emerge as such until discourse is ordered in a chronological sequence by the practice of alphabetic writing. On Sini's interpretation, practices temporalize, whereas for Heidegger it is time that is the condition of possibility of practices. This also means that, for Sini, the event itself is a sign; it is the event of a sign, that is, the event of a practice (and not of Being).

Over the course of his career, Carlo Sini has published more than twenty books. Among them are: *Il pragmatismo americano* (1972), *Semiotica e filosofia* (1978), *Passare il segno* (1981), *Kinesis. Saggio di interpretazione* (1982), *Immagini di verità* (1985), *I segni dell'anima. Saggio sull'immagine* (1989), *Il silenzio e la parola. Luoghi e confine del sapere per un uomo planetario* (1989), *Il simbolo e l'uomo* (1991), *Etica della scrittura* (1992), *Il profondo e l'espressione* (1992), *La filosofia teoretica* (1992), *Pensare il progetto* (1993), *L'incanto del ritmo* (1993),

Filosofia e scrittura (1994), *Scrivere il silenzio. Wittgenstein e il problema del linguaggio* (1994), *Gli abiti, le pratiche, i saperi* (1996), *Teoria e pratica del foglio-mondo. La scrittura filosofica* (1997), *Idoli della conoscenza* (2000), *La scrittura e il debito. Conflitto tra culture e antropologia* (2002), *La libertà, la finanza, la comunicazione* (2002), *Il comico e la vita* (2003), *Transito e verità. Figure dell'enciclopedia filosofica* (2004), *Archivio Spinoza. La verità e la vita* (2005), *Del vivere bene. Filosofia e economia* (2005), *Il gioco del silenzio* (2006), *Agostino e la scrittura dell'interiorità* (2006), *Da parte a parte. Antropologia del relativo* (2008), and *L'uomo, la macchina, l'automa. Lavoro e conoscenza tra futuro prossimo e passato remoto* (2009). Many of these books have been translated into Spanish (*El pragmatismo*, 1999; *Pasar el Signo*, 1989, *Semiotica y filosofia*, 1985), German (*Die Zeichen der Seele*, 1995), French (*La philosophie théorétique*, 1992) and one also into English (*Images of Truth*, 1993).

The present work, *Ethics of Writing*, contains the texts of two lecture courses held by Sini at Milan State University between 1989 and 1990. The format of the lecture course explains the tone of the discourse, which, albeit in a constantly high and scholarly manner, sometimes gives in to a more colloquial register. The book is comprised of two parts, the content of which has in part (and in its broad lines) been exposed in the course of the previous general presentation of Sini's overall project. More specifically, the first part, titled "Logic and Writing: The Content of the Form," addresses the question of the logical form, that is, of the possibility of correct representation. In particular, Sini asks the (Wittgensteinian) question of the relation between logical form and first philosophical, and then scientific thinking. The content of the logical form could not in fact itself be "logical," Sini argues, because such a move would lead to the syntactic and tautological formalism that affects most Neopositivist thought. Nor could the content of the logical form reside in Heidegger's "truth of Being" as originary donation and phenomenological manifestation of truth in things and beings. Were the matter as Heidegger claims, how could one move from phenomenological experience of beings to the form of logical judgment, Sini asks? Otherwise stated: how does "logic" (and thereby the entire philosophical-scientific thinking) arise? Here is where Sini's original journey begins.

He retraces the process that, moving from Parmenides to Aristotle, has led to the formalization and stylization in the use of signs. Through various references to Friedrich Creuzer's studies of ancient cultures, Alfred Kallir's monumental research on the invention of the alphabet, and the oralist school of Eric Havelock and its distinction between non-writing cultures and Western culture born with the invention of the alphabet, and in constant dialogue with Jacques Derrida's reflections on writing (with respect to which Sini develops a close and critical reading of *Of Grammatology*), Sini argues how it is only with the practice of alphabetic writing and reading (invented by the Greeks, inherited by the Romans, and still in use today) that the analytical-rational, that is, scientific-philosophical mentality characterizing Western culture could develop. With the invention of the alphabet, the iconic and symbolic character of writing has disappeared, and Western human beings have moved from a sacred and ritual dimension of signs (in which signs were deciphered more than read) to a purely communicative and pragmatic dimension geared to sheer information, in which signs serve for reading as quickly as possible without misunderstanding. The alphabet becomes a system of signs that enables the translation from a visual sign to a vocal emission. The concept of universality thus arises as the ability to transcribe any spoken language and any personal experience into a dimension where thinking and saying are void of all factual contingencies.

The overcoming of this cultural situation, which is the situation of our times, Sini provisionally concludes, requires not a new theory but rather a new practice of writing, that is, a different "ethics of writing," an alternative way of inhabiting writing. As ground of Western logical reason and its "deconstruction" (what Heidegger had named "destruction"), there is no unsayable Being or unthinkable universe, claims Sini, who on this point embarks in a long and deep confrontation with Derrida's notions of archewriting and archetrace. Simply stated, there is a concrete world of practices that cannot be exhausted in logical definitions, categories, or judgments as outcomes of alphabetic practice.

The second part, "The Tradition of Thought," concerns precisely the notion of practice. Specifically, it addresses the question of the identity of philosophy in relation to traditional thought and knowledge, and raises the issue of the end of philosophy and the encyclopedic models of knowledge, these being the topics at the center of Heidegger's famous essay "The End of Philosophy and the Task of Thinking." A very close confrontation with Heidegger brings Sini to criticize Heidegger's notion of *aletheia* as *Lichtung*, and to raise the question of what path is left open for thinking once one understands the relative and contingent nature of logical truths and the philosophical practices supported by them (philosophical practices are in fact the "historical" products of alphabetic practice). At this point,after an analysis of the nature of practices, especially philosophical practice, Sini formulates his own theoretical proposal, which is an ethical one: not theory (or a new theory) but rather the awareness of inhabiting theory as a practice is the possible solution and chance of rebirth for "theoretical" philosophy. Most importantly, this ethical solution seems the most viable also for our times of urgent need of an ineludible dialogue with other, non-Western cultures. The confrontation (made possible by the awareness that Western theory as the outcome of the alphabetic practice is one practice among many, one way of inhabiting the truth among many) among diverse concrete practices of life, discourse, and writing would lead to a profitable reconsideration of various forms of knowledge in the preciousness of their differences—differences that cannot be reduced to the alphabetic practice of writing and its will to power.

Silvia Benso

PART I

Logic and Writing

The Content of the Form

CHAPTER 1

The Question

1. *The logical form*. If one utters the word "house," writes it italicized or capitalized, or even sketches a house as children do, the meaning of these sounds, marks, and drawings is one and the same. It remains the same even if one says "*maison*," or writes "*casa*." There is something common to all this, a common *form* of word and thought enabling one *to signify* the house. The contents (vocal signs, written signs, alphabetic signs, drawings or hieroglyphs, and so on) change, but something in common makes them be signs of the same. This something in common is the "logical form."

What constitutes the logical form is the major question in Wittgenstein's *Tractatus Logico-Philosophicus*. The question is ultimately left unanswered, because one cannot *say* what the form of all possible contents is.[1] One cannot exhibit a *pure* form, a form completely void of a sensible content. Saying is a content which, to be able to signify something, must already be informed by that logical form one would like to see purely in itself, independently from the saying and from any possible content.

One cannot exhibit, one cannot see the logical form pure and in itself. Nevertheless, one can comprehend the meaning of such an expression. It confronts us as an objectively perceivable mental content. What is the *content* of such a logical form if considered purely in itself? We always think of the form of the content. Yet *is* not a "pure" form already itself a content? Does it not *have* the content of that "purity"? And what content does purity have as the form of all logical contents? What is, here, the content of the form?

2. *The logical science*. The logical form—yet what is "logic"? Logic is a branch of philosophy, like ethics and aesthetics. Its specificity as a discipline concerns the fields of true and false in relation to verbal enunciations and, more generally, in relation to knowledge. Discourse (*logos*) says: "The sky is overcast," "The stone is hard." The issue is to establish whether such assertions are correct: that is, whether they are true. Such an establishment constitutes the disciplinary, technical duty of *episteme logike*, the logical science.

Logic, ethics, and aesthetics concern the areas of "normative sciences";[2] they deal with the problem of true (and false), with the problem of good (and evil), with the problem of the beautiful (and the ugly).

Where the problem emerges, however, the question disappears (as Heidegger remarks); the question has left. By reducing logic to its *problem*, one does not answer the *question* of what logic is. We occupy ourselves with truth and falsity. We declare the assertion true because it represents the situation correctly, since it is *true* that now the sky is overcast and that, in general, the stone is hard. We devise subtle criteria to establish that and how it is possible to say the false (since it is not true that the sky is always overcast, and so on). Yet in all this hustling, we have erased and silenced the question.

3. *Question and problem.* In a lecture course he gave in 1937–38, Heidegger asserted that the word "question" designates those questions that are no longer asked as questions. As soon as philosophy becomes a discipline, that is, a set of disciplinary problems, it ceases to be that *fundamental question* that it was in its origin and in its profundity. Problems cover up questions, and provoke a misunderstanding of the essence of questioning.

Such a misunderstanding happened to philosophy very early, if it is true, as Heidegger claims, that the story went as follows: from questions one moved to their "fixation"; "frozen" questions were no longer asked as questions, since the case simply became that of finding the answer, maybe by transforming already available answers or by collecting and comparing handed-down opinions.[3] What is described here is ultimately the "dialectical" method, theorized and applied by Aristotle at the beginning of his "treatises." In this way, problems replaced the fundamental questions of philosophy. They became problems of philosophical erudition, and thus definitely truncated the real questioning, rendering it infeasible or impossible.

By starting the "tradition" of philosophy, that is, its "history," in the way it is still configured for us today, with its disciplinary areas and its problematic fields, Aristotle thus erased the philosophical *question*, the very act of its advent or "historical" event. We should ask ourselves, what is the philosophical tradition? As long as we do not ask, even the question of logic will have to remain unanswered.

4. *The time of truth.* "For a long time there has been logic as a discipline of scholastic philosophy, and in fact precisely since the beginning of Plato's school, but indeed only since then." Thus writes Heidegger.[4] This means that there was a time when truth had not yet reduced itself to the "unarguable" site of logic and its correct or incorrect assertions. There was a time when truth functioned as the fundamental question that is the act of birth of philosophy, of philosophical questioning.

This is precisely Wittgenstein's reversed path. He begins with the "logical form of propositions" to go back to the logical form as inalienable and

8. *The visible and the invisible.* Can one detach the form of the house from the house? Can one hold its pure form in front of oneself? Can one contemplate it independently from its bricks, its tiles, its beams, its architraves? One could say that the form gives itself to be seen, yet only in its content, or in the disposition of the content; it gives itself to be seen precisely as the *form of the content,* the form of a determined content. Is it really true, though, that one can "see" the form, be it *in* the content?

The fundamental Platonic question of, and distinction between, sensible look and suprasensible, or intelligible, look is rooted in this issue. Positing such a distinction, and on its ground inventing and constructing the "intelligible look" is, literally, the beginning of philosophical *episteme*—that is, generally, of science or logical science and its peculiar *logos.* Therefore, the entire "history of the West" is comprised in the cone of light of the invention of the idea.[8]

In its core, the extraordinary invention of the idea means that the sensible object (the house in flesh and bones, or in lime and bricks) is seen with the eyes, whereas the intelligible object (the form of the house, its design or intelligent end) is seen with the "mind." How the mind operates (and, therefore, what it is) remains a big *problem.* This is the specific object of logic, the philosophical discipline that must clarify how the mind sees, understands, and reasons—for example, whether, albeit in its own way, it intuits (the form) even though its perceiving is of a different nature than sensible perception; or whether any intuition is precluded to it, as, for example, Kant or Peirce claim, for analogous and yet different reasons.

9. *Mind and discourse.* One should beware being caught by these *logical* problems. One should stop one's questioning at the level of the form, of the form of *logos* because it is here that the form gestures to us and shows itself first of all. What is the form of the house? It is that configuration of bricks that allows them to function as shelter for humans, animals, and things. The form of the house is therefore *here,* in *this* discourse (*logos*); that is, as Plato says, it is in defining discourse, in *logos tes ousias.* The form of the house is contained precisely and first of all in the defining discourse that says: "to function as shelter for humans, animals, and things." Because of this [definition], one can say that squirrels "have a house" in the tree, and one can invent other analogous expressions.

The mind is thus discourse insofar as discourse itself is the (nonsensible) *logical image* of the house on the basis of which, starting from the problems of logic, Wittgenstein resurrects the original questions. "The house is white, but the roof is red," says discourse. Yet how can these purely graphic or acoustic signs, their peculiar syntactical connection, their succession in time or their location in space, *signify* the house, that is, provide an *image* of it? In what can these things *resemble* each other? What can the signs of discourse have in common with the thing they say? How could they *signify* without having something in common, without discourse (the mind) and thing (the house) having a "common nature"?

Looking at the form of discourse, on one side, and at the sensible form of the house on the other, one wonders what they might ever have in common, so that the one is the image of the other and signifies it. The problem has no exit, unless the question arises: what is the content of the form?

10. *Constitutive paradoxes.* Human beings have studied the form of discourse for a long time: its grammar and its syntax, the set of rules of denotative and communicative applications, the semantic rules, and finally, the rules of use, or pragmatic rules. Yet, the content of all these forms raises neither problems nor questions.

At most, the content is handed over to inquiries made by specific disciplines such as phonology, the study of writing systems, various semiotics, and so on. Instead of bringing us closer to the simple and originary question of the content of the form, however, with their characteristic and often very complicated abstractive problems these compartmentalized and empirical analyses take us far away from the question and cover it up, precisely because they appear to be busying themselves with the content and thereby transform it into a problem.

Neither do they realize, nor do they problematize the paradox on which they peacefully rest; that is, in their semiological and linguistic inquiries, in their study of phonic and graphic "matters" of language, they already use and put to use the very form (the logical form) and the very content of the form that is meanwhile the object of their analyses. This paradox is indeed constitutive of the question. Every time a science is asked a genuine question (for example, when cosmology is asked *what* "universe" *means*), then it realizes that the question *cannot* become the problem of that science. It cannot become the problem without the very science's collapse, that is, without the science's becoming itself the problem, and, even before, without becoming itself the question.

11. *The double mind.* The mind (the *nous,* as Parmenides already claims) is a nonsensible, intelligible, intelligent seeing. At the same time, the mind is discourse (*logos*). This duplicity of *logos* and *nous,* these two souls (noetic and dianoetic) of logic have never been composed or clarified completely from the perspective of their genesis. They continue to sustain the vacuous debate between "intuitive" and "reasoning" individuals.

In a logical sense, mental discourse is definition (*logos tes ousias*). It is a discourse referring to what is, that is, referring to the being or essence of a being. The mind "intuits" being because it possesses its definition (the essential discourse). In this sense, or through this means, being and mind have something in common: *einai te kai noein tauton* [being and knowing are the same]. What they have in common is something double: a suprasensible "ideal" form and a discursive "syntactic" structure.

In the *Sophist,* when he wishes to explain logical definitions, Plato refers precisely to syntacticity or *schematicity.* Like the grammarian, who knows which letters should and should not be linked to form a word, and like the musician, who knows which sounds should and should not be joined to form a harmony, the dialectician, that is, the philosopher, in his logical awareness knows which *ideas* should and should not combine in order to achieve the definition, the *logos tes ousias*. Logical competence is a classification of the elements and their connections. These elements are similar to the letters of the alphabet. Or *are* they the letters of the alphabet? What kind of unthought lies at the bottom of the philosophers' examples? The *reader* should open his or her eyes.

12. *Hermes' altar.* The mind, discourse, the logical mind and its definitions—one takes these *things* as obvious, "evident facts" that have always inhabited the earth and human minds. One does not realize the enormous Platonic construction of the "soul" (the logical or philosophical, that is, epistemic, soul).[9] Its intelligent light veils and blinds us to the point that inverting the order of elements comes spontaneously to us. On the basis of Plato's (forgotten, and therefore unnoticed) gesture, one thinks that the mind is the *cause of* discourse; one does not realize that, on the contrary, the mind *emerges in* discourse, in a certain mode or kind of discourse, and that it does not exist at all "before."

One must penetrate the Platonic light, and go through its enchanting circle.[10] An aid can come, for example, from the great and forgotten Creuzer. In Homer's language, and in the Homeric individual, there is no mind and, least of all, the logical mind. There are speech, heart, and breath, and Creuzer exemplarily shows the meaning of these connections.[11]

Additionally, the very "discoursing" of language is something that has been constructed and achieved; it is an event in the "history" of speech, not something originary. The ancient Greeks were clearly aware of this. In the god Hermes they honored the inventor of the alphabet and discursive speech (one should not overlook the acumen of this very essential connection). Thus, in archaic temples, they celebrated him with an altar as exemplarily simple as meaningful—a pile of stones laid one on top of the other to symbolize precisely the phonetic writing of the alphabet. Each stone is a letter; each stone is a step in the discursive construction of the expression.[12]

13. *The clothing and the way.* Originary language is *figurative,* Creuzer says. It offers "images of sense," and it offers itself in them. It is more writing than discourse, as it were. At this layer of expression (which still lies at the grounds of words; unnoticed jewel, *cosmos* whose splendor Creuzer's philology uncovers) there is no distinction between speech [*parola*] and writing. One does not yet differentiate between symbols devoted to hearing (*symbola phonetika*) and those destined to vision (*aphona*), says Creuzer. Here, words show and display, somewhat as does hieroglyphic writing, which is simultaneously sign, drawing, and sound.

This primordial language is ostensive, is an intuitive pointing toward [*mostrazione*]; that is, it is an act of indication. Its displaying is a covering with an image of sense. Therefore, this speech is *endeictic*—it is an *endeixis,* a term that also means "clothing," or "that which covers."

This originary language is followed by discursive speech, or *diexodos*, that is, flowing discourse (that flows through time), narrative speech (*muthos*). Literally, *diexodos* means "straight way" or "exit."[13] Thus, it means the direction, the end, the goal, the arrival point of a project, the aim of a thought that reflects with the aim of. . . . From the originary spatial sense of the way (which the term *diexodos* first signifies in an ostensive [*mostrativo*], indicative, or endeictic manner), one moves to the temporal sense of the "discursive exhibition through concepts"; that is, to the logical-defining sense of the "deduction that generates conviction." In other words: first, the minister-educator of humanity indicates, shows and lets appear the God who has been evoked in the sacral and cultural images that are at one with speeches and names, exciting presences and visions; then, he narrates, tells, argues, defines, and *demonstrates*.

14. *Discursive separateness.* Creuzer mentions a curious passage from Plotinus. In it, it is said that Egyptian priests knowingly chose hieroglyphic writing rather than phonetic writing because the latter generates considerations and judgments "according to a discursive separateness." This story is fictional, since the ancient Egyptians were in truth unaware of phonemes and alphabet, and they could not make the choice Plotinus attributes to them. Nevertheless, it is a very meaningful story, which shows that, after all, the Greeks were not completely unaware of the essential connections tying the practice of writing to the nature of the message, and to the nature of the mind that formulates and receives it.

Alphabetic writing is an indifferent means, or "intermediary." The eye overcomes phonetic signs, does not dwell and concentrate on them (it *must not* do so, if it wishes to read "fluently"). The eye *uses* alphabetic writing, this exemplary "technical means," by keeping it at a distance, away from the focus of attention. From here comes the peculiar "position" of the reader (the "discursive separateness"), and the connected function of *being subject* of and for this practice.

Conversely, in hieroglyphic writing and reading, identification and fusion with the figures are required. Here, to read amounts to contemplating the drawing "pathically" [*paticamente*] and "aesthetically"; that is, to interpreting it by sojourning in a participatory manner in its "image of sense," by being not outside but inside it, not far away but near. In this sense, the hieroglyph is a piece of "clothing," an indicative-iconic sign (as Peirce would say) that veils and unveils at the same time. It is impossible not to recall with how much problematic acumen in the *Tractatus* Wittgenstein too uses the examples of the hieroglyph and the piece of clothing in his search for the logical form of spoken and written language.[14]

15. *The jokes in the* Cratylus. The passage through the written sign (from the hieroglyph to the alphabet) has its analogue in the resounding body of the word, or spoken sign. For this passage, we have the exceptional testimony and document, so often misunderstood and neglected, of Plato's *Cratylus*. In it, names or originary words are said to be imitations (*mimesis*) of things; even better, more properly and concretely, they are imitations of actions concerning things.[15] Thus,

originary words are literally "images of sense"; they imitate and portray in the voice, through appropriate (mimetic) sounds, the action they designate.[16] It is true that this originary naturalness of language (whose phonically iconic signs are thus not at all conventional or arbitrary) has gotten lost, and has dispersed itself in the seemingly conventional multiplicity of languages. Nevertheless, the originary link between sound and image has not completely disappeared. It is true that when in Greek I say *reo,* in Italian I say instead *fluisco* and *fluire* [in English I say *I flow* and *to flow*]. Yet the conventional indifference between the "r" sounds and the "fl" sounds rests ultimately on the fact that, in a different and yet analogous, that is, not conventional but rather natural manner, these letters portray the action they designate. Thus, *fluire* is a vicarious image of *reo*; it is a similar and resembling, only apparently conventional alternative. Never could it happen that the sound *fl* might be replaced with the sound *pt* (evident sign of im*p*edimen*t*, arres*t*, s*t*o*p*, and obs*t*ruction), and that language could say that water *pt*ows.

Already in the *Cratylus* (which, since its irony is undoubtedly profound, does not at all raise questions and examples simply as jokes, as some have thought), we have the *passage to logic.* With a grandiosely revolutionary gesture, which overthrows and subverts an entire and very ancient universe of meaning, the dialectician, that is, the philosopher, takes no interest in the sensuous body of words, which he abandons and relegates to an immemorial past. Rather, he takes interest in the soul of the word, that is, in its logical meaning, that is, in the definition concerning the *ousia,* the essence of the signified thing. Therefore, the *Cratylus* is only one step away from the *Theaetetus* and the *Sophist,* for which it is the direct premise and introduction.

According to the *Cratylus,* the definition does not *imitate* sensuously (artistically, aesthetically). Rather, it establishes a *true* (logical, scientific) relation between word and thing.[17] It shows being through dialectic saying (*dialeghesthai*), that is, through *logos tes ousias* which is the very *logos* of truth.

One can see here very clearly the place from which Heidegger asks his question (that concerns precisely the truth or the truth of being). It is a place where everything has already been decided and has happened, and therefore a place that is unfit for a real genealogical understanding of logic. The definition abandons the disclosive "is" in favor of a copulative "is" that aims at establishing the logical connections between being and non-being. Yet, it is not by looking at "being" and its "truth" that understanding such a passage is possible. By opposing *aletheia* to *mimesis,* Plato makes a deeper and more complex gesture than what can be measured by an *aletheia* understood *à la* Heidegger, even if Heidegger's *aletheia* is a necessary beginning and premise for such a measurement and understanding.

16. *The ages of the mind.* A first or simply more ancient practice of *logos* is emotional and participatory. At this level, no properly logical mind is shown. One could talk of a sensual-gestural mind (although the term "mind" is not appropriate here, if one considers the abstract and, precisely, logical use we normally make of it). The primary task of the sensual mind is to name, to arouse names,

that is, to denote in a direct manner by indicating the thing and cutting it out, as it were, through gesture and name, or through the gesture that names. This evocative and indicative mind enacts a language that designs the world in its things in such a way that sound and writing are still intimately intertwined and plastic. This mind that knows how to name and distinguish does not know yet how to narrate properly.

Next is a discursive mind of a fabulative kind. It is a mind that tells stories and legends, but whose linguistic practice is still unaware of letters and writing. This mind does not know how to either read or write, even if its names portray and draw, and thus, in this more general sense, they write the things of the world. Such a mind puts to work its own acted consistency in language. It is a consistency that is linked to the illustrative becoming-narration of gestures and, more in general, to narrative practice. Vico would say that from the language productive of the gods' names one has moved to the heroes' language, which narrates their epic enterprises in the time of imagination.

Finally, from this narrating *epos* (where the narrator is the *Vistor*, the witness that tells the vision inspired to him by the goddesses of memory, of mythical oral memory), one moves to logical-dialectical *logos*, to discourse guided by logical image, which is one with the definition, the defining discourse. Yet how does this move happen? This is the issue.

17. *From the* odos *of wisdom to the* methodos *of logic*. In such a move, various components interact. For example, there is the ascent of *logos* to a suprasensible (circular, panoramic) vision. Parmenides names such a vision with the word *noos*. We are confronted with the advent of a discourse that overcomes the *pathos* of participatory, endeictic, naming and fabulatory speech.

The ascent represents a new *odos*, a new way of wisdom. It specifies itself more properly as a particular discursive way, as a well-defined *diexodos*, that is, as a method (*methodos*) of speech. It is characterized by peculiar signs (*semata*, Parmenides says) consisting in the formal non-contradictoriness of assertions and utterances. Initially, this contradictoriness is thought of as the concrete parting of the ways, a pair of paths one of which "says that it is," the other "that it is not."

The partition is schematized as a simple crossing of lines, drawn on an ideal writing board. The crossing appears then as an inverted "y" (λ). The contradiction, perceived as a parting of ways, translates into a scheme of writing whose procedure is "analytical," that is, "critical" and "dichotomous."

In other words: the speech that analyzes and judges (*krinein*) is not [the same as] the speech that names, evokes, narrates, or accompanies the action ("Off to the ships, Achaeans!" or "Off to the ships, philosophers!" as Nietzsche says). This analytical speech aims at forming a logical image or *mimesis* of things. The image is, more precisely, a *diagram* (as Peirce would say), a crossing of lines within a graph (within a "leaf-world," Peirce, again, would say); and this *is*, literally, the definition. For example, this is the prototypical definition pertaining to angling as it is advanced in Plato's *Sophist*:

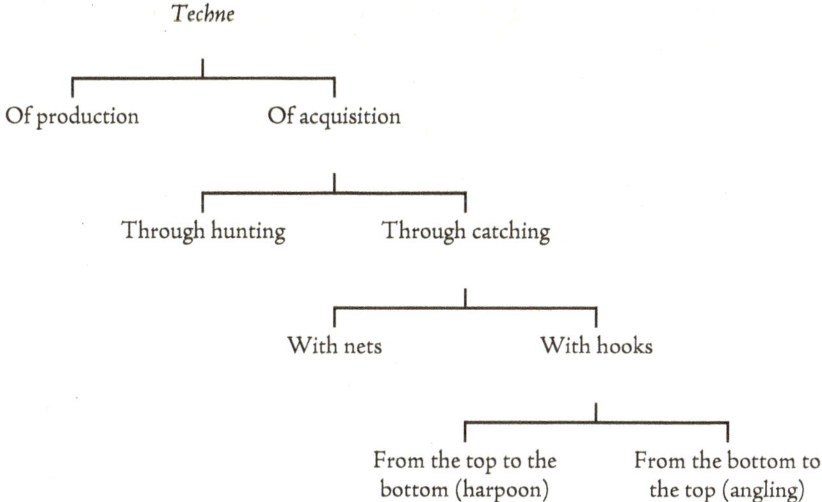

At the end of such an analytical procedure, we find the figures (*schemata*) of syllogism.

18. *Heracles' parting of the ways*. Prodicus, the sophist, tells the famous myth of Heracles at the parting of the ways. When at the threshold of adulthood, the young Heracles finds himself faced with the choice between two paths, that of virtue (*arete*) and that of depravation (*kakia*), depicted as two women of opposite qualities and different languages and aspects. The first path leads to good harmony (*cosmos*) and the correct use of social techniques; the second leads to vice, corruption, and the merely utilitarian, egotistical, and therefore disastrous use of the tools and products of civilization.[18]

The Greeks ascribed to Heracles also the invention of writing and the alphabet, which at the time ended with the letter "Y." Hence, the image of the parting of the ways, which schematically comprised within itself also the image of the tree of life, one of the oldest symbols present in numerous civilizations.[19]

With this intertwining of references, Prodicus clearly shows that he understands what is at stake in writing and the alphabet. They lead human beings to the parting of the ways where the very meaning of their lives, and more particularly of their civilization and social cohabitation, is at stake. As eminently human techniques, writing and alphabet venture the definitive exit of human beings from the circle of naturalness; thereby, they venture the opposite alternatives of a superior meaning of humanity or its complete destruction. For this, a peculiar *sophia* is required: that is, the formation of a dialectical mind capable of discriminating true from false good, the good from the opposite path. For this, *philo-sophia* is required. It is not a negligible detail that an ancient tradition indicates Prodicus as one of Socrates' teachers. By arguing ironically, and by defining maieutically, Socrates simply inverts Heracles' "Y."

19. *The leap.* The practice of language does not comprise within itself the definition, the defining practice, as an unavoidable necessity. This latter practice has in the former an ideal condition of possibility; however, its enactment does not happen by itself because of an intrinsic and "natural" evolution of *logos*. Numerous civilizations have ignored the defining practice and dialectical games of analytical *logos*; this has not prevented many of them from achieving high and sublime realizations.

Intertwined with action, pathic speech does not bother about contradiction, for example. Such a speech focuses only on *meaning*, which is intimately connected to *pathos* and *pathemata* ("passions," yet deprived of our psychologistic connotations). The god that is evoked (for example, Dionysus) can be both male and female, adult and child, meek and ferocious, having the sense of death and life, of chastity and orgy, of clouding and knowledge, and so on.

Precisely because of this, the question concealed by logic cannot be searched starting with truth. Heidegger claims that truth as *aletheia* must be understood as the originary disclosedness or unconcealedness of a being (and in truth, by naming a being and the being of a being as he does, Heidegger already says too much, and says it badly, since he clearly presupposes a typical *logical content* without questioning it; he presupposes *being in general*, that is a product, or, even better, the product of the defining practice of *logos*). Yet, Heidegger continues, logic translates the originary disclosedness into truth understood as "correctness" (*orthotes*) of judgment and enunciation. This assumes judgment as the place of truth and as an essential image of the thing. This is correct. But *how* does such a leap happen?[20]

20. *That and how.* Evidently something does not work. Between phenomenon (manifestation) and truth of enunciation there is a big leap of meaning, a heterogeneity of terms and contexts. It is not enough to remark *that aletheia* (disclosiveness) is not *veritas* (correctness as correspondence between *logos* and the disclosed being). One must then show *how* this difference determines itself; that is, what, differing, subtends to it. What is the similar *odos* within which the differing of the logical *methodos* determines itself? Between *aletheia* and *veritas* there is a hidden and deep continuity, which supports the passage from one to the other. Yet there is also a deep abyss that cannot be crossed on the edge of simple "truth."

The point is: how can discourse (*logos*) assume the meaning of logical enunciation, or function of logical image? If one says: "Off to the ships, Achaeans!" this has nothing to do with truth at all. The linguistic gesture identifies units of meaning ("off," "ships," and so on) and inserts practical, indicative, and orientating functions (like a stretched out arm or forefinger). Today one would speak of "illocutory" objectualities, for example. Even if one says "The ship is in the harbor," the meaning of this sentence is descriptive-denotative, or even narrative; it has nothing to do with truth.

In saying this, one could lie—one objects. This is true, but even the act of lying is a determined linguistic practice that has its pragmatic meaning within itself, a meaning that does not need the logic of truth to institute itself. Calchas could very well have tricked Agamemnon while remaining unaware of syllogisms and metaphysical assumptions on a "true being."

The general or universal question of truth emerges only when one asserts the *problem* of the Socratic-Platonic definition: what is ship, what is harbor, what is being? Thus, the "leap" is something occurring to *logos* and in *logos*. What lies behind the *problem* of logic is not the truth (disclosive or assertive). Rather, it is the emergence of the universality or purity that govern the formal character of enunciation (the "logical form" of the discursive image). Or better, it is not properly the form (which is the arrival point); rather, it is the *content* of the form, that is, that which logic employs (problematically), but which, by employing, it suppresses from its understanding, from its *question*.

21. *The recovered question*. Is writing, perhaps, the content of the form that logic elides and forgets? Is it the "scheme," that is, writing as *schematismus latens* [hidden schematism]? It is a fact that logic has evolved toward a more and more peculiar system of writing without ever "thinking" or worrying about the "weight" of writing itself. Conversely, it has flattered itself thinking of proceeding on the uncontaminated path of "pure" thought, of the "purification of *logos*" (purification from the "errors" of language).

Let us suppose that to discover how discourse becomes "logical," that is, to discover the content of the logical form, one decided to analyze, in speech, sound, voice, pathic-expressive materiality of accent, tone, and rhythm. In so doing, one would take a wrong path that does not lead to the goal. It is the path that, initially, Socrates takes up in the *Cratylus*, and on which he exercises his "irony" ultimately to set it aside and oppose it with the path, or method, of logical definition. This path has to do with the *pathic* (and, in this sense, disclosive) character of speech. From here, however, there is no passage to the logical definition, which conversely has to do with *schemata* (diagrams) and *elements*.

Schematization (it would be better to say "stylization"[21]), through which one proceeds toward an "elementary" and analytical thinking, is the characteristic feature of a practice connected with the introduction of the alphabet and alphabetic writing. Is the alphabet, then, the content of the logical form? Is this the secret that Heracles and Hermes hide within themselves? One should withhold the answer, and be content with having found the question.

CHAPTER 2

Writing

22. *The Greek literate revolution.* "May not all logical thinking as commonly understood be a product of Greek alphabetic literacy?"[1] Havelock encounters this ("radical," he says) question in the course of his essay concerning the "crisis that occurred in the history of human communication, when Greek orality transformed itself into Greek literacy."[2] One of the consequences of such a "crisis" is the birth of literature and philosophy: "twin enterprises of the written word, the first of their kind in the history of our species." The reasons for this birth (which are so often referred to Greek "genius," that is, to an explanation that does not explain anything) are to be found "in the context of what has been called the Greek literate revolution."[3]

Posing the question in terms of "history of human communication" and "history of writing" is, however, not "radical" at all. This is so because "history," "communication," and even "writing" are typical *effects* of a logical mind that is raised within and educated by writing. One should be patient with Havelock, and take all the good things he may offer. And his offer is not small.

23. *The conceptual word.* The invention of a conceptual language and lexicon can be tracked back to the Milesian school and in general the Pre-Socratic thinkers. As Havelock says, they took Homer's and Hesiod's language and endowed it with a new nonoralist syntax, thereby forging "the primitive theoretical language."[4]

The "discovery of 'selfhood,'" insofar as "separation of the knower from the known which a growing literacy favored,"[5] is a consequence of this invention. The climax of this process occurs in Plato with the invention of the soul.[6] The arrival of Platonism, meaning the appearance of a large body of discourse written in prose, [was] a signal announcing that Greek orality was giving way to Greek literacy and that an oral state of mind was to be replaced by a literate state of mind.[7]

[Here is the] paradox of Socrates' figure: "the one who does not write" (as Nietzsche says) is the teacher of philosophical writing. In truth, Socratic dialoguing (which is put in writing by his disciples) and dialectical research are something antipodal to the rhythmic poetry of orality, and are distinct also from the "long speeches" of Sophistic rhetoric, in which the *pathos* of argumentation does not yet achieve the purity of the concept. Socrates does not write anything, but he has read a lot and has reflected much on "writing."

24. *Ethics and morality.* Another consequence of the invention ("and a Platonic one") of writing was "the notion of a moral value system which was autonomous, while at the same time capable of internalization in the individual." For this notion, "the Greek enlightenment had laid the groundwork, replacing an oralist sense of 'the right thing to do,' as a matter of propriety and correct procedure."[8]

What is thus born with Plato, as Nietzsche intuits, is "morality" and the reasoning by "values" which, as Heidegger says, is antipodal to ethics, that is, to the originary *ethos* of ancient thinkers, and is conversely congruous with metaphysical subjectivism and anthropologism. The affirmation of the interiority of moral conscience and the unfolding of nihilism are thus one and the same process.

The *ethos* of orality is conversely a *practice*: [it is] the behavior that is "virtuous" (that is, efficacious, adequate, opportune in the literal sense of *arete* and *virtus*) each single time and in each single case. This behavior lies on the forefront. Ethics is not a theory, that is, a theory of morals and values.

25. *The saw, the hatchet, and the log.* The study of the revolution introduced by writing, that is, the consequences of the passage from the civilization of orality to the civilization of writing (which is progressively spreading all over the world), leads to verifying Vico's great intuition: that is, human beings have not always spoken and thought in the same way, and there neither is nor will there presumably ever be a single "mind," a single "human consciousness" fixed once and forever.

For years Alexander Luria (as Ong mentions)[9] studied the illiterate populations of the Soviet republics of Uzbekistan and Kirghizstan. He asked an illiterate peasant what a saw, log, and hatchet are, and in what ways they differ. The peasant replied: "They all look alike. The saw will saw the log and the hatchet will chop it." The illiterate peasant sees one single aspect (*eidos*) where we see many. This does not mean, as Ong claims, that the peasant cannot think. Simply, he thinks things within the unity of a function, within the unity of a *practice*, and has instead no interest for "purely logical forms [*schemi*]" and definitions.

The peasant would have said that also a fish, line, and hook have the same look, thus throwing us into astonishment. The most astonishing thing, however, is that we can no longer be astonished by that extraordinary operation, by that *practice* that Plato enacts at the beginning of the *Sophist*, when he "defines" fishing with hooks, thereby providing us with the prototype of all definitions and establishing the foundations for the logical mind and thought. That is, he operates one of the deepest revolutions in the domain of truth and human consciousness. One could say that for the illiterate peasant thinking is always within a situation within a practice. A specific *practice of thinking* does not yet exist for him. Therefore, neither does that abstract object that is thought exist.

It is likely that, to the question 'What is thought?' he would answer that to think is to speak. At least since Hamann, we have started to go from speaking back to thinking; that is, we have reinserted thinking within the practice of language, and thus we have started a backwards path so as to circumnavigate the continent of our logical consciousness.

26. *Doing, speaking, defining.* The poetry of orality and even Greek tragedy lack, Havelock claims, "any linguistic framework for the statement of abstract principle." One almost never comes across examples of "a conceptual subject attached to a conceptual predicate by the copula 'is.'"[10] "The propositional idiom with the copula which we continuously fall into is precisely what Plato wished the Greek language to be converted to, and he spent his entire writing life trying to do this."[11]

> Since Sophocles' day, much has happened to the speech of the mind and to the mind itself. While retaining the language of doing, of action or feeling in part, we have supplemented it, and partly replaced it, by statements of fact. The participles and the verbs and the adjectives that behave like gerunds have yielded to conceptual entities, abstractions, objects. Oral Greek did not know what an object of thought was. The Muse, as she learned to write, had to turn away from the living panorama of experience and its ceaseless flow, but as long as she remained Greek, she could not entirely forget it.[12]

Oral language (the character of which is eminently narrative) has an activist and dynamic structure. Its practical sensuality determines a "verbomotor" culture, "in contradistinction to the static categorical language characteristic of achieved literacy."[13] The language of oral narration speaks of things in relation to that which acts or suffers; it shows just actions, not *the* statically defined justice. This is in fact the objection Socrates constantly moves to his astonished interlocutors: "I have not asked you to enumerate various examples of good actions to me; I have asked you what the good is."

27. *The enchantments of practice.* One should not think, however, that matters are exactly as Havelock describes them. He observes with a scientific eye, and objectively studies the linguistic forms of poetry, tragedy, philosophy, and history. That is, he systematically employs (with the ensuing paradox) that "logical mind" determined by writing the genesis of which he wishes to reconstruct.[14]

Plato knew nothing of the effects of grammar upon thinking, and of writing upon grammar. He could have not formulated within himself the thought that Heidegger advanced in his *Introduction to Metaphysics*; that is, that in the Greek way of thinking "being," a privilege is assigned to the third singular person of the present indicative, that is, to the copula "is." We thus do not think "being" starting with "thou art," "you are," "I am," "they would be," "though all of these, just as much as 'is,' represent verbal inflections of 'to be.'" Therefore, our determined way of thinking "has not just dropped on us accidentally from somewhere but has dominated our historical being-there since antiquity."[15] (Heidegger is very far from understanding why the Greeks thought in this manner because of the arbitrary privilege he places on "language," *logos*, writing; that is, because he remains a "Platonist" on the essential issue).

Plato could not speak of an unmotivated privileging the third person. By exercising the dialectical, that is, philosophical practice of definition, he rather goes into ecstasies over its objects, that is, over the "suprasensible visions" ensuing from it. Plato attends the enchantment of philosophical practice. He inaugurates it, takes part in it, is subject to it (more than being the subject of it). It is we, in *our* practice and in *its* enchantment, who can perceive writing as lying behind Plato's ideas. It is only *for us*, and not for him, that what I am writing becomes true. This is, in turn, the truth of a further practice. Where and how to put an end to these Chinese boxes, that is, to the enchantment of these disenchantments?

28. *The logical practice*. In the *Metaphysics* and in the *Politics*, Aristotle de-scribes human beings; he does not tell what they do. He links the human being as subject "to a series of predicates connoting something fixed, something that is an object of thought: the predicate describes a class, or a property, not an action."[16] What asserts itself is the generic neuter ("the things by nature," "best of animals, worst of animals," and so on), which is rare in Homer and in tragedy. "In philosophy on the other hand, conceptual force was being assisted by this usage, especially as applied to the Greek definite article."[17]

Meanwhile, the verb "to be" "is used to signify not a 'presence' or a 'forceful existence' (its common use in oralism) but a mere linkage required by a conceptual operation."[18] This linkage *is* thinking as we understand it. The narrative practice has turned into a logical practice.

Here one starts to see how to fill the gap between *aletheia* (presence) and *veritas* (logical judgment). The "theoretical" look as "panoramic" look and as doctrine of being (Parmenides, Heraclitus) is the arrival point of such a gap. This result determines itself, however, within a practice of *logos* (certainly in connection with other practices) which is increasingly transformed and dominated by the practice of writing.

29. *The advent of prose*. According to Havelock, very few scholars ask what a "tradition" concretely is. Actually, it changes its characteristics according to different situations. Within the oral tradition, the transmission of *ethos* and forms of knowledge and their conservation across generations requires a peculiar use of memory, the characteristics of which are, for example, repetition,

ritualized recitation, rhythm and musical intonation (poetry), mimic action or dance, semantic parallelism, parataxis, the dynamic and emotional character of the contents, and so on. In general, "tradition in short is taught by action, not by idea or principle."[19] *Paideia* is eminently a practice and not a science (a scientific practice).

With the disappearing of the oral tradition and the affirmation of writing, not only does the ancient use of productive and creative memory disappear and is replaced with a reproductive and mechanical memory that simply learns the written text by heart;[20] moreover, the importance of rhythm and poetry in general severely weakens (it increasingly becomes an aesthetic game). To preserve itself, tradition no longer requires these tools, and this allows the affirmation of prose. "Prose became the vehicle of a whole new universe of fact and of theory."[21] One should add: this universe is *truly* new; that is, facts *literally* did not exist *before* the practice of prose, and *theories* could not be held *true* backwards, that is, for example, so as to explain a universe constructed on the basis of oral memory.

The passage to prose, *its* facts and *its* theories "was a release of mind as well as of language," Havelock claims.[22] This too should be understood *literally*: it is not a matter of a previous existence of the mind that is *later* liberated; it is a matter of the *event* of pure mind, that is, a practice of thought and speech that frees itself of the *pathos* of "archaic" speech. That is, [it frees itself] of the speech that *now*, for pure mind, becomes pathic and archaic.

30. *Public truth*. The advent of prose provoked "the creation of 'history' as essentially a prosaic enterprise."[23] This turning point (which is not the creation of "historiography" but rather precisely of history, historical human being and historical reality, because outside of writing none of them can exist) is perfectly exemplified by Thucydides, as Detienne explains. With history, the entire Western scientific mentality sets into motion: "the same opening toward the novel and the nontraditional, as it provoked history, also created philosophy and science."[24]

These are the roots of the formation of "public truth," [which is] infinitely on the way in its research (in its *theorein*), as Peirce claims ultimately repeating Socrates ("a life without examination is not worth living," asserts Socrates during his trial; this is the real birth of the theoretical man, Nietzsche comments).

Public truth, in which we are still entirely immersed, presents various correlative levels, which are constitutive of "pure" mind and subject. There is history, the practice of which causes the formation of an abstract prosaic subject that, through "documents," tries to create a perspective "external" to the events at stake, that is, something non-participatory but rather merely observational; in writing, such a something passes itself off as a truth of the events which is their happening in front of the historical look (*as if* they had truly happened in such and such a manner). Then there is philosophy, the practice of which determines the birth of a panoramic and theoretical subject that defines the truth in itself of all things, that is, translates things from the lived experiential dimension into the abstract logical definition (*as if* things were truly in this manner; and one should notice that the lived experiential dimension is not a primary given, but rather the result of peculiar practices of speech and writing).

Finally, there is science, which is the methodological focusing of the theoretical and historical subject. [Science] does not limit itself to reason *as if*; rather, in its modern version, it translates the "as if" into a "thus I want it to be." The universal descends to earth and roots there. That is, it becomes concrete, effective. The "idea" of public truth thus turns into the reality of our technical projects, informing therewith our very perception of experience.

31. *The universal form as particular content.* Such is the prosaic subject; even earlier, however, is the *subject* that emerges through the practice of writing. In orality, speech [*discorso*] flows [*scorre*] as a river, and the speaker is one body with it. Writing instead separates language from the speaker and translates it into an object, a visible and fixed thing. Standing against it, the speaker acquires its own separated relevance. It literally becomes a "self." Such a subject is not present in Homer and archaic poetry. As Havelock says,

> this in any strict sense only became true in the time of Plato. Achilles may have had a 'self' in our sense of the word, but he was not aware of it, and if he had been, he would not have behaved as a hero of the oralist vocabulary, a speaker of utterances and a doer of deeds.[25]

A maker of good speeches and a doer of good actions, Jäger says, according to the Greek notion of *arete* and ancient *paideia*.

There is no doubt that the "self" is a Socratic discovery, an invention of Socratic vocabulary, and that these latter are both made "textual" by Plato and his "strategy of the soul" (which is the very beginning of philosophy). All this confronts us with a disquieting result as far as the truths of our prejudices go:

> the concept of selfhood and the soul, as now understood, arose at a historical point in time and was inspired by a technological change, as the inscribed language and thought and the person who spoke it became separated from each other, leading to a new focus on the personality of the speaker.[26]

Our entire "faith" in personal individuality, as well as in democratic and Christian "values," is challenged at its roots.

Neither can we rest any longer on the trust that the universality of logical mind and laws is a "superhistorical" given, an expression of reason *überhaupt*. "Logical procedures" appear instead as a discovery of the civilization of writing, and not as something rooted in "human nature" since the beginning. That is, one can see how the logical form has a content; this is something contingent and not universal. Better said, it is the particularity of content that is the universal itself.

32. *The illiterate and the ignorant.* The universality of the subject of which Havelock speaks is to be related more to the "reader" than to the "writer" : "the civilization created by the Greeks and Romans was the first on the earth's surface which was founded upon the activity of the common reader"[27] and thus gave birth to a universal process of alphabetization.

With this process, being educated and literate become one and the same. Earlier, one could be educated and illiterate (the Greeks do not have words equivalent to "literate" and "illiterate": these were introduced by the Romans, who created a "culture" for themselves by reading Greek texts). Human culture (*Bildung*) changes its face and becomes *Zivilisation* (and lastly, in our times, *Weltzivilisation*). Today it is for us a given that "illiterate" means ignorant, backward, marginalized, and so on. With this turn, philosophy too changes; it becomes "philosophical culture," historical-disciplinary tradition, theory of texts and commentaries.

An effort is necessary to understand that what we think today with respect to culture is a result and not a cause: that numerous and highly developed civilizations were illiterate and made by illiterates; that the identification of culture and civilization with the possession of the alphabet is not a "beginning" but a "fact." As Havelock well says, to identify human culture and alphabetization is simply a "curious kind of cultural arrogance."[28]

One should think about this: the establishment of the relation between culture and alphabet, that is, the "fact of technology" of which Havelock speaks[29] (one could say and object much with regard to that "technology," since it is such only because we perceive and think of it in such a manner), entails a cost. It determines *a kind* of civilization, not *the* civilization but rather a *possibility* of culture which excludes and is detrimental to other possibilities. Great advantages as well as great losses and dangers ensue. It is not a matter of devaluing (what we have) or of regretting (what we no longer have). It is a matter of understanding, for example, the root of many of our interrogatives and problems.

33. *That strange thing that is reading.* The foundations and the first wonderful realizations of Greek civilization occurred in a pre-alphabetized context (which is something entirely different from today's non-literacy). As Havelock says, the Greeks began to read and write within a context of oral culture, so that Pindar and Plato were very close to complete non-alphabetization.

This remark seems odd, if one thinks of Plato's literary sophistication: a man who *knew* what writing means as very few do, perhaps as no one after him does. His activity as a writer is certainly of no small relevance. How can one explain such a wonder? Other, easier questions arise: with what material did he write, take his notes, correct, sketch outlines, and so on? And how many hours a day did he devote to reading and writing?

To exercise such an intense literary practice, reading must be on the front more than writing. Havelock is right: writing is not enough to have an alphabetized culture (history of writing and history of reading do not coincide); not the existence of a technique of writing but rather the number of people capable of reading defines the level of literacy.

The issue is all here: before the introduction of the Greek alphabet, writing is a "practice for the experts," a closed or esoteric universe, a job for professionals. In Greece itself one has to wait until the end of the sixth century and moreover the fifth century BCE to see the slow and progressive diffusion of a taste for reading, which only in the fourth century begins to expand in the whole area of the Mediterranean Sea. The ancients never portrayed the act of reading, and Aristophanes still puts onto the stage an actor immersed in reading only to the goal of having his audience, mainly composed of illiterates, laugh.

34. *The letters.* What is so peculiar to the Greek alphabet that it was the only one to allow for a civilization of readers? This is one of the issues Havelock has the merit of having clarified most convincingly. The Greeks were the only ones to invent visible signs endowed with univocity of meaning and reduced to twenty signs or a little more ("the ideal number for the 'democratization' of reading").[30] Thus the foundations were laid for the institution of an educational system that starts children reading in the age of their greatest mental malleability, so that reading becomes an unconscious reflex. We still belong to this circle of concomitant causes and consequences: writing, educational system, democracy.

No systems of writing preceding the Greek alphabet achieve such a result, although they approximate it in various degrees (that the alphabet was invented by the Phoenicians is therefore false). In general, such systems were "syllabaries": empirical attempts at reproducing the actually uttered syllables, with or without the use of signs to record those which, thanks to the Greeks, will be called vowels. The Greeks, instead, achieve the great leap of "idealization": they "dissolve"[31] the syllable into purely "ideal," "theoretical" components: that is, they invent the letters. "Although both 'vowel' and 'consonant' seek to describe sounds, they were coined only after the Greek alphabet made these sounds 'visually' recognizable as 'letters.'"[32] Speaking of vowels and consonants in pre-Greek writings is arbitrary, an undue retrocession of our mentality (which is derived from the use of the alphabet). In those times, they knew nothing about vowels and consonants; that is, these were not experienced or perceived as such.

For the same reason, however, it is arbitrary to consider the systems of writing that precede the Greeks as "a series of trial and error attempts" to reach the alphabet, as Havelock maintains.[33] One should rather think that each civilization gave itself the writing which it needed, which was congruous with its practices and its way of experiencing and perceiving life.

35. *The circle mind-alphabet.* The Greek writing system, according to Havelock, overcame the empiricism of syllables and concrete words "by abstracting the non-pronounceable, non-perceptible elements contained in the syllables."[34] Thus, it created "consonants." Consonants are "an abstraction, a non-sound, an idea in the mind."[35] The Greek system isolated this inexistent sound and gave it

its own conceptual identity under the form of what we call a "consonant." The Greeks invented aphonous, voiceless (*aphona*) sounds, or more precisely *hemiphona* (uttered half-way, semi-sonants, such as "s") and *symphona* (con-sonants, elements voiced "in company").

In truth, the Greeks created, literally, "a table of atomic elements"[36] that can be combined in innumerable relations and are fit to represent ideally any linguistic noise. The relation between atoms and letters is more than a mere coincidence. Everywhere in Greece we find the creation of new, purely theoretical *units*. It is in this way that the chronology of historiographers, the geometry of Anaximander, the conventional land partition introduced by Clystenes' democratic reform, and so on, are born.[37]

In sum, the Greeks made the "leap" (as Havelock says)[38] of abstraction. How are we to understand such a leap? We encounter here an evident circle: "abstraction," the "simple idea of a sound in the mind," the "mind" itself are constituted on the basis of the practice of writing and reading; they do not pre-exist them. We cannot explain the birth of the Greek mind by the alphabet and then turn the alphabet into a product of the Greek mind. But then, with what "mind" did the Greeks invent the alphabet? With the "oral" mind? To express oneself in this way is pure nonsense. There is something that does not work in this entire matter of the "leap," and even the ensuing questions sound equivocal or have the appearance of being ill-posed. Or should one resort, once again, to the "geniality" of the Greeks? There is still a lot of ground to cover, before one can see the ground of the question.

36. *Prometheus'* grammata. The creation of a perfect (or almost perfect) ideal system of representation of spoken language determines a consequence the importance of which can hardly be exaggerated: spoken language becomes an "artifact," a materially visible and manipulable "thing." Words and sentences become artifacts that render memory visible by objectifying it, Havelock says.[39] According to Aeschylus, this was one of Prometheus' gifts to humankind: *grammata*, that is, inscriptions or written letters. It is evident that the consciousness that is formed in oral communication is entirely different than the one deriving from the practice of reading and writing. The greatest effect of the changes induced by writing "was felt in the mind and the way the mind thinks as it speaks."[40]

A further consequence of all this is that, by materializing itself, language starts to become an object for observation and analysis. The sophistic age starts to be interested in grammar and etymology (that is, it started creating them), although the Greeks, being still so close to orality, do not give birth to a real linguistic science and philosophy of language.

It is a fact that ever since then we have considered language on the basis of its transcription, that is, we have considered it from the rebound and reflected image deriving from its being written. Thus, we equivocate and believe that this *is* language in and by itself (as Saussure too laments).

37. *The ambiguity of saying and knowing.* According to Havelock, it is only when language is fixed in writing that a reflection on it becomes possible.

> "The acoustic medium, being incapable of visualization, did not achieve recognition as a phenomenon wholly separable from the person who used it. But in the alphabetized document the medium became objectified"; it acquired, in the artifact, "an independent existence."[41]

Verba volant, scripta manent [spoken words are volatile, written words stay]. Havelock, however, expresses himself ambiguously. In orality one can recognize no "acoustic medium" (this is a notion proper to the logical mind, that is, to writing). The reason why one does not speak of language and [language] remains unnoticed is not its invisibility, the fact that it flows ungraspable in time rather than stay still in space. The case is not that *first* is language to be *later* recognized only when it is written down. It makes no sense to ask a person from an oral culture to reflect on "language" and tell us what he or she thinks of it (the Greeks, as well known, had no term equivalent to "language").

The practice of discourse of primary orality is something complex that does not sustain analytical disquisitions. Here to name, reveal, express, and even listen and see (sign, design) are intertwined in a unity of meaning, in a horizon of world that has nothing to do with analytical objects such as "language" (which is so evident for us who write), or communication, or similar.

The opening of world that voice and its autophonic rebound constitutive of self-consciousness make possible[42] does not fail and disappear within the visual and objectifying experience of writing. Such an opening goes on with *its* intentionality and its specific *doing.* Simply, at the level of *knowledge,* we assume it from the perspective of the practice of writing, its intentionality and logic. From here comes the ambivalence of our speeches: they do not know what they say, and do not say what they know, that is, what they do.

38. *The technical factor.* Through the alphabet, the Greeks became capable of transcribing accurately the complex content of spoken language. This was not possible through previous systems of writing; because of the uncertainty, generality, and complication of their signs, they could work only when communicating very rudimentary, canonical, and repetitive ideas (such as the formulas of cults, the encomium of the king, and so on), and more in general when the reader already orally knew the text which the signs suggested rather than transcribed accurately. From this comes, according to Havelock, the impropriety of the term "literature" in reference to pre-alphabetic cultures and their texts (such as the epic of Gilgamesh and similar).

In such texts, "the basic complexity of human experience is not there":[43] we have myths, legends, a few tales, proverbs, rituals, and parables; the characters are few and not at all well characterized; the whole thing gives the impression of an archaic monumentality. Nothing [here is] similar to the free richness of

Greek literary subjects, their critical, passionate, ironical, tragic, playful, and so on individuality.

Havelock's thesis is that this does not depend on the primitive nature of non-Greek populations and some sort of racial superiority of the Greek stocks; it rather depends on the "technical factor" of writing. The former transcribed only what the technical device allowed, that is, what they could transcribe, and not what they actually were and said.

It is possible that there is something true in this thesis, and yet its shortcoming is to presuppose always and everywhere an identical human nature and experience. This amounts to the shortcoming we have already pointed out, namely, that of conceiving of writing as a simple technical device (an idea that in its turn comes from writing) and of situating all non-alphabetic writings on an evolutionary scale, so that their only goal would be that (which they did not know they had) of approximating the goals of alphabetic writing (for example, the "democratization" of culture). Thus, if on the one hand Havelock refuses to consider the non-Greeks as "primitive," on the other hand he judges them incapable of giving themselves the writing that they needed in order to record their "human experience."[44]

The entire picture changes if we consider it through Creuzer's eyes. He identifies the specific archaic expressivity in symbols; symbols are neither tale nor myth (with characters, dialogues, and so on) but rather an image of sense that is plastic and monumental, visual and acoustic simultaneously, rich with enormous sacred pregnancy (hence, as Creuzer claims, the "tremendous seriousness of prehistory").[45] The impersonal monumentality and rigidity Havelock laments would then not be a deficiency coming from a mere "technical factor"; these would instead be precisely the expression of a completed human experience and of the conscious, and in its way perfectly successful, will to represent it.

39. *The technique determining the content.* If one considers carefully, though, Havelock's reasoning has an important aspect to it, since in its own way it raises a problem pertaining to the relation between form and content. He substantially claims that content (for example, the epic of Gilgamesh) is what it is because of the form into which it is transcribed (that is, pre-alphabetic writing). Such form is in turn what it is on the basis of its materiality, that is, its technical limits: thus, the content of the writing form (alphabetic or pre-alphabetic) determines the narrative content. Analogously, one could maintain that the content of the *Iliad* is what it is because of that form of transcription that is the alphabet (even if in truth the question is more complex, since Greek epic is an originally oral composition).

Havelock thus understands the problem, which I raise, of the content of the form ("the control of technology over content," he says, for example).[46] Yet the problem is badly posed, and the relative question is not adequately focused when we presuppose the content (that is, the alleged complexity of human experience, the "complex" human being, the "psychic" human being as universal given) and *on its basis we evaluate the form.*

Havelock does not free himself completely of an anthropological conception of writing. For him, there are human beings *plus* writing. There is no event of that sign which is writing and which thus is the human being in the specific and different modalities of such an event. He realizes that, for example, alphabetic writing determines the birth of "logical" (and then "psycho-logical") human beings, but he never thinks and pursues the radical meaning of such a discovery to its end.

Writing determines human beings, their experience, their consciousness and conscience [*coscienza*],[47] their speech. But then, what is "writing," so as to be able to enact all this? This is the real question.

40. *Alphabet and philosophy.*

> The introduction of the Greek letters into inscription somewhere around 700 BCE was to alter the character of human culture, placing a gulf between all alphabetic societies and their precursors. The Greeks did not just invent an alphabet; they invented literacy and the literate basis of modern thought.[48]

Havelock seems to realize well that the essential issue is not the alphabet in itself but rather "practice," its practice. It is [practice] which, after an ancient stage of expansion, declines during the middle ages, and explodes in the modern epoch thanks to the insertion of a new practice (of a further content of the form), which is the one made possible by the invention of the printing press.

Insofar as one considers it not as abstract theory but rather as practice (theoretical practice), philosophy too has had an uneven influence over times. Only through very long vicissitudes and tortuous paths could the potentialities contained in Plato's and Aristotle's thought manifest themselves little by little. Actually, they attain our present.

It is thus that the new writing system, as Havelock claims, has in the long run modified the human mental attitude, through a highly complex intertwining of practices. Writing in itself would not have sufficed. Within and thanks to its practice, the immense work of philosophy could occur as a "foundation" of rational humankind. This work has produced the encyclopedia of knowing (theology, science, and art) constantly redrawing its contours and contents.

41. *Alphabet and nihilism.* The essential character of the new writing system is its nature as "gimmick."[49] Unlike any other system, the alphabet loses all consistency and value in itself. The names of the Greek letters, which derive from Phoenician, lose track of their meaning; no one knows anymore that in saying "alpha" the ox is named, and so on. The form, too, takes up the greatest conventionality. As Kallir would put it, those which were drawings [*disegni*] become pure indifferent signs [*segni*]. As Havelock remarks, the alphabetic tool behaves

like an electric current in the brain, that, since childhood, has directly provoked the sounds of words with no other particularities accompanying or screening such function.[50]

Judging such a loss of meaning of the writing signs as a deficiency would be absurd, according to Havelock; alphabetization is possible only if letters annihilate themselves in themselves and assume only a value of transit and means, thereby favoring the fluency of a pure mnemonic procedure. [Judging it a deficiency] would be like charging glass with its transparency. Havelock is correct, but his correctness is entirely inscribed in the logic of efficiency of means and tool, so that he forgets or neglects the deep cultural consequences deriving from all this, although he indicates them in general.

With the advent of the alphabet and the transformation of the "human mental attitude," the entire world of the sacred and the cult progressively declines and disappears.[51] A utilitarian, economicist, instrumentalist vision of things emerges and imposes itself. Human being, the subject, its humanistic and transcendental (that is, first metaphysical and later scientific) anthropologism emerges. Disenchanted historicism and "logical" conventionalism of culture spread on the earth. The forming of habits becomes informing of souls, and truth becomes technical and performative. Values lose value, as Nietzsche claims; that is, they relativize themselves. The aura and face of nihilism, first tragic and titanic and then frail and resigned, appear. And so on. Truly, this is no small thing.

42. *Literature and law* [diritto]. As universal instrument, the alphabet allows for translatability into all languages. It posits itself in the service of communication among human beings and renders the immense continent of "literature" possible (starting with Roman literature, which imitated and transcribed Greek works); literature then provides the model for the education of Western human beings (the *bonae litterae*); today, this model is declining significantly, announcing a turn that disconcerts us and is hard to interpret.

Since the beginning, however, Greek alphabet also opens up another immense continent, which Havelock neglects: that of right [*diritto*], that is, the problem of *writing the laws*. Both in Greece and in Rome such a problem constituted a fundamental step in the struggle of democracy against aristocracy. As happened for truth, justice too changed its location. Earlier a word was true because of the authority of the one who uttered it (god, priest, sovereign) and later it became true, with Parmenides, because of the non-contradictory signs characterizing it (that is, because of its "logic" consequent to the logic of writing); analogously, justice, which once was just in function of its administrator (what the king does is *themis*, just, because the king does it; what is right descends from the king's act), later became such because it was fixed in writing.

With reference to what is written, anyone can be the judge of one's own cases, because anyone can read them, exemplified and provided for (what is not written is illicit, that is, not subjected to norms). This new justice (*dikaiosune*), which attributes to anyone one's own, determines first of all the figure of "everyone" (of the indifferent *equality* in front of the law), and then the distinction between what is "public" (the interest of everyone) and what is private (one's own cases). Justice is ultimately only that which can be written alphabetically (the "sentence"). In its greatest universality lies also its limitation, in its indifference its partiality, so that one could say: *summum jus, summa injuria* [the greatest right is the greatest injury].

43. *The content of the form as condition.* The alphabet is the instrument that makes the creation of "current prose" possible. This is not only a stylistic fact, but also an event that opens a new universe of meaning, a new truth and reality; as Hegel would say, the time of the "prose of the world" begins.

My question of content and form, and of the content of the form emerges again here. The *formal* revolution of the alphabet (which is determined by its "literal" content) directly affects the *content* of that which can be preserved. If one needs to preserve utterances on the basis of oral memory, then rhythm, meter, intonation, rhyme, and so on are the materially indispensable instruments to favor memorization. This is precisely what happens in the poetry of oral culture, which, like every culture, is concerned with handing down important utterances. This poetic technique conditions the content itself: speaking in meter allows saying certain things and not others, in a certain way and not in another. Even beforehand, it conditions thinking and what can be thought. That is, it makes one think in a certain way and not in another.

With prose, one has an instrument of universal recording that eliminates the need for memory insofar as it materializes it, translates it into a "thing" that is ideally always available to everyone, with no need for any specific effort. The relevance of such a revolution is immense, as we know. One should however consider carefully one issue (which Havelock tends to neglect): given its content (the "literal" materiality of the alphabet), *this* form too *conditions its content*. It puts limits on saying and thinking insofar as it posits them within *its own* limits, meanwhile rendering saying, thinking, conceiving in a different way impossible. The one who is trained to an immense reading and writing in prose can no longer think like Homer and Pindar; one's "logical" soul can no longer inhabit the truth and world of those souls. One can only remain within one's particularity, which is the partiality itself of one's own universal prose. This, however, is superstitiously mistaken for the "neutral" recording of reality in and for itself.

44. *Alphabet and knowledge.* In the revolution of prose, as Havelock correctly identifies, "a revolution was underway both psychological and epistemological."[52] The core of such a revolution concerns the birth of philosophy, historiography, and science, which are evident "products" of prosaic writing. This is precisely true both from a psychological and an epistemological perspective.

The form of philosophical, scientific, and historic "reason" is forged in prose and its content. The same is true for that "mundane" and "everyday" subject the psychology of which Nietzsche exemplarily describes in its arising event with reference to Euripides' tragedies (Socrates' *alter ego*) and novel.

In alphabetic writing, however, the statement "could lie around as an artifact"[53] that can be read any time one needs to. Moreover, on such an artifact one can carry out all those operations of verification, control, statistical measurement, data accumulation, comparison, and so on that are constitutive of the scientific practice itself.[54] It is because the readers place themselves *against* the artifact that they can acquire the "discursive separateness" rendering them cold, objective, disinterested, analytic, in a word, "rational." The age of knowledge begins.

45. *Gods and individuals.* Havelock remarks that alphabetic writing makes possible and favors the formation of original statements. "Previous transcriptions, because of the ambiguities of the script, discouraged attempts to record novel statements. . . . For what use were they likely to be, or what influence were they likely to have, if confined within the ephemeral range of casual vernacular conversations?"[55] Once again, he grasps something true, but then he considers it in an inadequate manner and upside down.

Only alphabetic writing produces, through its practice, "critical" subjects, that is, subjects that are separated from the tradition, at a distance from it, severed from its contents, aware of mastering language and using it as an expressive instrument for their own ideas, and lastly, conscious of having ideas, that is, theoretical and universally true visions denoting and explaining experience. The existence of *individuals* endowed with original ideas (this new figure of human being so well exemplified in Greek literature and art) is the product of complex practices; among them, the practice of alphabetic writing occupies an essential and leading place.

If we look at things from the other side, it is not that in oral culture individuals had no sufficient instruments to fix their original ideas, and therefore they abstained from this. Properly speaking, there were no individuals, instruments, or ideas. The practice of their tradition was made and occurred otherwise; the desire to be "original" was the last thing they could conceive and approve of. In that tradition the human being is not a subject in our sense, language is not an instrument, and truth is not an invention or a property of human saying. In that tradition, only the gods speak, think, and "produce." If we do not believe this and think that this is their own superstition, this is precisely the inevitable limit of our own thought and superstition.

46. *The cost of the alphabet.* Havelock often repeats that we must remember the price we paid for the edification of our culture on the basis of the Greek alphabet. We could in fact say that the content of the form of our writing directly determines the content of our culture and excludes all others. All this seems evident and it is opportune to emphasize it. Yet something is not convincing.

What, precisely, have we lost? If we reason in this manner, we think we are mourning some contents as such. As if we were to say: how good it was when there were gods. Yet, when there were gods, we were not there, in the same way as there was no grown-up in the world of childhood we fantasize we are mourning.

Contents are not there "in themselves": they are always functions of the form and of the content of the form. If we speak of contents in themselves and feel the actual and fascinating thrill of imagining them while we stroll along the narrow streets in Herculaneum or the fora in Pompei, this is precisely an effect of our historical culture and objectifying mentality. That is, [such contents] are the product of the content of the form within which we live our figure of being subjects and imagining abstract contents within which we fantasize to be able to live, and perhaps live better.

It is not a matter of "prices" we would have paid (*who* would be such payers?); it is a matter of the fact that we perceive the limits and problems of our culture and life and, to confront them, we have no other way than to think them, like adults, who want to understand their childhoods in order to clarify to themselves the nature of their problems, and in doing so they accept carrying to their limits the contradictions that characterize their bein Nietzsche intuits this too: to think of oneself one must dare think even against oneself, and finally against *thought*, exposing oneself to the circle thereby entailed.

47. *The price of clarifying.* Literacy has come out of a nonliterate world. Thus, according to Havelock, clarifying the oral cultures (which is ultimately his true topic) becomes a fundamental prerequisite in order to understand the written cultures.

This is an admirable proposal and actually educational. Here too, however, the circle emerges: one cannot avoid it and one does not do well if one hides this from oneself. How should we accomplish the "clarification"? Is it not evident that this can be done only on the basis of our written culture, its categories and truths? That is, that we study and reconstruct the "structures," the "essence" of oral culture as if we were to write it? Rather, precisely by writing ("documenting") it with our books and tape recorders? What will be, ultimately, the actual meaning of such artifacts?

Even beforehand: what else is the subject that wishes to "clarify" oral culture with analytic objectivity than the product of writing, a product that has arisen through difference from orality, and that now claims to observe, with its own eyes, the event of its own production? Is not this proposal the very effect of its own way of looking (and not something obvious and valid in itself), that is, of its "mind" and "mentality"? It is like Oedipus, who thought he was looking for someone else (the culprit) and was only denouncing himself.

48. *Mathematical writing and the invisible.* Without the practice of alphabetic writing, European science would have never been born. Without alphabet, and the mentality (the mind) deriving from it, scientific conceptuality, its terminology, and its definitions and classifications, would literally be unthinkable. Even beforehand, and at even a deeper level, the logical reasoning, the positing

of circumscribed problems, the orienting of research toward causes and effects considered in themselves, and finally the critical and unprejudiced questioning which are the essence and engine (the philosophical soul) of the scientific enterprise would not be thinkable.

As Havelock remarks, when the matter is counting, the alphabet is insufficient.[56] The principle itself ruling mathematical writing (that is, the *position* of figures, rather than the simple *succession* of letters) is different from the principle of alphabetic writing. Modern science is thus the product of two practices, both necessary and insufficient: alphabetic writing *and* mathematical writing. The Greeks knew nothing of the latter.

Both writings are a peculiar system of transformation of the invisible into the visible. One could say it better in this way: [a system] of *production* of the invisible and its transformation in an *ad hoc* visible. In the singularity of such process, in its common and differing gesture, are inscribed many enigmas and many possible answers to our problems and questions, which originated in the first invisible that Socrates invented when he spoke of the soul and that he then exhibited in his speeches and death. (The invisibility of Plato's ideas and the birth of science are simply the direct consequence thereof.) The content of such invisibility is the question that is here incessantly asked.

CHAPTER 3

Archewriting

49. *The where and the elsewhere.* When it comes to Havelock, the problem with which one is constantly confronted is essentially that he proceeds straightforwardly and non-problematically to trace a "history" of orality and writing. It is as if that which he has claimed and uncovered (the birth of the logical mind, historiography, philosophy, and science from the practice of the alphabet) were not something that renders vain, paradoxical, and absurd any "historical" or "historiographic" project and its alleged truth. To be able to speak and write about writing he would need, as it were, a second-level writing, an archewriting.

This is the starting point of Derrida's *Of Grammatology.*[1] Derrida is too philosophically sharp not to declare immediately, by the preface, that what he is going to do is "outside" all history of ideas, literature, or philosophy. The reason for this is obvious. These "readings" of reality are prejudiced by our writing, that is, by our "logic," which is, as it seems, the product of the *content* of a determined *graphic form.*

"Outside"—but outside where? What is the place of *Of Grammatology?* In what sense is its writing, or in what sense does its writing hint to, an archewriting? And how could this discourse be "true" without the claim of being "another philosophy of history for the education of humankind" (as Herder ironically used to say)?

50. *The three features of logocentrism.* What Derrida calls "logocentrism"[2] is nothing but our ethnocentrism implanted on a metaphysics of phonetic writing (that is, on a metaphysics that thinks it is posing the problem of being, when in truth it simply questions that which is concealed behind the copula "is" of judgment).[3] This ethno-logocentrism, the most powerful of all ethnocentrisms (and it remains to be asked *why* it is so), "is *today* in the process of imposing itself upon the world."[4]

One should forget for a moment about the *today* that one emphasizes in Derrida's text. One should instead consider the three features of the imposition

Derrida lists. The imposition implies universal phoneticization (exactly what Havelock, at the end of his discourses, wishes [to say] very frankly: to hell with the Chinese and their ideograms). Thou shalt not have any other "writing" *outside* of me. This universal phoneticization of writing "must dissimulate its own history as it is produced."[5] That is, first of all, it must assimilate any writing to its own concept of writing (and, to this goal, it must produce and in-form the mind with its practice). Then, from this perspective it can proceed to writing the "history of writing," definitely concealing behind it the contingent event, gesture, and laceration of meanings that have produced it.

This is nothing else, however, than the last mask of the "history of truth," and of the truth of truth, that characterizes the second feature: the ascription of the origin of truth in general to *logos*. In other words, there is truth, history of truth, and lastly history only because *logos* has imposed and fixed itself as "full speech" (full of meaning)[6] removing writing from its inside, and debasing it to being the outside of its inside. It is thus that "facts," previously *made accidental*, can be enlightened by the light of truth (that is, they can acquire meaning) and be arranged in a history, that is, according to sense[7] and an end.

The third feature is the concept of science or scientificity of science; that is, of *logic*, which is the very core of philosophy. It is philosophy (in its turn, the core of universal phoneticization, that for which it is absolutely true that philosophy *is* the essence of the West) that has always determined what "science" is. It is however also true, as Derrida claims, that the *practice* of science has never ceased to dispute the imperialism of *logos*, for example by increasingly resorting to non-alphabetic writing. One should in turn hold over the extent to which this is true, and the sense in which it is so.

51. *The logocentric epoch*. On the one hand, science presupposes the imperialism of the truth of *logos*, even only to posit itself as a "non-phonetic characteristic."[8] From this perspective, science is a "second intention symbolism." Yet,

> at the moment when the phoneticization of writing—the historical origin and structural possibility of philosophy as of science, the condition of the *episteme*—begins to lay hold on world culture, science, in its advancements, can no longer be satisfied with it.[9]

With these words, Derrida grasps very well the core of the issue. Yet what does "at the moment when" mean?

The challenge (of science) is ongoing (maybe it is "structural" to science; but then, what is the difference between science and philosophy in the unity of *episteme*?); only *now*, however, has it become evident as such. What does "now" mean?

Derrida of course asks himself this very question (although he cannot renounce the "now") since he immediately remarks that the traditional concepts of mutation, explication, accumulation, or revolution describe *styles of a historical movement* that (like the very concept of history) have meaning only within the logocentric epoch. And (one must add) this too is meaningful within the logocentric epoch, because mentioning "epochs" and thinking in terms of epochs (or even just disputing such a way of thinking) is already trespassing on the prohibition, insofar as, in its own way, such thinking reveals a historical conception. The *epoche* of being mentioned by Heidegger is, of course, no exception.

As Derrida acknowledges, this means that the project of grammatology as science of writing is paradoxical from the very beginning, and presumably impossible. It can be situated neither inside nor outside, neither in heaven nor on earth, neither above nor below, and it has no where.

52. *The* impasse *of grammatology.* Actually, the where of grammatology is an *impasse.* Its nature is as follows:

> the idea of science and the idea of writing—therefore also of the science of writing—is meaningful for us only in terms of an origin and within a world to which a certain concept of the sign (later I shall call it *the* concept of sign) and a certain concept of the relationships between speech and writing, have already been assigned.[10]

"Sign," "speech," and "writing" are objects of the practice of *logos,* of the logical mind, which, in turn, is a product of the practice of phonetic or alphabetic writing (we can summarize it thus, in a simpler, clearer, and more explicit manner). Turning these three objects into questions, as grammatology wishes, amounts to circumscribing an *impasse,* since they literally do not exist (thus conceived, that is, as concepts) if not within that which is to be questioned.

There is nothing to do then except to expose oneself to the *impasse,* in faithfulness to the "world of the future." Unfortunately, [the future] announces itself as a "danger" and "monstrosity," that is, in the form of a subversion of "constituted normality."[11] It is this future, as world to come, that makes relations and values of sign, word, and writing tremble. One should therefore let thinking "err" in view of this world of the future.

This sounds fine, yet one should not renounce one's suspicions. What is the future? What is the world to come? Is this not already the most common of "normalities"? And is it not normality, *this* specific normality, that which is the most monstrous, so that *not* to recognize this constitutes the danger itself?

What does resigning to "erring" mean, if not a reassertion of the logic of truth? Truth vanishes only if erring is welcomed as a radical being in error (this neither Heidegger nor Derrida seem to be willing to do) because error is truth itself, and is part and parcel with truth.[12] But then properly there is no longer error. According to what unit of measurement, in fact, could one say that one departs or approaches, gets lost or gets saved, moves forward ("enters") or backward? In real *impasse* there is no longer above or below, right or left, forward or backward, stillness or movement.

53. *What lies underneath it all.* A historico-metaphysical *epoch* must ultimately determine the totality of its problematic horizon as language. Thus Derrida, like Heidegger, claims that today all ways of thinking lead to language. The terms "language" and "writing" undergo a real inflation, which ranges from art to cybernetics, from semiotics to biology, from communication science to neuronal messages, and so on. Everything speaks, everything writes, everything transmits information, and so on.

This terminological inflation is the "symptom" of a shifting or drifting of sense. "Everything that for at least twenty centuries tended toward and finally succeeded in being gathered under the name of language is beginning to let itself be transferred to, or at least summarized under, the name of writing."[13] At the end of the "epoch," hierarchical relations are inverted: the outside challenges the inside, the servant challenges the master, writing challenges *logos*.

There remains the "everything that." What is this "everything?" What is this "that," which first pressed to be seen as language, lastly to move toward writing, but which (obviously) is neither language nor writing? Is it perhaps archewriting? Can we allow that it enters the scene under the guise of what is profound, of substance, of *hupokeimenon?*

54. *A "now" which is not now. Today* things are as follows: the old hierarchy, which considered writing as the signifier of the signified, as the fallen secondary level of the secondary level that *phone* already is when compared to the real and proper signified, *now* shows itself in its inversion. In truth, writing comprises language within itself. Ever since the beginning, the play of signifier affects the signified (so that *today* the play reverts to itself); the rule of signs and the very concept of signs vanish. *Today* the Western concept of language reveals itself as the disguise of a primary writing.

Primary? Derrida immediately corrects himself. It is not a chronological priority. It is a "more fundamental" writing than the writing that, "before this conversation, passed for the simple supplement to the spoken word."[14] It is a prior that is always there, beyond the temporal threshold, and that retains within its circle the entire language, which *now* appears as a guise or kind of writing.

If that is so, what *now* happens is the evidence of a timelessness [*senza tempo*] retaining within itself the time of logocentrism. This privilege is not an "error" one could have avoided; rather, it is something that "has necessarily dominated the history of the world during an entire epoch, and has even produced the idea of the world, the idea of world-origin, that arises from the difference between the worldly and the non-worldly, the outside and the inside, ideality and non-ideality, universal and non-universal, transcendental and the empirical" (the body and the soul).[15]

It is *now* that all this becomes manifest. Yet this *now* cannot have a temporal, chronological, or historical meaning because it confronts itself, or us, with a timelessness whose primeness, by being always already present, is beyond presence.

This is exactly what Derrida can neither say nor think. It is his insurmountable *impasse*. He continuously repeats: "today," "now," and he bites his tongue.

55. *The end of the book*. Logocentric metaphysics dominates for "nearly three millennia,"[16] confining writing to the role of a technique, a spokesperson for full and originary speech, for the speech that, in living presence to itself, has its first manifestation in the breath and in the echo of its self-conscious listening to its own speaking. This domination cannot erase, however, the originarity of *primary* writing. Fatally, this reemerges (as remorse, or as that which has been removed).

One would want to ask: what is the "privilege of hearing oneself speak,"[17] the rebounce of the voice without which (Derrida knows this very well)[18] no self-consciousness could ever arise? It is not a simple error. Is it maybe something structural, that is, epochal, historical, or what else? There is no answer. Because of the way he has set things up, Derrida cannot give an answer, either *now* or later.

One begins to understand meanwhile why *now* what has been removed comes back: because *now* one begins to discern the "death of the civilization of the book."[19] "This death of the book undoubtedly announces (and in a certain sense always has announced) nothing but a death of speech (of a so-called full speech) and a new mutation in the history of writing, in history as writing."[20] One should note the new, refined bite of the tongue: in history *as* writing. Indeed, Derrida has to say "mutation" (one has to talk, somehow). No correction can do it. Mutation can only refer to a history (or "archehistory"?) *of the* (of what?), which comprises within itself history *as*.

The death of the book can be seen in the facts that (according to Derrida, ever since the beginning dissenting) mathematical writing increasingly surmounts through scientific domination, and that the practices of information, cybernetics, taping, and so on confront us with strange handmade articles, in which even the voice becomes a "thing," for example as recorded voice. Therefore, at the moment when phonocentrism is about to impose its rule everywhere, it limits itself by itself, shows itself as something "finite," "epochal," "historical," "contingent." An anthropological variation. This would be the sign of an even deeper mutation. It might be so. But for now one can see no real "mutation" in what has been said so far. One can only see a further *externalization* of the logic of the alphabet, which from papyrus moved to medieval codices, from these to the press, from the press to computers, laser printers, Xerox machines, and so on.

Does all this make no difference? Of course it does; but one must know how to think the difference, and how to situate oneself in it in the proper way.

56. *Images and things*. The traditional notion of sign is founded on a "natural resemblance"[21] between soul and things. The affections of the soul (Aristotle already claims this) are "natural" images (common to all human beings: *sensus communis*) of being. This is the point. Derrida understands it well, and thus his entire meditation addresses that which is most important to think *today*, but

not that which is most essential in such importance: that is, the two notions of "resemblance" and "image." These remain substantially unthought, and therefore they are taken as obvious and non-problematic.[22]

There is another, equally essential issue on which Derrida does not meditate: that is, "things." The affections of the soul, he claims, constitute a universal language, a complete transparency. Between being and soul, things and affections, there would be a relation of translation or natural signification. Derrida knows well that it is Plato who institutes this relation and on its ground establishes the "signs of the soul." His attention is completely focused on the hierarchical institution of these signs, that is, on the "spiritualization" of meaning (what I call "strategy of the soul"). He challenges this "spiritualization" and the subsequent logocentrism. Yet, he has nothing to say about "things": they are there, silent and unarguable, outside (inside? outside–inside? inside–outside?) the soul.

The Platonic gesture, though, is double and complementary. On the one hand, it institutes images as place of the soul, spiritual signs. On the other, and as an immediate consequence, it institutes *tà onta*, beings, "things in themselves," which stand against images. Hence, the non-problematic "realism of the common sense" of all of us who live in the mode of the subject, that is *subjected* to Plato's gesture and invention of the world. We cannot call into question images without adding that *there are no* things.[23] By extending to them the notion of sign, Peirce has indeed proceeded further than Derrida and his ambiguous and partial contestation of the sign.

57. *Signifier and signified.* Tradition implants the first conventional symbolization, that of the voice (*phone*) or *logos*, on the natural resemblance between soul and things. The spoken language is thus the first sign or the first *signifier* of the spiritual *signified*. The written language (and any other deriving or depending graph) is a second-level convention, a signifier of a signifier, a further *means* of worldly expression and removal, something to which no constitutive meaning can ever belong.

Ever since then and forever after, Derrida claims, the notion of sign implies within itself the distinction between signifier and signified, according to Saussure's terminology (and despite the fact that he sees in it two faces of the same leaf). Thus, the notion of sign *depends* on a phonocentrism that is, at the same time, a logocentrism (institution of the "originary spirituality" of the signified): "absolute proximity of voice and being, of voice and the meaning of being, of voice and the ideality of meaning."[24]

Derrida proceeds at full tilt to the conquest of the enchanted castle of sign and to its complete devastation. The crux of his attack strategy is the "difference" *between* signifier and signified, a difference that can belong neither to the one nor to the other, a difference that is "older" than either and is already put to work in their distinction, which thus becomes unthinkable within the very distinction. Derrida, however, completely ignores the notion of sign and sign relation in Peirce. Such a notion does not rely at all on a dyadic difference, but rather on a triadic differential circle. The truth of the sign as well as the secret of the West and its "question" (and hence its, that is, our "problems") are inscribed within *this* relation. What happens, at this point, to Derrida's "difference"?

58. *The* aporia *of the heterogeneous.* Since to speak is to "hear oneself speak" (autophonics), which is the very same principle of self-consciousness and presence to oneself, then phonocentrism determines the meaning of being in general as presence.

From this privilege assigned to phonocentrism (to hearing oneself speak) there derive, according to Derrida, certain "subdeterminations" characterizing Western *episteme.* One could also say, thence derives Plato's ontology, which at bottom rules Western knowledge. Such subdeterminations can be listed as follows: presence of the thing to the look as *eidos*; presence as substance-essence (*ousia*); temporal presence as punctuality of the now (*stigma, nun*); presence of the *cogito* to itself; co-presence of the other in the *cogito* (intersubjectivity).

The picture is suggestive and altogether convincing. Yet Derrida has too much of an easy way out. He should explain and show to us how, from the centrality of *phone*, one moves to the privileging of the look as the site of "theoretical" truth. How do these heterogeneous gestures become joined in designing the place of truth? Moreover, how can "substance" come into the evanescent fluidity of the voice and its echo, which is "light as air and equally ephemeral" (Havelock)? Additionally, what does temporal instantaneousness have to do with the presence of the voice to itself? Are time and voice perhaps the same thing? Perhaps that the infant that hears its own screaming (obviously without knowing that it is *its own* and that it is a screaming) experiences something properly temporal? Or, to come to an understanding of temporality, does one need a peculiar tempography, that is, a writing whose principle is well distinct from *phone?*

Derrida does not commit himself to any analysis of gestural expressiveness or what I call "corporeal graphemata."[25] Perhaps he does not deem it necessary. Perhaps (and this is more likely) he deems it impossible because any analysis of "phenomena" (any "phenomenology") contains already in itself the privileging of *phone.* In this, he has his reasons.[26] Yet, his cautious non-exposure to the *aporia* and contradiction of gestural expressiveness has the strange result of consigning him to them without hope.

59. *Semiology and theology.* The epoch of *logos* debases writing to a fall into the exteriority of meaning, Derrida claims. This depends on the inaugural distinction between *signified,* which would be something mental, spiritual, ideal, and *signifier* (acoustic, graphic, "material"). This distinction molds the other distinction, fundamental for the entire history of metaphysics: that between sensible and intelligible (body and soul). Thus, the Western conception of the sign (and of any signification) is completely akin with what Heidegger calls onto-theo-logy. In other words, every presence (every sign) is always conceived on the model of the eternal self-presence of god as primary place of meaning and *logos.*

As Heidegger recalls exemplarily, the problem of "natural resemblance" between mental images and *"extra mentem"* things is solved as follows: *in mente Dei* (in his infinite intellect) are the ideas, that is, the signifieds, of all things he has created; through its illumination by the divine active intellect (*lumen naturale*), the finite intellect perceives the form of things that, through god, is common to both things and one's own intelligence.

Derrida is absolutely right to remark that, when linguists and semiologists (and then anthropologists, sociologists, and so on) accept the difference between signifier and signified, they already accept the metaphysical difference between sensible and intelligible, and the whole onto-theo-logy: precisely they, "who believe that the scientificity of their work begins where metaphysics ends."[27] Semiological science cannot maintain the difference between signifier and signified, that is, the very notion of sign, without referring to an absolute *logos*: "The sign and divinity have the same place and time of birth. The age of the sign is essentially theological. Perhaps it will never *end*. Its historical *closure* is, however, outlined."[28]

It does not look as though semiologists, or all scientists in the human sciences in general, are at this point minimally intentioned to listen to, and understand these statement. And yet one should be even more drastic and remark that the *whole* of science (for example, even neurology or astrophysics) is essentially "theological" (and God knows if, and when, [science] will begin to realize it). To make such a claim, the Derridian analysis of sign is necessary, but not sufficient. For example, such an analysis does not clarify the institution of the "panoramic look" without which no science can come to be.[29]

60. *What is the sign?* In Western tradition, the order of the signified is never contemporary to the order of the signifier, Derrida claims. The signified belongs to the domain of spiritual and pure ("formal") meaning that always comes "before." It cannot refer to any "material" (that is, meaningless) fact or to any "trace." Thus the signifier, which is mere reflection or inversion, is always a little below, a little detached, a little "after," even if by the time "of a breath" (as it happens with the voice). By unifying signifier and signified, the sign constitutes thus the unity of heterogeneity.

If this is true, then one cannot subject signs to the defining question of philosophy. One cannot ask "What is the sign?" One can only reject the very question that would like us to reply that the sign is that thing which. . . . The sign is not a thing, and its being cannot be a simple presence (a fact) that can be signified by the copula "is," since by signifying in this way the sign has already come into play. The sign, then, can signify everything except itself (and thus it is "the only ill-named thing that escapes the question of philosophy"), since one cannot apply a proper signifier to the pure signified, which is always presupposed. One cannot retrace (and thus define) the signified of the sign, since any trace (any predicate) refers to the signifying of the signified. It is non-objectifiable.

One could add that the very same thing occurs with the god of theology. One cannot define him. His absolute and infinite being does not sustain the determinations of finite thinking. Saying that God is good or powerful properly does not mean anything (except our foolishness, Spinoza would say). To seek a way out by adding that, of course, it is a matter of *absolute* goodness and *absolute* powerfulness does not solve anything. Extending a quality to infinity so as to make it congruous with God's infinite nature renders it vain as determined quality, as Hegel remarks (so that we have no idea of what infinite goodness would be. It is the absurd claim of defining something by something indefinite and indefinable). Alternatively, if it maintains a reference to the finite determination of goodness, then, no matter how great such goodness, it is nevertheless heterogeneous in relation to supreme or infinite goodness (the infinite and the absolute do not sustain delimitations or determinations).

The same is true for the sign. Whatever one says *about it*, it "is" not *the* sign. Rather, it already has the sign within itself. We are in it (as the human being is in God). This perhaps explains our frenzy to talk about it, but does not justify the claim to be able to do so "with good sense."[30] If philosophy is semio-logy, then it is theo-logy, and it is already inscribed in its failure.

61. *The paradox of deconstruction*. According to Derrida, Nietzsche is the first to realize that the ideal priority of the signified (on which the whole Western metaphysics is based) does not hold. There is always some reading, some "writing," some "text" that precedes the *logos* of truth and the pure signified. There are always more "originary" *operations*[31]—although this cannot properly be said because the thought of the origin and the originary is a typical consequence of the thinking of *logos*, of thought and "logical" truth.

Analogously, it is not the case of inverting the situation by assigning primacy or priority to the signifier. To mention a signifier is already to belong to the logic of the sign, so that to challenge such a logic by praising the function of the signifier is pure nonsense. Signifier means reflection, exteriorization, incorporation of the signified. It makes no sense to talk of a signifier more originary than the signified because this of which we are speaking, whatever it is, is certainly not a signifier. The "text" of which Nietzsche speaks, then, is neither a signified, nor a signifier, nor anything that can be thought or defined within the dualistic logic of the sign.

According to Derrida, what alone is left is then to *distrust*

> the very idea of the sign, the 'sign-of' which will always remain attached to what is here put in question. At the limit, therefore, that thought would destroy the entire conceptuality organized around the concept of the sign (signifier and signified, expression and content, and so on).[32]

Derrida has constantly devoted himself, with obstinate insight, to this "destruction."

The problem is that by distrusting so tenaciously, he in truth distrusts too little. By trusting distrust, he entrusts himself to the traditional notion of sign and its Saussurian version. All his deconstructing actually states and restates: you shall not have any other sign outside of me. Derrida walks his deconstructive path in relation to this notion of sign, that is, by accepting its "mentality" and measure. To operate the destruction of the sign, Derrida can only remain *within* the sign, and be precisely "attached to what is here put in question." Hence, the "destined" paradox of deconstruction and its language; hence, its programmatic "closure."

62. *Underground itineraries.* Derrida never comes into the open to breathe some fresh air. Having barricaded himself inside the Saussurian edifice of the sign, and being busy deconstructing it from the inside, he is like someone who, having arrived by train to the station, immediately enters the subway, and never exits it again. It is almost as if he had never exited the train station. Where could the town be? He reads signs and directions: piazza Castello, piazza della Repubblica, via dei Giardini, via Garibaldi. . . . Where are these "things"? There is no other trace of them except that of their gloomy signifiers. The town is a hallucination.

Derrida never relies on the "ingenuity" (in all senses) of experience. Having criticized, with solid arguments, the phenomenological appeal to the "things themselves" because it is invalidated by the assumption of Platonic *logos* and voice, he drops also the anti-intellectualistic sense of the appeal itself. He claims that Nietzsche's importance lies in his appeal to "operations." But then he neglects to look at his own operations, being content with introducing them as a reaction and a (somewhat desperate) countermove against the operations of metaphysics. It is as if metaphysical categories were the only possible way of thinking life (*where* and *when*, however, has this been decreed?), so that the demonstration of their incapability would amount to the demonstration of the unthinkability of life itself.

Derrida thus believes that the experience of signification, signified, and sign (an experience we continuously have) can be determined only within *his own* difference between signifier and signified, and that one cannot do anything with this difference except show that it is unthinkable and impossible. The very idea of returning to look at experience, at its way of signifying, at its and our operations—the very idea of coming out of the subway once and for all—probably would seem odd to Derrida, and this to say the least: where would he go, if there is no longer any land? Yet, maybe the land has not been "informed" of that which has occurred to it, and the town ignores its having completely turned into subway signs.

63. *The being that is not nothing.* Heidegger speaks of the "voice of being." This is a dangerous and ambiguous metaphor in which Derrida smells an odor of phonocentrism. Heidegger himself, however, corrects himself. It is an unarticulated, silent, mute, insonorous, a-phonic voice. The voice of the sources cannot be heard. The same ambiguity affects "being" (a word more metaphysical than

any other). The being of which Heidegger talks is never a signified (a being), and thus cannot have a signifier either. Thus it "escapes the movement of the sign,"[33] which is the greatest compliment Derrida can offer. If that is all that is at issue here, though, it seems to me to be rather modest.

What excites Derrida the most is the "history of being," which in Heidegger is the self-giving while at the same time self-withdrawing of being in a certain guise (a historical guise). What withdraws itself, however, has no guise. I would say that it is the rebound of its fall (of the fall of any guise) subsequent to its donation (its eventuation). Derrida emphasizes the issue from the perspective of the guise, and therefore what subtracts itself is *nothing*: "nothing escapes the movement of the signifier."[34] Being is dissolved into its historicity, with no residue. It does not have an ontological place for itself. Rather, it is an integral part of ontic historicity, and moreover, I would add, of the movement of the latter (its befalling and falling). This is exactly what Hegel claims, *pace* those who today think that the "decline" of Heideggerian being marks the advent of a new hermeneutic modernity or postmodernity of thinking, which would no longer be "dialectical," "authoritarian," and so on (Derrida is not among them, because if he were, I would not address him here).

The difference between being and history amounts to nothing, precisely as nothing is the difference between signified and signifier (it is neither a signified nor a signifier). The latter difference is, in fact, a model also for the former (as it is a model for the traditional difference between god and the world). The whole problem lies in that "it is nothing";[35] that is, the problem lies in taking for granted that there is nothing to be said about nothingness, and that it should be thought only starting with determined contents (which are something that is not equal to nothingness and that nothingness can thus not be, so that it is precisely nothing, that is, nothingness). But how could we have determined contents without nothingness? What if they were exactly the same as nothingness?[36]

64. *The provenance of grammar.* In Heidegger, the historical finitude of being manifests itself well in its being tied to language. Western metaphysics is the result of the domination of grammar (of Greek grammar), which privileges the copula "is." Yet, the claim that, when compared to the universality of the notion of *language* [*linguaggio*], a language [*lingua*] is *a* language [*lingua*] and as such it is a contingent historical fact—such a claim can be made and thought only as a result of the domination by Greek grammar and its consequent "logic." Havelock shows very clearly that the affirmation of copulative judgments and all linguistic grammatical analysis occurs in Greece only with the age of Plato (and not earlier). Our "hidden provenance" (as Heidegger says) is all here, or is to be thought here: it is not a Greek mystery of being.

On the train of Heidegger, Derrida asks what constitutes our history and what has produced transcendentality itself: that is, the form as condition of the content. Thus, Derrida too in his own way asks what the content of the form is. Here, he seems to find it in the "grammar of being," that is, generally, in writing and archewriting. For him, this is synonymous with that which is outside *logos* and has forever challenged it from its inside. Thus his "content" (of the form) remains vague and moreover ungraspable. That is, he does not ask at all on the basis of what content the form of *logos* and of logic has configured itself. Rather, he tries to speak of something "other" (without succeeding or being capable of succeeding).

To refer to grammar (of being) is, in turn, insufficient. One could ask: can there be a privileging of "is" without the analytical-ideal decomposition of the voice into the letters of the alphabet? How can one come to understand that "would be," "was," "has been," "will be" *are* all "forms of the verb to be"? Is the practice of the alphabet not the plot and the grid within which grammar and its science ("its discipline") can become visible? Even to ask how verbs come to be articulated as they are in Greek (which is not appropriate for all languages) is a complex question for which reference to either grammar or the alphabet would not be sufficient. There is an epic, lyric, and dramatic use of the oral form whose contents already push toward these forms. Then there is the additional push of the practice of writing. Derrida, however, takes "voice" and "writing" as general, that is, *vague* terms, and thus he unwillingly consigns himself to metaphysics.

65. *Truth on the cross.* Transcendentality denies itself to all objectification and thus to all writing, Derrida claims. Therefore being, which is not a being, cannot be portrayed. Yet, one does write "being" and this writing *is* portraying it. At a certain point Heidegger, shrewd, thought of barring it, of letting one read the word "being" only under a cross (and added that this is *not* a purely negative "sign"). Derrida comments:

> this deletion is the final writing of an epoch. Under its strokes the presence of a transcendental signified is effaced while still remaining legible. Is destroyed while making visible the very idea of the sign. In as much as it de-limits onto-theology, the metaphysics of presence and logocentrism, this last writing is also the first writing.[37]

This is fascinating, though one should take a step back and consider that not at all the very idea of the sign, but only the idea of the sign as transcription of the voice is destroyed. That is, what is destroyed is precisely the vicarious and degenerated sign that Derrida criticizes, and that he derives from the practice of alphabetic writing. Yet certainly the sign is different than this "idea." The sign is the place of fundamental *questions* such as reference, distance, rebound, event. These are questions that no cross can delete or silence. How does the experience of distance occur (that is, how does experience occur)? What does reference mean? The transcendental was an answer. Let us cross it out; there is no lack of reasons for doing it. One should not, however, indulge in fantasies. It is more urgent to expose oneself again to the questions.

Does this all-important question of the non-representability of being not refer ultimately to the fact that the voice, the vocal gesture cannot be written?

The voice articulates knowledges of the "writings" of the body and the world, the "know how to do," and "know how to say." It is preliminarily necessary, yet not sufficient in order to "know how to write" in the sense of alphabetic or current writing. As I have shown in *Il silenzio e la parola*, by determining the intersubjective rebound of the answer, the voice lets the "is," "being" resound as "public truth," as truth "for everybody," whose place, being ideally ubiquitous (everywhere and in every place), takes up the meaning of the ultrasensible and non-representable. It is on the ground of these experiences that metaphysics elaborates the notion of transcendental, translating a *practice*, an *ethos* of the eventuation of the world into the superstition of onto-logy.

66. *Of old and new snares*. In Heidegger, being is no longer a transcendental signified. By writing and crossing it out, it becomes "a determined signifying trace."[38] This signifying is not a signifying, however, since it does not belong to, and does not reflect a signified. That is, it becomes something *unheard-of*. How to let one hear that the "being" one utters is crossed out? And, similarly, how to let one hear the "a" in "*différance*"?

It is odd, but one really has the impression that Derrida falls into his own trap (and not without pleasure). He claims that, insofar as the sign is a differential relation between signifier and signified (S/s), then the trace that distinguishes them can only have the meaning of a signifier (precisely as trace, line of demarcation, boundary line, and so on). This signifier, however, is *not* a signifier. One cannot assign a signified to it. Thus, this signifier cannot be "said." Nevertheless, one has written it. And on this, one could truly say a lot.

Since Heidegger's being differs from the difference between signified and signifier, then being is the difference itself (in Heideggerian terms, the differing from presence and of presence). This *différance tout court*

> would be more 'originary' (than the relation being/a being), but one would no longer be able to call it 'origin' or 'ground', those notions belonging essentially to the history of onto-theology, to the system functioning as the effacing of difference.[39]

One should slow down. Who has ever said, and where has it been decreed, that "origin" and "ground" are to be reduced to *the way in which* metaphysics has thought of them? And that they do not contain within themselves additional possibilities of question and meaning? Should one perhaps erase such words from the common and philosophical vocabulary? (And, to tell the truth, one is not even able to do so, since one does nothing except utter and evoke them, limiting oneself, when one remembers, to crossing them out.) Let us not fall into our own trap.

67. *The trace*. What is the "trace"? One can imagine any opposition (difference), and the trace is already there. For example, let us imagine the opposition

between conventional and natural. What is conventional *is not* natural. How does one establish the "is not," however? What is natural is such with reference to what is conventional, and what is conventional is such with reference to what is natural. The *possibility* of posing the difference is the coming into play of the trace. Analogously, if one says that the voice is the natural aspect of speech, and writing is its conventional aspect (as Saussure and Havelock quietly do), the play of the trace has already occurred in such saying.

This means that the trace is the opposite of the metaphysics of presence; rather, it is its challenge, Derrida claims. There is never a full, "natural" presence, but always a "wholly other" that announces itself in its difference, something (let us cross it out immediately) that is neither identity, nor simplicity, nor resemblance, nor continuity, an irreducible absence, the absence of "another *as such*." The trace is thus "another origin of the world"[40] (which is neither origin nor originary because in every origin it is already there).

"The trace must be thought before the entity,"[41] because it is *through it* and *in it* that entities unfold themselves in their differences. Yet, to think of it is a major problem (it is *an issue*), since it conceals itself behind every entity. It is no more conventional than natural, no more physical than psychic, no more biological than cultural, and so on. It has always already "become" (be-fallen) without being in itself unmotivated (it could only be such in relation with what is non-unmotivated, what is "natural;" yet, it is the trace itself that traces these oppositions). Rather, it "is indefinitely its own becoming unmotivated,"[42] that is, it is the letting itself be seen in a present entity that is such only for another, or has its motivation in another (the natural in the conventional, and so on).

I would say that the trace is the de-cision, the "incision" of having always already decided, or of having been drawn into the drawing. It is the event of the sign.

68. *The play of the trace.* The sign plays in the trace, and the trace is a play of signs. The "thing itself" is a sign and plays in the sign (as Peirce understands). This play does not happen *in* the world. Rather, it is the very play *of* the world (as Nietzsche says with the image of the child). The "seriousness" of the transcendental consigns itself to the *paideia* of writing mentioned in Plato's *Phaedrus*. Thus, "writing is a game within language."[43] It inhabits its interior, ever since the beginning, with its being or rather becoming unmotivated.

This "immotivation of the trace ought to be understood as an operation and not as a state, as an active movement, a demotivation, and not as a given structure."[44] Where does Derrida truly take upon himself the burden of the extraordinary opening that is announced here in his words? Where, and how, has he taken thinking ("thinking the trace before the entity," as he claims) to the height of that operation, of that active movement he here evokes and invokes?

What, is one blind? Are deconstruction and the whole game of writing that derives from it not exactly the active demotivation here suggested? The active emptying out of metaphysics and its transcendental and naturalistic motivations?

No, it is the one who so claims who is blind. To practice the theoretic deconstruction of metaphysics is still to consign oneself to the practice of metaphysics, be it in its inversion. It is a remaining subjected *to* such a practice. It is not at all a self-exposure to the *question of practice* (of this, and of any other). It is not a matter of practicing deconstruction rather than construction or other things. The matter is that of the essential bond that ties together all threads of Western knowing and doing, that is, the bond of theory *and* practice (Aristotle's *Metaphysics* begins precisely from this assumption). It is a matter of the kind of knowing that is implicitly at work in every practice, and a matter of our active ability to practice its opening.

69. *The absent writing.* Originary, natural, "intact" language never existed. It has always been contaminated by writing. Here it is not a matter of alphabetic writing, but of the writing of the trace, and of its originary differing. Ever since its beginning, speaking is already in this difference, for example with respect to the expressive gestural manifestations of the body (as Merleau-Ponty would say), and then within its own interior, as spacing, pause, breath, inarticulate sound, and so on.

This writing, more originary than the common concept of writing, is "archewriting"; it is that for which language has always been writing. According to Derrida, the term suggests that such a notion communicates with the vulgar concept of writing, which has imposed itself because of the historical dissimulation of archewriting:

> desire for a speech displacing its other and its double and working to reduce its difference. . . . Repression of the most formidable difference. It threatened the desire for the living speech from the closest proximity, it breached the living speech from within.[45]

This archewriting will never become the object of a science. "It is the very thing which cannot let itself be reduced to the form of presence."[46] Yet in some perhaps indirect way Derrida has presented it. This is like putting something on stage, and then denying having done so. How not to remark that all this has the very same nature of the sign? Not only is the "thing itself" a sign, archewriting is as well. There is also a more disquieting perplexity: is naming something that cannot become an object and let itself be seen in the world as a worldly thing not the very strategy of the soul? Or is it not negative theology, which is the very institution of the metaphysical transcendental (which, not by chance, Derrida will try explicitly to exorcise, differentiating it from his own thinking)? That is full presence though, one might say. Yet what is the difference between absolute presence and absolute absence? In themselves, they give no sign of themselves, they do not refer to, and do not inscribe themselves in, any distance. How can one distinguish them? On the ground of what signs can one differentiate them?

70. *The scheme*. Archewriting is "at work" both in graphic and non-graphic substance and expression, Derrida maintains. It is "the pattern uniting form to all substance,"[47] to all graphic matter or other. And it is what makes possible signification, sign function. In our terms: as *scheme*, archewriting is the content of the form. What "scheme," though? And how would it be "at work"? Derrida's brilliant insight renders itself vain because its proceeding is "vague." Scheme, form, matter, language, and writing are taken as vague objects, that is, as by-products of the logical form, which thus is left to act undisturbed. It remains unnoticed that it is to this very form that one should ask the question of the scheme and its content.

As a condition of any linguistic system, archewriting cannot be part of the linguistic system, cannot be situated as an object within its field, Derrida maintains. This does not mean that archewriting has a real place *elsewhere*, that is, *another place* that can be assigned. It is not there and it is not non-there. As such, it is an (irresolvable) *problem*. Yet it is not a *question*; that is, it is not the opening of the look onto an "operating" that puts to work not *language* (which does not exist) but rather "the linguistic system" as determined object of a determined practice.

Grasping neither the meaning nor the place of the question, Derrida is led back to Husserl, that is, precisely there where he would prefer not to stand. Since it has been addressed vaguely, his question of the scheme is reduced to that which Husserl would have called "animation" of *hule*, of matter. Having crossed the soul out, Derrida writes "archewriting" in its place; yet this is only the nonsoul of the soul, that is, nothing more than a deletion. The "sign function" remains unexplained. The problem of the "signified" is such that it cannot even be posed correctly as a problem. This does not depend on its *nature* but on the difficulty of asking the question correctly.

71. *The archetrace*. The archewriting is nothing else than the trace, yet thought of as archetrace. The trace is not something empirical (an empirical mark) that, according to the classical pattern, would come from a full presence, that is, from a non-trace. It is rather an originary *trace* and in this sense an archetrace. It is the origin of the origin. Yet, "that concept destroys its name": "if all begins with the trace, there is no originary trace." Derrida also claims: "the origin was never constituted except reciprocally by a nonorigin."[48] The problem is that he does not realize what he is actually saying.

At the origin, there is not full presence, but deferment. Deferment hints to an origin that is not there (what it defers to is still a deferment). This *situation* is the archetrace. This means, Derrida claims, that grammatology can "no more break with a transcendental phenomenology than be reduced to it."[49] This is admirable honesty. Derrida needs the origin as non-trace so as to cross it out while letting it be visible (like Heidegger's being). It is *this* origin that grounds the discourse of the trace as non-origin; that is, it grounds the thinking of an archetrace and an archewriting. Had phenomenology (metaphysics) not talked of an origin, Derrida's discourse could not *take place*.

Grammatology is thus, necessarily, a *second-order thinking*. What a primary thinking, a thinking that is in practice and at work (including the *work* of the second-order thinking), is remains unthought. That one may *experience* the origin (if not, wherefrom this word?), and that the question is what one can truly experience, all this is left in silence.[50] Or better, it is left to primary thinking. Primary thinking would have exhausted all that one could say about the origin; all that remains for us to do is to show that such a saying is meaningless.

This means, however, that the only way of thinking the origin is that of saying it as full presence, completely self-present intention, soul and spirit. One can only think the unthinkability of such thinking. Derrida is very far from seeing that, when he claims that "the origin was never constituted except reciprocally by a nonorigin,"[51] precisely *then* does he attend a truly alternative primary thinking. That is, he attends the thought that the origin is the edge of the trace, of the very empirical trace, that is, of the concrete practice that is practiced in this saying and writing. He attends the thought that the origin is the *ethics of writing*. In my jargon: [the origin is] the symbolic edge as finite and determined putting-to-work of the sign.

72. *The possibility of the other side*. The trace is a "pure" imprint: "the *pure* movement which produces difference." The (pure) trace is the difference. "This difference is not more sensible than intelligible." It "permits the articulation of signs among themselves"[52] (in the phonic or graphic context). It "permits the articulation of speech and writing."[53]

What is interesting, here, is not the usual tactics of *nec . . . nec* (neither sensible, nor intelligible). This tactic is a total assumption of the strategy of the soul and of its characteristic oppositions; it is an unarmed dependency on its logic, so that to say *nec . . . nec* neither asserts nor shows anything more than to say *et . . . et*. What is interesting is the *articulation*. With this term, once again Derrida comes close to the question of the content of the form: "Difference is therefore the formation of form. But it is *on the other hand* the being-imprinted of the imprint."[54] The form is "on the other hand" an imprint, that is, a content. This "on the other hand" shows how Derrida is, at the same time, on the good path and in an *aporia* (because of the very fact that he does *not* realize to be on the path, on the way, and that there is a way). He takes the "on the other hand" as the equipossibility of an alternative whose terms ultimately erase each other. If one says that the trace is a form, immediately the latter disappears. *A* form can only be an imprint. If one says that it is an imprint, how can one understand it, in its unity of sense, in its identity, and in its meaning of "imprint," in any other way than from the perspective of the form? *Nec . . . nec*.

If one asks Derrida whether, perhaps, the content of the form is writing, he answers: yes and no, it is archewriting, something that has a relation with writing and the trace, but that meanwhile is neither writing nor trace. Thus, he never truly thinks the possibility of the "other side," which is exactly *this* being imprinted in writing (in *this* writing), the occurring of a practice whose determined content is the articulation of the form (of this determined form of writing, which is "purification" of *logos* in the alphabet and of the logical mind). It is not a matter of choosing between "pure" and "impure" (form and imprint), but rather of realizing what constitutes the putting-to-work of "purity."

73. *The articulation.* The differing of difference is an articulating.

> This articulation permits a graphic ("visual," or "tactile," "spatial") chain to be adapted, on occasion in a linear fashion, to a spoken ("phonic," "temporal") chain. It is from the primary possibility of this articulation that one must begin. Difference is articulation.[55]

Derrida is here inspired by Saussure and his theme of the *articulus.* It is not the sound in itself, the pure act of the vocal system that makes a language. Rather, it is its "articulation," that for which the phonic chain is divided into syllables, which aggregate in meaningful units or in distinct words. It is the imprint that *decides* and *excises* by codetermining distinct (articulated) signs and the relative distinct ideas (from the famous "amorphous masses" of sound and thought).[56] The problem is to understand how such a correspondence occurs, that is, how the one-to-one translation, *articulus* to *articulus*, of the signified into the signifier, and *vice versa*, happens.

Derrida limits himself to remarking that all this presupposes an *a priori*, articulating differing that no articulated sound or graph of writing, and thus no concept, can express. [It presupposes a] "pure" difference that underlies any "impure" work or "fact" (that is, those *facts of difference* that the "positive sciences of signification" such as linguistics can only describe *a posteriori*, after the fact).

In articulation, however, this is not at all the issue. The issue is that of showing at work the *scheme* that factually translates phonic expressions into the idealizing distinctions of the alphabet. It is only on the ground of *this* operative scheme that objects (objects of thought, meanings) such as *the* language, *the* writing, *the* difference can arise. To degrade difference behind the alphabetic scheme and to let it work unreally as its "presupposition"—this is a nonsense from which derive all the paradoxes Derrida comes across (*nec . . . nec*). Indeed, Derrida's archewriting is the radical questioning of the place from which Havelock advances his stance on writing. At the same time, though, and despite its extraordinary merits, it is a sterile and inconclusive questioning.

CHAPTER 4

The Content of the Form

74. *The genealogy of the logical mind*. The question I ask about logic does not concern the truth, whether understood as correctness of judgment or manifestation (*aletheia*) of a being and of being in a being. The question concerns the content of the form. Such content lets itself be seen in discourse, and especially in defining discourse. The form or the logical form of the house ("to function as shelter for humans, animals, and things") shows itself here, and not in alleged suprasensible intuitions or hyperouranian illuminations.

This means that in logic and its subsequent problems (as in metaphysics and its "theories" of being) the *form* of discourse is taken as *given*. One inquires into its structure (syntax), its denotative relation (semantics), and its use (pragmatics). Yet the content of this very form, its self-constitution in a practice, its becoming, all this is not researched, does not cause any problem, and does not arouse either wonder or question.

One proceeds as if discourse were "originary," that is, obvious; as if, in the way we inhabit it and know of it, it belonged to the domain of things that ever since the beginning have been certain, real, open to everyone and for everyone. If one has not reached it yet (like the child or the primitive), this is because of one's psychological or ontological insufficiency, or because of an incomplete development of one's being, which therefore remains foreign to the reality of true things that are valid ideally for everyone, and that one needs to access for an adequate knowledge of oneself and the world.

What we are truly missing is a genealogy of the logical mind, that is, of the path of the mind, of its self-purification, and even earlier of its self-constitution *within logos*.

75. *Pathic speech*. It is Creuzer who (if we do not consider Vico) first elaborates a genealogy of the mind through language, symbol, and sign. In this sense, he speaks of an "originary" speech that would be, at the same time, figurative and ostensive.

Figurative: speech is here one and the same with "bodily acts" (with gestures, as Merleau-Ponty claims, or with *praxis*, as Marx contends). It is an expression of emotions, not in a "psychological" sense (since there is no *psyche*, no psychic subject yet), rather as moved and motivated by disclosures of recognitions and world manifestations. This gestural speech offers "images of meaning." It does not distinguish between signs geared toward hearing (*symbola phonetika*) and signs geared toward sight (*symbola aphona*). It touches, recognizes, hears, sniffs, and so on in the concentration of only one revealed "meaning." Heideggerian *aletheia* undoubtedly has to do with this level of experience and encounter. Yet, insofar as it is thought of as truth of being and its manifestations in a being (with all the painstaking metaphysical and post-metaphysical work that follows), its opening immediately closes and is misunderstood, and any possibility of genealogy, even as question, disappears, vanishes, collapses.

Secondly, this speech is *ostensive*, that is, indicative (*mostrativa*) and endeictic; it shows by pointing (*endeixis*: the clothing, that which clothes providing indications). It is a designing and signing the world, as hieroglyphic writing or ideograms still show at much more advanced and articulated stages.

With respect to this originary (or, of the origins) speech, which still lurks behind the look of the child and its first drawings, so sharply studied by Merleau-Ponty,[1] one cannot speak of "mind" or "soul" in a Socratic-Platonic sense. Homer mentions speech, heart, breath; there is, however, no soul or mind in his vocabulary. The originary speech is "pathic," tied to the *pathos* of the experience of the world.

76. *The play of gestural acts.* If (from *our* perspective) we wanted to disentangle its intertwining, then to explain how pathic speech weaves together several meanings, blended in only one "image of meaning," would be rather complex. This would mean to render [pathic speech] the object of an objectifying consciousness that, while still presupposing the inhabitation of such a speech, nevertheless dispenses of it and situates itself outside of it.

In general, one should show, for example, how the gestural acts of sight and touch encounter the world and come in contact with it, thereby instituting an originary field of peculiar "objectifications." This gestural play of seeing and touching is simultaneously "graphic" and "autographic." It delineates world itineraries and horizons as corporeal vicinities and relations of background and foreground. At the same time, however, by posing the world at a distance, this play bounces back and constitutes the perceiving tactile and visual body, thus designing its place and boundaries, its subsistence and consistence.

On the other hand, more than an encounter with [or] a provenance from (the world), hearing and voice are an invasion by the outside and from the elsewhere that circumscribes the imperceptible point of the hearing Self (of the same Self, for example, that screams without properly "knowing" it, or knowing it only insofar as, having been rebounded outside, it "hears itself" scream as reflected in the voice). In sounds, the elsewhere speaks, and the voice is always the voice of the *Other*. It is only through the complex gestural acts of communication and discourse that the Other becomes "impropriated" (rendered proper to oneself, made one's own by the answer of the Other) [*impropriato*]. This is what one calls "learning how to speak." It is a voice that rebounds on itself and constitutes the speaking Self; which later will learn to speak silently to itself, only then becoming an "it-self," a member of self-conscious (conversing) intersubjectivity.

Hence the illusion of the abolishment of the Other and the outside that accompanies the interiorization of the voice (illusion that Derrida correctly denounces). By speaking directly to myself ("thinking"), I grasp myself in the self-conscious fullness of "meaning" originating from "me" with no need to pass to the *outside*. This is true as for the constituted result, but not for the constituting genealogy, which is promptly forgotten.

That the Other is already at work in the voice with its worldly "writing" does not imply at all [the Other's] ungraspability and unachievability as principle. Analogously, the illusions deriving from the experience of the silent voice do not erase the originary constitutive character, belonging to the voice, of self-conscious subjectivity. Oddly, even Derrida forgets to question these genealogical evidences, transforming the Other into a metaphysical *monstrum*.

77. *Discursive speech*. Intertwining and interacting in the most complex manners and determined situations, gestural acts and their practices constitute the horizon of the world and the irregular boundary of the body, with its openings and its rebounds. This is a center that is always invaded by the Other's "exteriority," and thus is always reactively capable of projecting itself onto the Other, making it the object of its *praxis*. That which is totally invaded by the world, made of world, coinciding with it, is also the peripheral return point lowering the world to its own object and image, with an "Empedoclean," rhythmically pendular movement.[2]

In pathic speech, *praxis* is on the foreground. To recognize, touch, point, mark out—all this is a showing the world and letting oneself be seen in it. Here sounds as emotional accompaniments, screams, and modulations are not yet preeminent. The originary objectification is essentially "practical." It is a *knowing how to do* that is not yet properly a *knowing how to say* if not as instantaneous, instinctive naming.

The germ of "general" universality and "logical" objectification (discourse or *logos*) lies in the *knowing how to say*, that is, in the voice. Coming from the outside for everyone, hearing and voice are experienced exactly as a "for everyone (that which is said *to* everyone and is said *of* everyone). That is, they are experienced as the communicative tool *par excellence* that creates "ideal" images of meaning, invisible places, unachievable "objects," intangible "things." All these are available to everyone and for everyone; they are schemes of reply as places of a *praxis* common to everyone.

Discursive, and not simply endeictic, speech flows and imposes itself through this venue. It is the unfolding of the current speech that constitutes *discourse*. It is the straight way (*diexodos*) that proceeds by succession (syllable after syllable, word after word, stone after stone) and accumulates *muthoi*, speeches, and tales according to direction, end, and goal. Beside taking place, now the images of meaning *make the way* projecting a beginning and an end. They think of *itineraries* and put them to work in *discourses*. The originary silence of the world is forever broken and forgotten, even if the voices get continuously and forever lost in the sidereal spaces.

78. *The three steps.* As one can see, a genealogy of the logical mind must acknowledge three major steps. First, there is a stage in which the so-called mind (that is, so called by *us*) is one and the same with a pathic-disclosive naming, whose character is eminently sensual and gestural (and only marginally "sonorous"). More than indicating, this mind marks out and draws, and at the most names, but does not narrate.

Second, there is a stage in which the mind coincides with a narrative speech that imagines and projects. This mind does not know how to either read or write. It is an "oral" and poetic mind, strongly tied to the "moving" *pathos* of the speech that discloses things and events of the world and expresses such events in tales, myths, and epic narrations. This is a mind whose discursive "coherence" (whose *methodos* insofar as *diexodos* or "meaningful" straight way) is all acted; that is, it is tied to that concreteness of gestural acts and *praxis* that makes the Russian farmer say that saw, hatchet, and log have only one *look*; that is, they aim at the active unity of the same practical goal.

Creuzer and later Cassirer identify two sub-stages of this second stage: first, the formation of myth as spoken and phantastic translation of "prehistory's" plastic symbols, images of meaning, and originary metaphors. Then comes the formation of heroic legends, that is, of a quasi-historical *epos* that progressively "humanizes" the originary word of the gods.

Finally, there is the third stage, in which the properly called mind emerges. The mind imposes itself in its three institutional (disciplinary) forms of history, philosophy, and science. Here, human beings begin to "reason with a pure mind," experience a new figure of truth (*the* truth), that is, another mode of their characteristic "being in error."

79. *Dialectical truth.* The "golden place" where the logical mind emerges and shows itself is the definition (defining practice). Plato entrusts it to the *dialectician* (the one who is an expert in discourses, who, like Socrates, practices *dialegesthai*). The dialectician (that is, the philosopher) takes no interest in the *body* of speech. He pays attention only to logical meaning; that is, to the syntactic and semantic function of the sign. In the *Sophist*, this is shaped after *koinonia*, after the communality of *genera*, according to being and nonbeing (identity and difference). This way, the "is" becomes explicitly copulative. It loses disclosive *aletheia* and acquires *orthotes*, correctness of enunciation, that is, *veritas* of judgment. Here one enters the domain of the "true relation" between word and thing. The ability to establish such a relation is what constitutes the logical mind (in general, "rationality," which from Aristotle to Descartes to Kant

becomes the mark of "humankind," that which characterizes the human being "as such").

The *Cratylus* takes care of "disembodying" speech. It recognizes the "pathic" ("mimetic") character of the originary speech through Socrates' "ironic" etymologies. But then it explicitly puts them aside. The philosopher must pay attention to the definition of the essence (*ousia*); that is, to logical purity, accessible as such only to a logical, pathically purified soul.

The *Cratylus* thus represents an essential step from the archaic to the modern use of *logos*. The move censors sound, imitation, plasticity of speech and removes them as "inessential" (coherently, since they do not concern the logical essence, which, nevertheless, asserts and shows itself *because of/through* this removal). For the same reason, Plato censors poetry—it is pathic ("oral," Havelock says) and its *diexodos* is not logical. Its discourse obeys the rules of rhythm, metrics, and melody (which are ostensive elements) and not the demonstrative rules. Poetry and philosophy are antipodal in their *methodos*.

Resurrecting *aletheia* in place of *veritas* (with the connected ambiguity of the question of being) is not sufficient to explain how all this happens. The leap can be covered only by asking the question of the (logical) form and the content of the form.

80. *The formalization of discourse*. The leap is something that happens to and in *logos*. It concerns the constitution of the defining *logos*. This process unfolds from Parmenides to Plato. Its evident character is the *formalization* of *logos*. Attention goes to the form of discourse abstracted from the content (which is assumed only as exemplary, for example, "Theaetetus flies" and so on). Not *that* something is said (its event), but *how* and *what* is said (its meaning) matters.

The *how* finds its main formalization in the "is" and "is not," that is, in the affirmative and negative character of the copula, an alternative that Parmenides already poses as insurmountable—*tertium non datur*. This formalization has its archaic precedent in the image of the parting of the ways, exemplified in turn as the tree of life and then "stylized" in the letter Y. The *odos* that decides of "sense"[3] becomes the *methodos* of the truth of thinking, according to the alternative "true/false" and the connected formal plays of being and nonbeing (if "a is b" is true, then "a is not b" is false; but if "a is b" is false, then "a is not b" is true, and so on).

Naturally, Parmenides does not yet think in terms of "affirmative propositions" and "negative propositions." That is, he does not yet think in terms of logical relations like the Sophists and Plato (who is properly the creator of the "logical relation"). Parmenides stands halfway between an *odos* disclosive of being (being and disclosure of being, *noein*, are the same) and an *odos* that is being formalized and raised to *methodos* through contradiction (nonbeing cannot be said or thought). Or at least so does Parmenides appear to us.[4]

81. *Discourses in line*. In Parmenides, the new form assumed by discourse is contradiction (you cannot say "that it is" and "that it is not" at the same time). The

content of this form is still the archaic image of the parting of the ways, of the *odos* of wisdom, which is transferred and transfigured from the context of the deception (*apate*) practiced by the gods to mortals' detriment to the context of logical and mental error (human beings with two heads saying both yes and no). This first step, this Eleatic opening, which Zenonian dialectics perfect and make explicit (if you take the wrong path of the parting of the ways, you find yourself in *aporia*, with no more path), achieves its complete expression in the *linearization* or *schematization* of discourses.

This is the main task of sophistic antilogy, which, according to the tradition, was started by Protagoras. It consists in building alternatives to discourses, in making them go in opposite directions. One says that Theaetetus is walking. I show that he is flying, and to anything one says, I will show the possibility of claiming the opposite by following a line or a scheme of considerations that leads in an opposite, contrary, and, even more, contradictory direction.

This discursive form (whose content is the method of contradictory linearization) still applies to traditional "pathic" contents. Hence comes the sense of an unheard of, de-sacralizing criticism of tradition. For example, the sophist approaches anti-logically the questions, "Is Helen truly guilty?" or "Should one love the one who loves us, or the one who does not love us?" Against common sense, and for the joy of the fools, he undauntedly demonstrates not only Helen's innocence, but moreover that the second alternative, advising to love the one who does not love us, is more convenient. He can do so, however, only because his provocative schematization of discourse is still logically imperfect. Beside the reasons for scandal and social revolution, his success depends on the fact that his interlocutors are completely ignorant, as much as and more than himself, of a complete schematization of logic.

82. *True sound.* In order to linearize discourses completely, first of all one has to render the terms homogeneous, first by instituting them as "terms," that is, as arrival points of a structural analytics of the "parts of discourse."[5] This is exemplarily delineated in the *Theaetetus* where what a noun is, what a verb is, and so on gets established.

To render terms homogeneous means to assimilate them to being (making all of them identical or akin to being) even when they remain different among themselves. This is precisely Plato's "Eleatic" operation. Its tool, its practice or realization is the definition. It must say the being or essence of the thing; that is, what a being is "in itself," for example, the horse "in itself," which means the "mental" horse. This mental thing is the object of a "suprasensible vision" (it is not the sensible vision of this horse) to which the *true sound* corresponds. This is not the pathically resounding speech but rather the silent discourse of the soul. What is sensible works only as an *exemplum* on which to practice dialectics.

The silent discourse of the soul is simply the translation of empirical names into a linearized scheme of relations where one line proceeds by inclusions (living beings → animals → mammals → quadrupeds → horses). From this line, at every inverted Y crossing, other lines depart by exclusion (vegetables, fish, bipeds, oxen, and so on). What one "sees" is in the end nothing properly sensible. It is not the image or the iconic figure of a horse (which we could still recognize in a typical ancient Chinese ideogram). Not because of this, however, is the vision something hyperouranian or mysterious. Simply, one can see the unfolded (logical) defining scheme where the terms occupy a geometrical place of inclusion-exclusion (*tauton-heteron*). That is, they stand in spatial relations, in topographic itineraries that enable the logical tours of discourse. This is the lit and safe labyrinth of true and false judgments (and connections), which have thus been fixed forever after.

Deriving an important corollary from all this is possible. When Plato says that the idea of the Good, which enlightens the eidetic *huperouranion*, has no being or *ousia*, he merely ascertains that it cannot be defined because of the simple fact that it cannot be transcribed, that is, spatially situated in the relational linearization of the defining path. In fact, it is the end [*la fine*] of the path or the goal [*il fine*] of the logical *diexodos*. One should meditate a lot on this.

83. *The change of voice*. The process of linearization and transcription of the voice occurs in the practice of alphabetic writing as well as in the practice of logical definition. To find one's way in this process is a very arduous problem that requires the most complex genealogy mainly because the voice is the sign par excellence. Yet escaping it is not possible. Ignoring any question thereabout, Derrida ends up confusing *the* voices and *the* writings. He speaks about *the voice* while remaining general, and, moreover, while attending a logical superstition.

The voice that names while disclosing pathically and the voice that designates the universal object available to everyone are not the same (they are not the same practice of speech). Pathic voice accompanies the originary, objectifying gestural acts (sight, touch, and so on) that disclose world and body. This way, it emphasizes *distance*. That is, it gives a disclosive sound to the surprise for the world that touches me, making me shiver, or that invades the visual horizon, or the acoustic field, and so on. Pathic voice plays in the rebounds of world and body, which distance by nearing and *vice versa*, in that practical attendance to the events of the world that is experience. Universalizing voice (linguistic-communicative voice) works completely otherwise. It names and evokes not distance but rather *absence*. It makes itself a sign of the *invisible* (and inaudible, untouchable, and so on), since it is a sign of a being that is valid for anyone, of the universal being or concept. Universalizing voice says "horse." This is something that is not encountered in experience unless as everybody's organized answer, in which that which the definition will make explicit is implicit. This is nothing else than the scheme of general and vague recognition. This voice renders a being "mental."

The potentialities of the voice are extraordinary. It promotes the articulation of experience, since its gesture is highly "general," non-"specific"; that is, it is available to signify all other gestures and their related beings. One cannot see that which properly belongs to touch; one cannot hear that which properly belongs to taste. The voice, however, has no specific objects. It does not encounter the world. It does not disclose it. It does not come from the world. Rather, it issues from the Self rebounded on itself. The voice makes that which is unheard of occur, creating a class of beings *ex novo*. There is no specific rose where the voice names [it]; therefore, all roses can generally take that place, in virtue of their supreme interexchangeability. Because of this, because of its iconic poverty, the voice is the sign par excellence.

84. *Evocation and the body of the voice.* In a originary and complex unitary (synesthetic) gestural expressiveness, voice, sight, touch, and so on *design* things plastically (iconically) at a level that is simultaneously ideo-grammatical. Having arisen in the pathic encounter with the world, the voice develops within itself a supreme *evocative* (that is, in its way, mimetic) function because of its constitutive generality. In its free naming and in narration, the voice evokes sight and touch. The move thus occurs from plastic symbols, from the immediately disclosive images of meaning, to *muthoi*, to the properly called words, and later to narrations, as Creuzer and Havelock explain in different and complementary ways. For this reason, archaic epic moves and educates to action.

In such evocative function, the voice is still balanced between the pathic (poietic and poetic) element of its own sound, which is born in and with action, and the universalizing element of its evocative naming. With the progressive loss of the body of words, the voice "spiritualizes" itself and aims at the simple function of "meaning," that is, of logical *logos*. The climax of this process becomes manifest in the "silent voice" (*aneu phone*), that is, in the pure vocal gesture, translated into a conceptual definition. This happens through the linearization of writing, of alphabetic transcription, which is first spelled out and then itself transposed (exceeded) in that virtuosity that the practice of silent reading is. This is what properly constitutes the "soul."

In this practice, sight and touch are also subordinated to linearized transcription. In their practices and their *designs* (as in the pictograms in the caves, and so on) they do not transcribe the distance of the world. Rather, in their mere *signs* they transcribe the absence that the voice has named, that is, the artificial, non-iconic body of the universal voice, that is, of the soul.

85. *Body and soul of writing.* One can observe the process of linearization and transcription of the voice at work in that complex practice of writing culminating in the alphabet. About this, Alfred Kallir's studies are particularly suggestive.[6] From originary drawing (which is already a complex transcriptive practice that goes from three to two dimensions and uses graphic conventions containing very little that is really iconic), one witnesses a progressive schematization of the figure. The originary drawing thus becomes, little by little, a conventional, completely unrecognizable sign.

The originary "D" of *domus* ("house") is, for example, at first a realistic representation of a domed hut, with the rectilinear side as a basis ∩. Later, the figure loses all particulars and by turning inserts itself into the ideal line of writing. The drawing [*disegno*] loses its *soma*, the iconic body of the image, and becomes pure sign [*segno*]. The originary unity (*symballic* [*simballico*], as Kallir says) of sound, vision, and image of meaning, this disclosive "concurrence" that Creuzer too mentions, is completely resolved. The purely visible sign becomes silent ("con-sonant"), and refers only to a letter of the alphabet.

This entire process of graphic practices implies a transfer of the meaning of eye and touch. In drawings, they concur *constitutively* to the meaning of the figure. The eye leads the hand (which, even earlier, had led the eye by inspecting the world), which transfers into plastic-iconic lines that which has been lived experientially. However, in the process through which the drawing acquires meaning and value of linguistic sign, of representative for the phonic sign, for the mere sound of the word, eye and touch lose their primitive, constitutive character and acquire a purely instrumental one. They function as *vehicles* of speech or, more precisely, of pure voice.

Correlatively, the voice is de-somatized in turn. It becomes a-pathic (as it never is in the speech of non-alphabetized or scarcely alphabetized peoples). It goes from "poetry" to "prose," so to speak, and drops its "musical" inflections. Precisely through sign representations and alphabetic transcriptions, the exquisitely universal and idealizing potentiality of the voice is enucleated and exalted. The reduction of graphic signs to a line of pure atomic succession determines their definition in terms of pure and abstract *elements* (vowels and consonants). The practice of the alphabet defines the voice analytically. The alphabet is thus an active principle of classification that organizes an ideal totality (language) in its differential elements as constitutive and recurring parts identical with the totality. From this moment, our current experience of the voice and *logos* changes too and acquires a new, "logical" meaning.

86. *Epic universality.* One must carefully consider how the universalizing character implicit in gestures and the practice of the voice gets translated. First, it expands in a community of oral practices. The men belonging to this community sing and tell their myths and legends of gods and heroes by representing them in "poetic" and "epic" enterprises. This strongly pathic speech evokes and commemorates the communal *ethos* of doing and saying, loving and suffering, for everyone; that is, for all *participants* to that community. In this manner, such a speech asserts its universalizing ability within the particularity of practices that accompany and constitute it and which it itself co-constitutes by raising them to the universality of evocative transmission, that is, of the "tradition."

Understanding firmly that the voice speaking in oral epos *is not the same voice* that gives itself to be seen in alphabetic writing is very important. Derrida does not literally *see* the issue, as if it were obvious and not in need of meditation and questioning. When he speaks about the voice, Derrida refers only to one linguistic signifier, which is the product of the voice of writing, or the reflection of its instituting practice. Thus, he remains prisoner precisely of the voice he wishes to deconstruct.

There are many voices and many signifiers that properly are neither "voices" nor "signifiers" (which are objects produced by the logical voice). There are also many practices, with *their* complexities and *their* objects. Thus, behind the linguistic signifier there is not the trace or the archetrace, as Derrida naively believes and would like us to believe. [Behind it] there is an unlimited antiquity of practices, an immense genealogical, phenomenological, phenomenographic adventure, to which Derrida remains blind. Rather than Rousseau, it would have been better for him to read Vico.

87. *Logical universality*. When the universalizing potentiality of the voice translates itself into the practice of alphabetic writing, what the latter makes visible is not the event-things, the character-places of the epic story. Rather, it is a matter of the "literal" objectivity of meanings. Free from the pathic-expressive context of "historial" [*istoriale*] evocation (from the context of the story plastically illustrated in the resounding voice), the word is *rendered* in its purified and ideal elements, that is, in its *letters*. Thus, one has a universality abstract from all contexts.

The "ideal reader" is thus progressively formed, the one for whom reading is no longer to look at and contemplate the written body (as in the hieroglyph of the origins, and so on); rather, [reading] is to direct oneself to the logical meaning through [the written body] and its conventional transparency. The "literal" or "literary" subject, of which Havelock speaks, is born. All this occurs in the simultaneity of the intertwining of practices, since one should not think that *first* is pure voice, which *then* subjects writing to itself and thus renders it alphabetic: or exactly the opposite. In a certain way, the "mind" that has *devised the idea* of the alphabet is the same mind that will devise the idea of logical definition. This mind does not preexist, however. It determines itself within its own alphabetic and defining practices. These, in turn, modify and specialize themselves out of the results, the "objects" that they themselves promote. This could be clarified further only by thematizing the question of *practice*, its nature, and its complex problems.

It is important to notice that by instituting logical universality, *this* voice has every reason to pose itself as archontic, master, of *its own* writing. Challenging this right without understanding how it has constituted and affirmed itself generates only equivocations and confusions. It is not a matter of going back from the "domesticated" writing of letters to an imaginary archewriting. The matter is that of retracing the path that, from plastic writing, has led to linear writing thus transforming the evocative voice into alphabetic voice. What must be objected to "pure" voice is not its primacy over alphabetic writing. Rather, it is the fact that it remains blind to the work of writing as transcription: that is, to the effectiveness of the content of the form (of *its* form) of which it is itself an effect. Not writing, or archewriting, but rather a succession of practices that "pure theory" does not know how to think is what precedes the voice. Derrida's deconstructionism leaves all this in the shade: that is, it leaves everything as it was.

88. *Rhythm and time.* Alphabetic writing does not transcribe and reproduce, *sic et simpliciter,* the "time" of spoken voice, its phonic or signifying succession, as Saussure erroneously thinks.[7] The issue is much more complex and different.

First of all, one should notice that the so-called temporality of epic speech is not simply linear. It is ruled by *rhythm,* and precisely thereby the *pathos* of action is reproduced. Every action, in fact, does not unfold through discrete, homogeneous, and empty units (it looks like this only to the photograms of an *a posteriori* analysis; that is, to the light of a further, decomposing practice). The action has rather a *sense* [*senso*],[8] which opens and closes rhythmically and is ruled by end and project. Thus, for example, one does not walk abstractly on the homogeneous line of time (thus walks a robot); rather, one walks according to a phasic rhythm whose direction and intention is determined, e-motioned (motioned by a participatory *pathos*) every time. In its turn, epic speech is a continuous self-interpreting that comes and refers on the basis of blocks of emotions proceeding episodically in a circle, backward and forward, and not in a unidirectional series. This "ethical" time (or time of *ethos*) could be defined as plastic, or symballic [*simballico*] time.

Conversely, alphabetic writing inscribes its ideal (apathic) elements, which are a depository of objective and universal signifieds (not of senses), on a homogeneous line. Precisely this linear transcription implies a specific *temporalization.* Such is the content of that form of time of which we generally have the "idea," and which we quietly exchange for a "real thing," a fact, or an obvious component of the world as it is in itself.

89. *The constructed reality.* The ideal line of writing is made of homogeneous points whose only relation is abstract succession. This relation is more spatial than temporal, and in any event static, crystallized, rather than hermeneutic. As a matter of fact, nothing happens to the point simply because of its location before or after another point. It is only a crossing, a vehicle of the transition that enables the inscription.

The punctual character of the line, which is common to both alphabetic writing and definition, could already be indicated as *the content of the logical form.* Thus, the spatialized linear temporality would be the essential *trait* of logical *logos.* I mean that, by temporalizing itself analytically (a-rhythmo-geometrically) in the line—in the scriptural and defining line—*logos* becomes indeed "logical." It acquires the objective, "formal" universality that belongs to impersonal, logical truth.

Truth understood as correspondence between judgment and thing would therefore have the content of a "construction" as its foundation. This is the construction of an (a-rhythmo-geometric) *realitas geometrica* [geometric reality] that is made of abstractly homogeneous, linearly disposed points. It is a writing of reality that is valid universally and objectively.

The truth of judgment is only the last stage of this construction. The linearized meaning of *logos* "adapts itself" to the "logical" ("in itself") character of things. Indeed, these are things that have been previously *reduced* within the linear scheme of the definition; that is, they have been reduced to its punctual and geometric elements. Judgment has forgotten all this; to say it better, it has never known it. It rules and legislates *over* this onto-logical construction that is the invisible foundation of its logical edifice.

For this reason, the Heideggerian opposition (*aletheia contra veritas*) is not efficacious, and does not explain anything. It does not show the hidden foundations; thus, nobody is convinced. Imperturbable, logic continues to rule sovereign, certain of its good right. It leaves *aletheia* for the nostalgic and the sentimental. To dislodge *veritas*, one must uncover its underground practice.

90. *Tautological reality.* The essence of logic is time, that is, linear time. This is the same as saying that the essence of logic is the line. Its elements are 1+1+1+n. It is the unidirectional flowing of an atomic unit ("number of movement"). From here, one can understand the ultimate reason of the principle that has always ruled logic (principle of non-contradiction)—one cannot affirm and deny the same thing, one cannot say "A" and "non-A" at the same *time* and in the same *sense*. This universal rule of "logical" *logos* is a formal principle whose *content* is the chrono-logical linearity of alphabetic writing.

Confronted with such a statement, common sense is flabbergasted. Indeed, it does not think of the alphabet. It thinks that the principle of non-contradiction is the very principle of "reality." That is, it thinks what metaphysics has thought, informing of itself the common mentality of "logical" Western human beings. And here one must be very careful and realize clearly the core of the issue. What metaphysics and common sense think is *absolutely* true. That is to say, it is *tautologically* true. As a matter of fact, the notion of "reality" ("reality in itself") is the logical construct that is in its turn grounded on "public" a-rhythmo-geometric temporality; that is, on that which is true universally for all human beings of pure voice or, which is the same, of alphabetic transcription. By "reality" one means that which can be inscribed *univocally* in the linear, a-rhythmo-geometric grid—that is, the public and incontrovertible *facts* to which science refers ("it is either A, or non-A; *tertium non datur*").

Experience is hostile and rebellious to the will to transcribe everything into this grid. But metaphysics, and the henceforth deriving common sense, have an answer ready, which is complementary to the overall strategy of the soul. It is the psycho-logical answer for which public facts are coupled with "private" and "subjective" facts—dreams, fantasies, suggestions, and similar. These are a "minor" reality, or an "imaginative reflection" of true reality, which later psychology (fully developed into a "science") explains in the same way in which public facts are explained—that is, with the same transcription that makes public truth occur, for example, by transcribing dreams into "cerebral" terms ("performative" manner of accomplishing Nietzsche's wish of "a more true dreaming").

The matter gets complicated unpleasantly when the incontrovertible univocity of public facts finds itself contradicted, unexpectedly and inexplicably, in the experiments of quantum physics. As a matter of fact, today this is a major *problem* for science. Maybe, in the long run, it will encourage [science] to revise the question.

91. *Chronological univocity.* The issue is as follows: insofar as the line creates a succession of exactly identical and empty points, then the value of the transcribed *logos* assumes that of its "position" as its only character. This being before or after the foundation is what Wittgenstein calls "propositional space." Divesting itself of all pathic-sensual content, logical meaning has no other content except its being positioned dia-grammatically through a linear alternative of "is" and "is not."

For example, one writes "Socrates is Athenian." Here, ideally the line doubles in the Y alternatives:

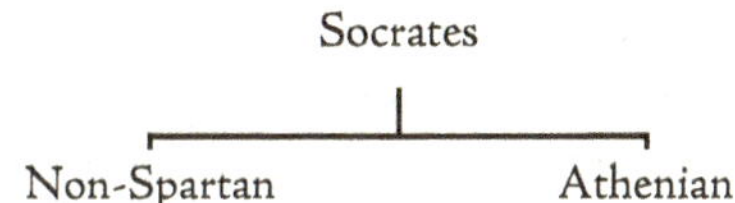

This overall place ("Athenian+Spartan") doubles in turn: "Greek," "non-Persian." This overall place doubles once again: "human," "non-animal." "Human-animal" doubles in the alternative "organic being," "inorganic being," and so on. At every point of the line something "is" (is transcribed) in topological relation with what "is not" transcribed (exactly because the former *is* transcribed). The point of the line of writing illuminates a point of the overall topology of being and nonbeing. The moment it illuminates the former (by transcribing it onto the line of writing), it does not illuminate its opposite.

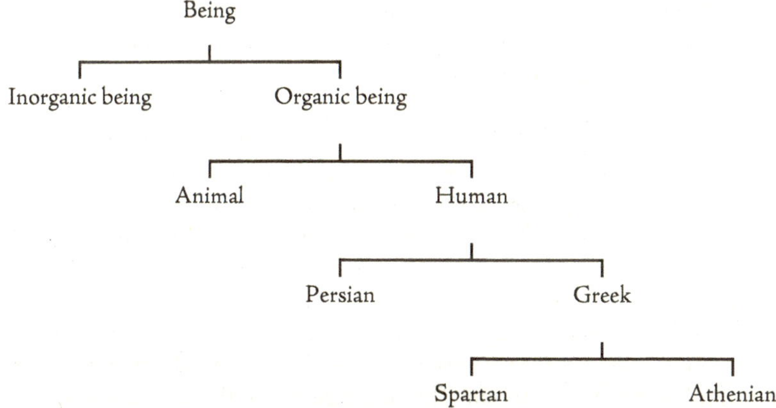

At the same *time* when one writes "Athenian," one cannot *mean* "Spartan," and not even "Persian," "animal," and so on, insofar as they are contrary to the topological line of simultaneity (*tauton*) "human," "Greek," "Athenian." The "logical" sense of an assertion is its ability to be situated at a defined point on the graphic line, a point that is defined by its chrono-logical univocity. *Now* one says (one has written) that X is Athenian, or that X is a beggar. To make somebody believe that X is, at the same time, the goddess Athena, is a matter for the poets. That is, a poetic saying.

92. *The proper sense*. One must understand "sense" analogously (at the same time and in the same sense). It refers to the homogeneity of successive units (1+1+1 . . .). The points of the assertive line must be homogeneous. They concern the "is" and "is not." That is, they are concretions or graphic representations of being. It must be *the same being*, though. What is written must be placeable on the same side of the topo-graphic scheme.

If one asserts that X is a beggar, one cannot mean that X is a god or a goddess. One can mean that it is a man dressed up as a beggar, since "beggar" and "man" attend the same topological line. Conversely, "god" and "goddess" belong to a different sense of being, to a different region or topology of beings. Thus, one can "logically" expect to encounter a beggar (or, more generally, a human being) and to have a conversation with him. But one cannot nourish the same expectation with respect to gods and goddesses simply based on the fact that Homer tells of divinities dressed up as beggars. This expectation is not "logical," and now we know why. It is forbidden by the univocity of sense of the points of writing, after which the logical mind and its definitions of the "sense" of reality are modeled.

The truth of myth becomes thus incompatible with the truth of *ratio* [reason], and the former is reduced (by *ratio*) to the terms of "poetic fantasy" and "superstition." This means only the following, though: the practice of letters (that by which what is asserted must be taken "at the letter," that is, in a univocal and "proper" sense) makes other and different practices of sense infeasible. Moreover, it makes us think that there has always (or in itself) been a proper, or literal sense of words and things, whereas this sense cannot be if not within, and as a consequence of, alphabetic writing.[9]

93. *The calculation of sense*. If one pays close attention, one notices that the chrono-logical (chrono-graphic) reduction already contains in itself the principle of the homogeneity of sense. In the punctuality of the "is" that is now asserted (and from which comes that metaphysical privileging of presence, on which Heidegger and Derrida have variously commented without achieving its depth) is implied a univocity of sense. Were the asserted sense equivocal, it would be solved in a chain of successive assertions (of "is").

As Peirce remarks, the premises, major and minor, of syllogism are built on the ground of the same criterion. They must be two; if there are more than two, one must build concatenated syllogisms. This is necessary for other reasons, since the premises must contain the whole of what *one knows* on the inferred issue. Only on the basis of these conditions can the final conclusion be logically valid: that is, non-contradictory and unambiguous.

If one says that of "a" one cannot predicate "b" and "non-b" at the same time, one has already implicitly said "and in the same sense." The second condition derives in fact from the first, if one considers that time (chrono-logical and chrono-graphic linearization) is not a mere container for the assertion. Conversely, it is the condition, material and then formal, of the logical definition. That is, of the topological disposition of the logical meanings of words in their own sphere of being, in the correct and appropriate crossing of "is" and "is not." The chrono-graphic and topo-logical univocity implies in itself the homogeneity of sense of that which is asserted. Better, it is the institution of this very homogeneity; that is, of the chrono-logical and topo-logical value of words insofar as they say *the* truth (Hobbes is still concerned with this terminological homogeneity in order to make logical "calculation" possible: "human+animal=rational," and so on).

To confuse "senses" means not to realize the places of the "ontological" (topological) belonging of words—that is, at which successive point or crossing of the line they should be situated. Therefore, Leibniz could legitimately claim that if there is a conflict of opinions, it is worthless to discuss. One should take paper and pencil, and write. The conflict will resolve itself by itself, then. [Leibniz] could indeed make such a claim because the writing of his logic has turned mathematical, so that his writing is an exact calculus. It does not look, however, as though many Buddhists have become Christians following this path or method.

94. *Point and line.* What does one mean when one says that the line is made of the succession of ideal points? The line is the chronographic transcription of the voice. At every point of this line, the de-somatization of speech occurs. The point is *here* and *now*. Yet, the here (by idealizing itself in the point) loses all reference to the context: that is, to gestural acts and expressive gesticulations, let alone the surrounding world that is lived pre-categorically (as Husserl would say). And the now loses all reference to the hermeneutic rhythm of interpretation: that is, to the sense of speech that plays between provenance and destination.

Determined by the abstract (geometric) coordinates of mere presence and simple succession, the point is thus ubiquitous by its own nature. Identical to any other, it is valid for everything and everyone. Thus the point represents a concentration of the voice taken in its "spiritual" universality: that is, abstracted from any "corporeal" character of speech and the practice of language. In sum, one could say that the point is the universality of the voice taken in its purity, that is, de-somatized and transcribed.

Thus at every point the line of writing turns the voice into what *is* and is valid for everyone. The point is the concentration of the universal voice that is every-where for every-one; that is, in every place; that is, always *elsewhere*. The point is the idealized concentration of the non-temporal "signified." The other side of such transcriptive practice is, necessarily, the "signifier." This is not at all the "natural body" of the voice; rather, it is a representation of "pure" voice, a voice that has been emended of its oral-gestural practice and has been reconstructed within the abstractly chrono-graphic scheme of the line of writing and defining topology. Behind the linguistic signifier is neither the *full and living* voice nor the trace or archetrace. There is the ideal (idealizing) line of writing.

95. *The invisible voice.* With its ideal points, the line is a displaying of the invisible of the voice. The voice, one can say, is *by itself* invisible. However, in the originary *logos* it is not such, insofar as it is symballically [*simballicamente*] associated with the event of the world in a visible, tactile, audible semblance. Indeed, it has within itself the feature of originating from outside and elsewhere (with respect to the where of the transmitter). By acoustically bouncing from the unaware transmitter, it transforms it into a Self: that is, into a participant to the "public" word resounding for everyone as place of the ideal community of those who speak. This community is certainly invisible (like the Self, which is part and reflection of it), since it is the mere principle of that which is valid for everyone and everywhere—that is, the principle of "meaning." This meaning is implicit in any work insofar as it is "said": that is, elevated "to the work of everyone and all," according to Hegel's beautiful expression.

It is precisely the line, and the line alone, however, that displays the invisible of the voice. By displaying it, it shows the invisibility that, earlier, was not realized as such; that is, it *assigns* it its invisibility.

The line alone enables the self-objectification of the universal trait or character that is implicit in the voice. The line displays it *as* invisible, that is, as "suprasensible," by its very own self-definition as "sensible," as signifier. This means that the line lets it be seen as abstract from any practice—except, of course, the practice of writing. On the other hand, this is exactly what is not realized, not taken into the line of consideration.

96. *Proper and improper.* Any representation of the point is improper. It is the mere signifier of something non-representable. The point is, in fact, the "here" that comes/issues from the "beyond," that is, from the "Other" (from the generalized Other, as Mead says; from the community of everyone's answers to the voice resounding for everyone). The point is always "beyond" its "physical" representation. It is *meta-ta-phusika*. Consequently, that the voice configures itself as something suprasensible and thus constitutes the very principle of the soul is not an ungrounded "metaphysical" claim, a lie or an illusion. Rather, it is the necessary effect of a certain practice, its form, and the content of its form.

Leaving ideological discourses and ghost chases aside, one should focus on the fact that the point drawn in the line is the *conventional re-somatization of the pure and panoramic voice* (which resounds everywhere and elsewhere). It is a giving back to the voice a body, after having taken it away from it (after its "purification"; as a matter of fact, however, these two moments or movements are two sides of the same trait).

That any representation of the point is improper means that what is proper to the point is its non-representability; that is, its universal publicity: its being for everything and everyone. It follows that representation is an "impropriation" [*impropriarsi*], a rendering proper to oneself what is proper to the Other or the beyond. It is to show the "genus," "the generalized Other." That which is "public" is in fact *proper to itself* [its own, *suo proprio*], not *proper to me* [my own, *mio proprio*] (that is, "private," as the other, residual side of the public).

The proper or literal character of language is thus the consequence of a transference (*metaphor*) from the invisible to the visible of alphabetic linearization and logical definition. This means that that is literal which is . . . literal. That is, that which can be transferred into the content of this form. This is nothing else than *truth* "properly" called, which means, written. The form of truth is a tautological effect of its writing.

97. *Sense and nonsense.* The point is the making present of the eternal present of the panoramic voice "now." The signified is topological (it is a universal scheme). Conversely, the signifier is chronological; it is a "sensible" succession of now-points. Hence derives the very old logical distinction of the two aspects of the "mind": intuitive and discursive (*nous* and *dianoia*).

The point is the omni-temporality of the signified that has descended into the temporality of the signifier. It is like the ideal center of a circle of manifestations, according to the "classical," circular image of time. The concrete practice of this transcription is the insertion of the point into the line and as line. The progress (of writing) is opposed to eternal recurrence. Directionality as homogeneity of points of the line (points twisted free from all "sense"), that is, the feature of *diexodos*, straight line, method, is what prevails in the practice of writing against the disclosive character of *endeixis*. In its pro-gressing drift, this carries with itself the schematic immobility of the signified.

We therefore experience two constant traits of "progress" as a typical figure of our "civilization" (*Weltzivilisation*)—its necessitating and unstoppable character (since we are inscribed in a practice of writing and reading that increasingly dominates and transcribes into itself all practices, "making them true") and its evident lack of sense, which is, in turn, an inevitable consequence of the affirmation of directionality (of *methodos* over *odos*).

One must observe carefully these "necessities," without any ideological enthusiasm or nostalgia. The matter is not that of acknowledging that "sense" is not of this earth, as Wittgenstein does, for example. It is a matter of understanding how the land has become "this land," in which, by excluding sense, the linearized direction has produced a new experience of truth: *the* truth divided into sensible and suprasensible. The former is visible, yet nonsensical; the latter would be sensical, yet cannot be seen.

98. *Three traits.* The "procedure" I am showing is terribly complex and difficult to grasp in its entirety and in its particulars. One must have a really stubborn confidence in writing to nourish the nonsensical claim of being able to transcribe it, as I am doing. Yet, one should try to think these three moments.

Alphabetic writing is a writing made of "elements"—"letters" (which today and more "scientifically" we call "phonemes," and so on), to which correspond the Platonic *eide* of the defining process (the alphabet is itself a principle of classification and definition; better, it is the "practical" model thereof, in which one can read the content of the logical form in general).

Through this writing practice, the very notion of ideality emerges (the "ideal" letters, the ideas as the essence of beings). One should recall what is said in the *Sophist*: as the grammarian knows which syllables should and should not relate to one another, so does the dialectician know which ideas should and should not be connected in a definition.

The ideality that is achieved is omni-temporal insofar as it is the result of the concrete, operational temporality of drawing, which, however, remains unnoticed. It is enacted, but not known. The sensible result of drawing (these strokes of the pen, and so on) is thus seen as a transcription, or conventional somatization, of ideality; it is the abstract succession of points, of "instants," which, in the empirical and temporal conventionality of the signifier, "represent" the ideal non-temporality of the signified.

99. *Mysterious transcriptions.* As we look at the issue in inverted terms (that is, starting from our undisputed "mind" as readers and literary individuals), we are under the impression that rather mysterious things occur in writing. For example, that there occurs a transcription, moreover an incomprehensible one, of the ideal space of the signified into the time of the signifier, and also of the invisible voice into the visible marks of writings.

The ideal space, however, is itself an effect of writing, the object of a gestural practice that proceeds through discriminations and graphs, according to the scheme of Heracles' parting of the ways. It is thus that *pure, elementary* places occur—that is, places subjected to the simple alternative of yes or no, being or nonbeing, identity or difference.

The voice, which is transcribed into marks that are by now only conventional, [marks which are] to be seen so as to be heard, does not preexist elementary writing. Rather, it is itself an effect thereof. This voice (as Saussure clearly sees) is simply a differential scheme on the basis of the relation identity–difference (that is, Hegel would say, according to the form of the disjunctive syllogism, a figure that completes and sums up the entire development of logic). The written "a" has no real or ideal "a" immediately behind itself. It is the mere difference with respect to "e," "i," "o," "u." It is identical to itself only insofar as it is different from the other vowels (and *vice versa*). In this differential scheme, each vowel is not a temporal sound, but an ideal place of interconnections. The written "a" does not refer to any spoken "a," but rather to the pure differential idea of the place of vowels.

In general, one can say that precisely the practice of linearization, as producer of the homogeneous (the homogeneous in discourses), enables the correspondence (and thus the inscription) between the ideal space in the time of the signifier and the voice in the marks of writing. The operation produces *both* sides simultaneously. There is no real transcription of the one into the other as it *seems* to us, because our way of reasoning is itself an effect of that operation. Thus, the mystery is a little less mysterious, and the miracle a little less miraculous.

100. *Invisible writing.* The writing line is the giving of a body to the voice, which has been purified by the linearization itself, that is, by enumerating it in its elements. Thus, it is the construction of an *artificial body,* a representation of that which is heard (not of that which is seen, since its marks are conventional and indifferent, unmotivated—or, at least, thus we think they are, having forgotten that we have linearized, that is, "stylized," them, drawn them with the stylus).[10] Therefore, it is a representation of the *invisible* (the silent voice is not seen and properly is not even heard).

Being a representation of something invisible, alphabetic or phonetic writing becomes itself, in a certain way, invisible. One does not look at it, one must not contemplate it. Rather, one must overcome it. One sees *through* it. One does not properly see it because there is nothing to be seen, not only in it, but also behind it. In reading, the look does not aim at a seeing, but rather at a "meaning" [*voler dire*] and a "meant" [*detto*]. More exactly, or properly, reading (like writing) aims at the unheard and inaudible of the said—that is, at the logical meaning of words (at their *proper sense*).

This meaning does not and cannot have a phonic body because it is that which has been pronounced for everyone or is the pronunciation of everyone (beyond the contingencies of the signifier, that is, beyond the immotivations [*immotivazioni*] of the different pronunciations or graphics). It can only have a "spiritual" sound, tone and voice of the soul: that is, a silent discourse within oneself, from oneself to oneself, without intermediaries, as Husserl says.

101. *The silent knowing.* The voice "disembodies" itself through the idealizing practice of alphabetic linearization (and already by saying "the voice" one is mistaken because before this practice there is no "voice"—which is one of its typical objects or products. Rather, there is the abyss of an immense intertwining and "antiquity" of other practices). This "pure" or purified voice re-embodies itself (almost a Pythagorean reincarnation) in the signs of the idealized writing of the alphabet (and, not to fall into a new mistake, one must try to understand these two moments as one single moment and transition). Alphabetic writing makes visible (conventionally, that is, precariously) the sound that cannot be seen (the inaudible and unheard). It is the signifier of a voice that is, in its turn, signifier of pure voice.

One must keep this circle in mind in its entirety. It explains why (as it has been said) the best, the most expert reading is silent reading. [Such reading] proceeds by "panoramic," "topological" gazes. It *grasps* meaning. It does not proceed spelling out, where the "mechanism" (that is, the originary operation, the content of the form) is still perceivable, so that the scheme, the plot gleams through. The one who reads in this fashion has not yet reached the kingdom of the pure mind and the revelation of its truth. Therefore, to impose itself, truth requires concealment and oblivion. It requires interior and exterior "emptiness." The one who has not yet *forgotten* is banished into the figure of the "rough" and "ignorant" individual. It is like the simple devotees of Saint Ambrose, who were amazed at seeing him read in silence.

In conclusion, alphabetic writing holds in itself a memory that neither those who are naive nor those who are knowledgeable (the "literary" and "educated" individuals) can read. It holds a secret that they cannot detect. It shows and discloses (but for *what eyes?* This indeed is not clear) the idealizing operation of linearization by "pure" elements," pure points that, in succession, compose the ideal line of writing.

102. *The problem of the line.* The operation of alphabetic idealization shows itself in its products, and simultaneously (like any other operation) hides itself in them. It remains blind to itself, and thus it arises as *problem*. It arises as "metaphysical" problem; it is more correct to say, however, as *the* problem of metaphysics.

First, one does not see *what* problem. What problem can arise from the line, insofar as it enumerates elements in its points? The line is the simple succession of its points (1+1+1+n) as places of the "defined" and "literal" truth. But what is *succession*? How can it *occur*? The problem of the line is *movement*. Indeed, the issue can be stated also as such: the problem is *time* as figure of movement. Now, finally, one understands, because one knows very well that *time* has always been the enigma of metaphysics, whether in the figure of the soul or in the figure of the history of being.

The enigma of movement is the very enigma of *praxis* insofar as it arises from the world, attends to it, projects it outside itself and objectifies it, distancing itself from it. It is the enigma of any gesture insofar as it breaks into two parts the omnipervasive presence of the universe. In its point of balance, that which was one becomes two—in the semblance of provenance and destination, or in the form of the before and the after, as we are more accustomed to say. It is the enigma of that which happens and which has happened.

Let us consider only the enigma of *this praxis*, that is, the one that draws lines or writings that are disembodied in their punctual elements. How can this very simple thing that is the *passing* from one point to the other occur? How can the very passing of this gesture and "mark" occur? And, on the other hand, how could there not be points, these simple elementary presences, since the line represents and discriminates exactly that which *is* (and *is not*), that which is real in "itself," insofar as it is valid universally for everyone, regardless of any *pathos*, that is, of any idiosyncrasy and error? One discovers the strength and depth of Zeno's question, and how binding his problem still is.

103. *The paradox of thinking.* The problem is all here: the line cannot represent the movement that constitutes it. This amounts to say that we cannot *think* movement, given that thinking is to define linearly. That which is not definable topologically and punctually in its linearizing elements (more simply said, that which cannot be *written*) is not thinkable. To put the graphic ("alphabetic") scheme to work, and to think logically, that is, in a truthful manner, are the same.

One can see this clearly: one cannot pass from one point to the other because, to be represented (and thus thought), this passage requires an infinity of points. One can look at it also in this other way: being ubiquitous, that is, non-coinciding with its own defined sign, the point is in-finite, or in-definite. In any point one may want to indicate, there are still infinite points. For the same reason, the suprasensible being (that is purely thought) cannot be defined, cannot be delimited. Rather, it must by necessity be infinite, as Melissus concludes. But that means that it can be neither thought nor thinkable.

Being cannot fall, or be-fall, into movement and multiplicity. The attempt at understanding this problem (at saving simultaneously being and the "phenomena") is the problem of dialectical *logos* from Plato to Hegel. It is the problem of metaphysics, which specifies itself in the problem of the relation between the sensible and the suprasensible, time and eternity, soul and body, truth and error.

The irresolvability of the problem does not lie in the paradox implicit in the claim of joining that which is heterogeneous (soul *and* body, and so on). Rather, it lies precisely in the opposite—that is, in the inability to understand that these terms are homogeneous and tautological (that the sensible exists *for* the intelligible, and *vice versa*); that is, they are products of the same gesture of inscription. To understand this, one must abandon the problem and return to the question. To be effective, this cannot be formulated in the terms of the problem (being *and* time; voice *and* writing). Rather, it must be formulated in the originating terms of this writing *praxis*. That is, in the terms of the content of this form.

104. *Alphabetic writing and mathematical writing.* The Greeks thought of numbers a-rhythmo-geometrically, that is, starting with point, line, and figure. The number is a spatial unit, an ideal region (*chora*). One should say and meditate a lot on this. From this characteristic fact derives the limit, as one says, of the Greeks' scientific knowledge, of their *episteme*, which is logico-argumentative, discursive, and demonstrative. Conversely, there are no grounds on which to attain a mathematical science of nature in the modern sense. Certainly, many more differences should be emphasized. There is a difference, for example, between Plato's and Aristotle's *episteme*. The first being, in his own way, a mathematician, aims at ideas-numbers and the geometry of being. The second aims at argumentation, *logos*, and chrono-logy.

In general, though, one can say that the *content of the ancient logical form* is by now clear. It consists in the *defining linearization of the voice*, in its linear punctualization. This content refers back to that immense opening that was the event of the gesture and practice of alphabetic writing. This was an extremely complex event, whose complete comprehension would require first of all a confrontation with the general theme of practices.

With this, one should not think that the entire content of the logical form (and mind) has made itself evident exactly because mathematical writing followed the originary "geometric" (a-rhythmo-geometric) writing. Derrida claims that this writing has always, that is, since the beginning, challenged the writing of *logos*. But he is greatly mistaken. Such writing has not existed ever since the beginning; on the other hand, its analysis would be extremely complex.

On this point, Havelock has the better insights. He remarks that our number system (an Indo-Arabic invention introduced in Europe around the twelfth century) is a convention based on ten symbols and the adoption of the position value of figures that are read from right to left (units, tens, hundreds, and so on). This system "supplanted all previous number systems just as the Greek alphabet supplanted all previous writing systems." When joined with the technique of the Greek alphabet and the press, this invention, "which [in its turn] converts the invisible into the visible," is the ground for modern science. "If either invention were to be subtracted from our story, it is difficult to see how modern science could have arisen."[11] The contribution of the alphabet is essential and decisive for scientific conceptuality and classification. Yet, when the issue is counting, the alphabet, its definitions, and its names are insufficient. Public truth requires here an additional writing, whose secret refers back to a peculiar content of the form. Without an understanding of this clue, even the modern problem of technics will remain, presumably, unattainable.

105. *Beyond metaphysics.* Mathematical writing has led metaphysical *logos* to its extinction. Galileo claimed that the world should be transcribed into mathematical characters, assuming that the divine mind, and, by reflection, the human mind are in their turn inscribed in a mathematical logic. Once again, the object was exchanged for the cause. Yet obviously this did not preclude its practical effectiveness.

With respect to this epochal event (whose content would require a peculiar question and a specific reflection), two things must be kept in mind. The first is that mathematical writing is a practice that inserts itself within the alphabetic practice and its logic. In the West, it is practiced by "literary" individuals, so that it serves their metaphysical way of conceiving of the world and truth, what is visible and invisible, what is ephemeral and valuable, theory and *praxis*. In this sense, mathematical writing is itself metaphysical (one should think of the complex and peculiar relation between mathematics and theology),[12] and it is precisely the one that uncovers and brings to completion the "will to truth" (that is, to power) of metaphysics.

On the other hand, mathematics is a practice of writing that contains within itself the germs of the "overcoming of metaphysics," both as *production* of the invisible in the visible through experimentation, and as transformation and inversion of the relation between theory and practice. Understanding these two results requires not so much a new theory (a new truth), as a new *praxis*. Provisionally, one could say that it requires an *ethics* of writing.

PART II

The Tradition of Thought

CHAPTER 5

The Tradition of Philosophy

1. *The two circles.* One says the tradition of thought; but one also says the tradition of philosophy. What does one mean? How do these two expressions differ? How do they not?

One should imagine two concentric circles. The wider designates the tradition of thought. The smaller, internal to the former, designates the tradition of philosophy. This sketch means that the tradition of philosophy lies within thought and is its expression. This is plausible. This is clearly Parmenides' "thought"; however, he was not situated within the philosophical tradition (rather, he inaugurated it, if it is true that his thinking originated philosophy). It is also true that the meaning, the sense of Parmenidean thinking is a typical problem of the philosophical tradition. One cannot think of it outside the tradition of philosophy.

One should now imagine the same two concentric circles but invert their designations: the wider symbolizes the tradition of philosophy, the smaller the tradition of thought. This sketch means that a tradition of thought can occur only within the practice of philosophy, its history and tradition. This too is plausible and well grounded.

The situation could not be any more ambiguous. What do the expressions "tradition of thought" and "tradition of philosophy" properly mean? What does one mean by them? What is the criterion or the legitimacy of their distinction or assimilation? How does one establish a priority between them?

2. *The two souls of philosophy.* Philosophy does not exist outside its history, that is, outside its historical and historiographic tradition. There is a tradition of philosophical thought because there are philosophy *texts.* Philosophy persists and transmits itself through books, so that one always or mainly philosophizes on philosophers (from them one learns to philosophize and then one continues "criticizing" them). *Pace* Husserl, philosophy seems to originate more from books then from "the things themselves."

In general, philosophy is a tradition of words (with its own difference if compared to literature and poetry).[1] Philosophy relies on speech. It occurs in an act of speech, in a definite linguistic practice or linguistic signs. This is so in two senses.

First of all, there is an oral practice and tradition. It predominated in ancient schools, but it is still very much alive and present. One should think of the practice of lectures, seminars, conferences, and in general the living dialogue among philosophers and all those who deal with philosophy.

Had it relied only on the oral tradition, however, probably philosophy would not have survived; at any rate, it would not be the way it is today. One should think of the influence of philosophical writings: treatises, essays, commentaries, and so on. These writings deeply shape and modify philosophical thought. They are not mere transcriptions of its oral practice, not even when it looks as though they are, as is the case for Plato's dialogues. Writing is an essential component of philosophical rationality. It affects its contents, not only its form.

On the one hand, philosophy is a peculiar practice of speech, a practice of discourses (it is not a prophecy, an oracle, a prayer, and so on). On the other, philosophy, that is, this practice of speech, relies heavily on a practice of writing or *doxography* and the peculiar tradition deriving from it.

3. *Philosophical clichés*. In the *Phaedrus*, Plato considers writing unfit to transmit philosophy. Only the living word, endowed with a father, can teach wisdom and educate the souls.

In the *Seventh Letter*, Plato narrates how he led Dion to philosophy through "conversation" and "persuasive discourses." Later he went to Syracuse to educate the tyrant Dionysius. He was scarcely convinced about the project, but he did not want to "look simply like a speechmaker" (and not a doer of good deeds). Unfortunately, he found out that Dionysius and his friends "were imbued with philosophical clichés." Dionysius listened to Plato for one single night, and, pleased, immediately composed a written piece—evident sign that he has understood nothing.

To study philosophy is difficult, Plato claims. One must listen to a teacher show the wonderful path (*odos*) of philosophizing, and meanwhile one must strive to walk it alone. This aim must permeate all daily practices and the very meaning of living. This is completely different than a "coat of clichés," in which those "who are not true philosophers" delight. "Thus, the one who is serious avoids writings of serious matters." Philosophical writings benefit only the very few who have understood that philosophy is a practice of life and a personal search. To the others, they are of no help; not having understood what philosophizing means, the others misunderstand the content and corrupt it.

Additionally, words and definitions are imperfect tools to express the essence of things. One should keep in mind the "inadequacy of speeches" to grasp the core and dynamic of thought, especially when they are written speeches, that is, frozen and petrified in "unmoveable speeches"—unlike oral speech, which, even in its unfitness, at least walks with thought.

This is very good. Yet, what would we know of Plato, today, without those "unmoveable speeches" which, luckily, he never ceased to compose, in a generous, even more, extraordinary amount, during his entire life? He devoted himself to them with the most "serious" of care and attention in style, detail, and as a whole.

4. *The alienation of writing.* What consequences derive from the fact that philosophy is a practice of speech that however transmits itself mainly through writing? Is it legitimate to read in this the roots of the "alienation of philosophy," that is, the loss of its originary "intentionality" as a consequence inherent in the very fact of writing?

Husserl thinks something similar in *Crisis of European Sciences*, Appendix Three. The living voice of the soul gets embodied in writing. Thus, it maintains and transmits itself in an *objectification* that distorts it, and favors the misunderstanding and oblivion of concrete philosophical subjectivity. This is a fall into "naturalistic objectivism" that carries with itself the entire Western science. Not forgetting itself in writing, recovering, and reactivating itself is necessary for the subject.

Where does the living voice of the soul, the philosophical subject, come from? Is it not, evidently, a construction of Platonic writing (with its written interpretation of Socrates' speech and life?) And where does Platonic writing come from? Was there really "first" a practice of philosophical speech, and "later" its written translation? In truth, there already was a practice of alphabetic writing that, by its nature, influenced the origin of rationality and the philosophical "soul." Within this practice Socrates and Plato were able to think the way they did and on its basis assert the difference in discourses (specifically, they elaborated defining speech, which is unthinkable without writing, scheme, or trace). And even before this, there existed the practice of writing rhetorical discourses, in relation to which Plato's philosophy establishes its own difference. It is Phaedrus himself, in the homonymous dialogue, who gives an example of this [practice], which then unchains Socrates' unparalleled irony. One knows something of this [practice] when one does exactly what the diligent Phaedrus was doing: when one keeps one's books, reads them assiduously, and tries to learn them by heart, if not "rhetorically" at least "logically."

5. *Event and tradition of philosophy.* Here one faces a clearly ambiguous situation and plot. One will admit that there must have been, at least hypothetically, a primordial event, that is, an event primary in order. Such is the practice of philosophical thought. Actually, this hypothetical premise reveals itself only in a practice and tradition of oral speech. The [latter] maintains and transmits itself only through writing. Thus, it is the intertwining of these two traditions that originates philosophy, its tradition, and its history.

Philosophy is thus, and at the same time, a (completely hypothetical) premise and a (highly ambiguous) result. If one considers it as an *event*, philosophy is a premise. It is the happening of a world opening consisting in the institution of an attitude or habit of thought having its own disclosive horizon of meaning and related truth. However, if one considers the *meaning* of this event that is philosophy, then one realizes that it manifests itself only in the tradition of spoken and written words, and in itself it is nothing except this very tradition.

Several questions come to mind. How can there be a practice of philosophical thought *before* a certain practice of *logos* (for example, the practice of defining *logos*?) How can there exist such a practice *before* the transformation of orality into alphabetic writing, that is, into an abstractly linear and elementary reasoning that proceeds by schematic alternatives and homogeneous idealizations? In sum: is there first philosophy, and later its historical tradition? Or is it the very tradition, with its ambiguous intertwining of orality and writing, that determines the cultural form and practice *we* name philosophy?

6. *The infinite work*. What are philosophical texts? If one considers them carefully, they are like islands that have survived the ocean of events. They are islands that would remain inhospitable and unknown without the myriad contributions of an immense doxographic, philological, hermeneutic, and, finally and therefore, historiographic tradition.

One should strive to recall the colossal, infinitely minute and tortuous work, marked by often fortuitous and almost miraculous events, that today enables us to read one of Plato's dialogues, Aristotle's *Metaphysics*, or Plotinus' *Enneads*. One should think, for example, of the enormous work of reconstruction, made of patient erudition and interpretative geniality, that today enables us to speak of Pre-Socratic philosophy, or, maybe better, thought even in the absence of so-called texts.

One should invoke the image of thousands of individuals who, in widely varying epochs, historical, material, and psychological conditions and circumstances very distant from and incomparable with one another, between a war and a famine, a plague epidemic and an invasion, in daily struggle with want, disease, and death, hindered by hatred, love, and fatigue, have tenaciously gathered, copied, emended, preserved, transcribed, and finally commented on the *Timaeus* or the *Sophist*, the *Pyrrhonian Discourses* or the *Confessions*, and so on. The question comes to mind, what was so precious in philosophy to provoke such tenacious and repeated efforts, on the side of individuals so diverse among themselves, of very different customs, beliefs, practices of life, hopes, ambitions, and desires?

One sees now this infinite chain of Interpreters (as Peirce would say) that unfolds throughout centuries. It is still at work in the ways of our times, and its truth extends infinitely. We, who practice philosophy, *are in this chain*, in this human wave of endless antiquity. Yet how are we in it?

7. *Sense and nonsense of culture*. Without this powerful and industrious interpretive chain behind us, no one of us could be in philosophy and practice it. Each of us is in philosophy only by virtue of a continuity/difference of practices of which each is, directly or indirectly, the product, and of which each is deeply made.

We live all this directly in the exercise of the cultural practice that today characterizes us, though generally in the most complete oblivion or unawareness of its origin and meaning. We rely without question on the university practice of studies, on the *praxis* of publishing and communication, on the modalities of conferences, articles, reviews, interviews, and so on. In this passive acceptance, in this non-reflective exercise, we find ourselves in the constant and unnoticed danger of being led very far away from philosophical intentionality and experience, or at least away from the question of their meaning. We find ourselves exposed to obtuse narcissism and complacency in our intellectual exercise and "cultural figure."

Analogously, we tend to philosophize on texts directly and non-reflectively, forgetting that the *Parmenides* and the *Enneads* have not always been those "cultural objects" we now tend to believe they are, and that in them an indefinite set of diverse practices (well beyond mere theoretical and historiographic interpretation) have concentrated and sedimented. We often take for granted this entire sedimented, "categorical" work, as if its results were the text itself in its "pre-categorial" reality (assuming it ever had one).

The situation is not much different if we think of a text of a century, or some few years ago. These texts too are islands immersed in an ocean of life and events. They are the, often occasional, coagulation point of their authors' numerous practices of thinking, writing, daily life. They are islands in a "current" that needs to be continually reactivated and crossed, if one wants to land and orient oneself.

8. *Scientific historiography.* One could object that we are not as unaware as we have been portrayed. As opposed to many others in the past, we do possess and practice a particular approach of textual reading and interpretation. It is the *historiographic method.* Its scientific effectiveness and awareness enables us to say and remember all that has been said on the tradition of different practices, islands, currents, and so on.

That is correct. The Alexandrian philologist, the medieval monk, the humanist, and the erudite were certainly unaware of the modern historiographic method. At the most, they did monumental or antiquarian history, but not critical history, as Nietzsche would say. This historical method, which imposed itself in the nineteenth century starting with Hegel, Dilthey, and so on, in our century has come to configure itself as rigorous "historical science." Like any other science, this practice assumes a public, panoramic, disinterested, "objective" look and turns it, for example, on the tradition of philosophy. Historiographic science configures itself as quest for the *truth in itself* of the past through the activation of an objective look and always perfectible techniques of objectifying inquiry. We thus have a history of philosophy that is a rigorous scientific historiography of philosophy, or that at least aims at becoming increasingly such.

This fact needs to be considered carefully because it does not seem that we can set it aside any longer. Since the advent of scientific and even experimental cosmology, we cannot seriously tell stories, myths or metaphysical-theological inventions on the origin of the universe; analogously, we can no longer read an author naively as if he or she were alive. For instance, we cannot dialogue with Descartes as we would do with a contemporary of ours without asking ourselves the "scientific" question of [Descartes'] objective historical location. As cosmology seems no longer capable of escaping the "public truth" of physics and its technical instrumentations, so does the philosophical tradition seem unable to escape the "public truth" of historical science.

9. *The eternal recurrence of the same.* The modern reduction of philosophical tradition and hermeneutics to the technique of historiographic understanding and interpretation has several merits. It contains an element of (we think) indispensability, which should be clarified and understood too. Yet one should also consider what surprising paradoxes and derailments accompany, silently and inadvertently, historiographic interpreting and its application to philosophy.

The first issue is that the historical look (that is, the historiographic method and technique) seems to elide itself paradoxically. Historiographism, in fact, elides the historicity of its own event, since everything is historical except historiography. Historiography can change the features of its interpretative technique and the specific contents of its methodical structure, but cannot change the historiographic-critical attitude itself.

Having become "scientific," historiographic practice cannot abandon the presupposition that constitutes it. It cannot even discuss or think it, since it should do so from within its own methodical categories (since it does not have any others). These very categories, however, constitute the presupposition that should be thought and challenged. Thus, historiography can only indefinitely perfect and strengthen such a critical-objective presupposition.

On the margin, one could remark that this is precisely one of the (if not *the*) essential feature) of technics and of all techniques: self-production as the eternal recurrence of the same. In this, as remarked earlier, the very element of "historicity" is paradoxically erased.

10. *Historiography and philosophy.* One should also consider this: historiographic-scientific thinking and interpreting are clearly a way of thinking. They are *a* determined event with its own defined birth and circumstances. They are the direct consequence of *a* [certain] philosophy. Yet historiographic interpreting claims to be and actually posits itself as absolute and insurmountable.

Historiographic practice is *a* practice among many possible ones. On the basis of which legitimating criterion (a criterion that may not be internal to its practice because that would constitute a vicious circle) can it establish its own superiority, the grounded reason for its preference? Moreover, historiographic practice is a direct consequence of the originary distancing of a *critical* look (and not, for instance, a *mythical* one) on the world and human beings, distancing that was brought about by philosophy.[2] But how can historiographic practice be able to judge philosophical practice insofar as it is a typical and necessary product thereof? How can it posit as its own object that very practice of thought of which it is itself part and result?

Lastly, the simplest, most evident, and most indubitable consideration: definitely, philosophers have not philosophized in order to make historiographic practice possible and provide it with material for its methodological appetite. Thus, and as a conclusion, philosophical historiography appears as extrinsic, decentered, and incongruous in relation to philosophical intentionality.

Heidegger, too, asserts this in his own way. Philosophical historiography (*Historie*) is not capable of truly thinking the historicity (*Geschichte*) of philosophy and its tradition. Insofar as it is methodologically scientific, it proceeds by *problems*. All problems, however, have the peculiar feature of eliding (by translating it into their own logic) the *question* out of which they arose. Philosophy, on its part, is itself the epochal event of questioning. The practice of philosophical historiography would ultimately eliminate philosophy itself. (At this point one should reflect on a very widespread oddity: the current multiplication on the part of Heidegger's fans of historiographic studies on Heidegger's thought).

11. *The untimeliness of philosophy*. That today philosophy takes up the predominating habit of historiography derives also from its need to justify itself "scientifically." The same should be said with respect to its widespread self-presentation as specialized logic and epistemology.

Once born as *scientia scientiarum*, as queen of sciences (metaphysics); in the modern age *Wissenschaftslehre* thanks to the Berlin masters Fichte and Hegel; finally "fundamental ontology" in Freiburg with Husserl and Heidegger; today philosophy, "theoretical philosophy," seems to endure in universities only thanks to the *inertia* of the tradition. It is a entity alien to the current *universitas studiorum*, which is founded on increasingly pervasive specialization. It is a discourse and practice that cannot be qualified "scientifically."

"You must give yourselves a *qualification*, join a specific discipline." This is what the expert colleague, half caring and half condescending, tells the theoretical philosopher. "How can you think of getting research funds and teaching positions? *What* research? *What* teaching? *What* is the topic of theoretical philosophy? What is its issue? It is not historiographic, it is not logical, it is not epistemological. . . . Today *philosophy* as such makes no more sense. Today there is science."

What can one answer? That the person confuses the problem with the question? But the person understands the question only in terms of a problem, and *therefore* philosophy as such appears to him or her as empty and amounting to nothing. From his or her perspective, things are *exactly* like this. Meanwhile, though, by assuming the habit and the mask of historiography or logistics so as to give itself scientific dignity and decorum, and claim for itself a peculiar "usefulness" and a serious bustling in research and teaching, philosophy sinks.

Rather than salvaging itself, it fades into its disguise and *because* of its disguise. How odd—by *qualifying itself* philosophy disappears.

12. *Absolute historiography.* What does "philosophical tradition" mean, then? For us, today, this tradition coincides with historiography, with the history of philosophy. It is in this "figure" that we practice and learn the philosophical tradition; this seems to us to be absolutely *obvious.* To know philosophy amounts to studying it historiographically. Yet, the point is: is to know, explain, teach philosophy in a historiographic guise also *to comprehend* philosophy? Is it to be comprehended (compenetrated) in it?

As we have seen, there is more than one reason why one should be doubtful about this. One could summarize the reasons in this way: first of all, because historiographic interpretation is definitely not the only way in which philosophy has handed itself down and maintained itself within the tradition. It remains true however (and one should keep this very much in mind) that it is precisely the historiographic habit that makes one certain of this. One can see clearly and with the assurance of many details that philosophy is a practice of spoken and written words that has known different modalities of manifestation and operation. It is known and documented that the medieval monk is one thing, the seventeenth-century scholar another, and so on. Yet all this is taught precisely by the historical look and historiographic practice. This opens up a problem, and, even more important, a question, that cannot be avoided.

Meanwhile, one should think also about this: by positing itself as a method, as unique and absolute, that is, as an undoubtedly "true" interpretive technique, the historiographic interpretation cancels its own historicity. It tells the objective truth-in-itself of the past. Yet exactly because of this, by distancing itself from the past, by alienating itself from it, it can never become "past," it cannot pass. Its panoramic eye that tells the events (and which was itself *an* event) has no "eventuation" if not in the form of an infinite perfectioning.

13. *The double look.* If one formulates issues of delimitation, origin and meaning in relation to the historiographic look, one is immediately led to irresolvable paradoxes, since these issues cannot even be thought and formulated within historiographic categories. On the one hand, we *are* the historiographic and historical look. We absolutely do not have another look that may be valid universally for us. Yet, on the other hand, we are no longer such a look because we are raising a doubt that locates us at its border. Where are we, then? And what are we?

The fact remains that the historiographic look is internally paradoxical. It is the typical product of *a* philosophy, and yet it posits itself as a universal (supposedly non-metaphysical) method claiming to be able to comprehend the entire philosophy and its tradition. Moreover, ever since its beginning, this look has been "predestined" for the advent of that "critical" reason that is philosophy itself. It is the product of philosophy (rather than being outside of metaphysics):

how can it claim to judge philosophy and describe correctly (that is, to understand truly) its practice?

Finally, and one should recall and never forget this, philosophical historiography, its possibility, and its practice are not at all the goal [*il fine*] of philosophy. No philosopher has ever thought and written with the goal of contributing to the history of philosophy. Thus, philosophical historiography is a practice that is incongruous with its object. This concludes the summary.

14. *What thinking is.* How would things be, were one to consider, at least in a preliminary way, the "tradition of thought," that is, of human thought in general, assuming that, in comparison with philosophical thought, it were broader, preexisted, and continued to subsist? What is the relation between the practice of human thought in general and the practice of philosophical thought? And first of all, what is the specificity of philosophical thought in comparison with thinking in general?

One cold answer that such a specificity is "logic." In fact, Plato identifies philosophical science (*episteme*) with dialectics or the defining art of speeches. Aristotle perfects it in the *Organon*, that is, in the method of truth that is, precisely, logic.

All this refers to the *content* of peculiar practices, within which the practice of alphabetic writing assumes a decisive importance for the constitution of the "logical form" of discourse and thinking. Nevertheless, can one be said to have shown in this manner the event and meaning of the philosophical *habit* and *disposition?* Plato himself would object to this, and Aristotle would too. One would not be able to find a way out were someone to ask, was it alphabetic writing that created the "philosophical mind," or was it the philosophical mind of the Greeks that created the alphabet? Or with what mind did [the Greeks] create the alphabet finally to arrive at logic?

One cannot avoid the ambiguous and obscure question: "What is thinking"? Why is this question ambiguous and obscure? Because "what is thinking" is a typical philosophical question (a *problem* of philosophy, rather than a question about philosophy and thinking in general). In what other way could one answer, if not by examining what "thought" is in Plato, Aristotle, Descartes, Kant, Hegel, and so on? One can answer only by giving birth to a "history of philosophy."

This is an upsetting result. This history of philosophy (an instance of the "history of philosophy through problems," as one says) would place thought simultaneously inside (as object of inquiry) and outside itself (as that which comes in every sense before any historiographic practice and questioning). Historiographic thinking should necessarily be something else than the history of that thought that it itself studies and describes "objectively." Lastly, this historiographic thinking should historicize itself too. That is, it should acknowledge that what it says about thought and the history of thought has only a contingent and provisional value; that is, it is not true. With the exception of reasserting that there is nothing else to do except to proceed on this path, with this method, *adinfinitum* without being able to understand why or in which sense what we will say in one hundred, or one thousand years will have more value, more truth than what we say today. That is, without being able to understand why we continue to walk this path that, however, we cannot renounce.

15. *The threshold of the origin*. It is difficult to imagine anything more troublesome than the problem of the origins. What was the originary gesture of thought and of its self-constituting as a handed-down habit? What was the originary gesture of philosophical thought and its tradition? Before any attempt at an answer, one should however ask: how can we think these originary gestures, these thresholds?

Let us assume, for example, that with Parmenides philosophical thinking had its actual beginning. Parmenides, then, stands at the threshold. That thinking of his that produces the famous poem is necessarily pre-philosophical and originates from a tradition that is not that of philosophy. In fact, in the poem there is no mention of "philosophy." Parmenides certainly does not think of "doing philosophy" in the same sense that this expression has assumed starting with Plato, and that has become decisive for us.

One can think of Parmenides, however, only on the basis of the philosophical tradition that he inaugurates, that is, beyond its threshold. How can one think the threshold itself? With what thought? More generally: is a thought that attempts to think the origin of philosophical thought still philosophical thought? Or is it not? To what point is it determined by the philosophical tradition from which it certainly comes?

16. *The thought of the end* [della fine]. The same question arises if one speaks of "conclusion" or "end." Wittgenstein, for example, tries to think the "logical form" of philosophy, tries to define and circumscribe it. Therefore, the act of thought that thinks the *Tractatus* is not the same philosophical thought of which the *Tractatus* speaks. Yet, without the presence and burden of the philosophical tradition, a work such as the *Tractatus* could in no way be conceivable.

As one can see, we are caught between the *alpha* and the *omega*. The difficulty in talking about the origin presents itself in the very same way if one considers the end [*la fine*]. We cannot locate ourselves beyond these limits, because all attempts always fall back on this side. Our only way of being, our only possibility is to locate ourselves *between* these extremes. Yet the extremes themselves are somehow mentioned and evoked when we locate ourselves with reference to them. Can we perhaps doubt our being within the philosophical tradition? Is it not obvious that this tradition had an origin? Is it not possible that, in the same way in which it had an origin, it will also have an end? The same happens with thought. The philosophical practice is certainly not the first intelligent human practice. As Aristotle remarks at the beginning of *Metaphysics*, human beings, moved by the need to live and the desire to know, elaborated some knowing much earlier, and in many other ways [than philosophy]. How did this tradition of forms of knowing and, in a certain sense, of thoughts originate? (One should not fail to notice that) we are still within the scope of that Aristotelian remark, except that where he proceeded by assertions and recognized matters of fact and problems, there we encounter doubts and questions.

How can one talk about the end [*la fine*] of philosophy? What kind of thought is the one that thinks the end of philosophy? For many reasons today it seems legitimate to confront thought with these problems. Yet as soon as one truly focuses on the question, then one experiences the inability to think it—that is, to situate our thought at the level of its height or, if one prefers, of its depth.

CHAPTER 6

The Task of Thinking

16. *The transforming answer.*[1] Heidegger wonders about the problem of the end of philosophy together with the question of the future task of thinking once philosophy has reached the end.[2] Yet what does it mean that philosophy, in the present epoch, has reached its end? And what task is reserved for thinking at the end of philosophy? What is the "matter" [*cosa*], the question (*Sache*) that concerns it?

Heidegger has well estimated, before anyone else and better than anyone else (except perhaps Derrida, or maybe Deleuze) the aporetic and disorienting character of these questions. Hence, he is prudent. He knows, for example, what one should *not* expect if one truly confronts the question. "The questions are paths to an answer. If the answer could be given, the answer would consist in a transformation (*Verwandlung*) of thinking, not in a propositional statement about a matter at stake."[3] The answer (if one can even talk of an answer) cannot consist in simple propositions asserting: philosophy and its tradition is this; its end is that; the "matter" or the task of thought is that other. The answer consists in the transformation of thought, so that it inhabits the questions differently. I would say that the answer is "ethical" and not "theoretical."

This, too, is not void of difficulties, however, and Heidegger proves that he knows this very well with a simple parenthetical. The question about what constitutes the "matter" of thought has inevitably a "critical" nature. It originates from a reflective, "theoretical" distance, and is immediately inclined to become a problem. Now, "to what extent [does] the *critical* question of what the matter of thinking is, necessarily and continually belong to thinking?"[4] In what sense is it a questioning that remains philosophical? In what sense does it surpass it and extends itself "beyond" (and thus also before, circumscribing both the *alpha* and the *omega*), that is, beyond the end of philosophy? All this is in no way clear.

17. *The completion.* Heidegger puts the issue in these terms: philosophy (metaphysics) thinks the being of beings, that is, the ground and reason why beings presence themselves, thus becoming *objects* of representation, knowledge,

manipulation and ("logical," I would add) elaboration. Ground and reason are successively conceived in many forms: as first cause, as transcendental possibility of the objects, as dialectical mediation of absolute spirit, as historical process of production, as will to power that posits values. The "history" of metaphysics unfolds from Aristotle to Nietzsche.

Today we witness the end of this history. As a matter of fact, no one develops great metaphysical systems any longer. Why? Is it perhaps a matter of decay and impotence? This is not the case. The issue is that of philosophy's coming to its *completion*; that is, it gathers itself in its extreme possibility. For philosophy, to come to its end (*Ende*) means to fulfill the totality of its revelatory circle, gathering itself in its place (*Ort*).

Since metaphysics is mainly Platonism,[5] the completion configures itself as reversal of Platonism (Marx, Nietzsche, Sartre). This extreme figure of philosophy makes it such that today any further philosophy would only be an epigonal rebirth. In the time of completion, it is a mistake to expect the development of new philosophies having a style similar to those of the past (such styles remain similar even when they revert, relativize, weaken the originals; the reversal of Platonism is still Platonism). Today we indeed have a great number of these epigonal philosophies: they fill the pages of newspapers (they make the news), conference programs, and publishers' catalogues. They "make culture," and yet they remain epigonal, that is, meaningless if considered from the perspective of the "matter" of thought. They do not attain the only and authentic current possibility of thought (and thus they are not a serious "matter"): the ability to think its own end.

18. *Special knowledges.* What concretely happens in the completion is the final imposition of a feature that has been essential for philosophy ever since its beginning: the development of sciences; their separation from philosophy; the institution of their autonomy. One should think of the issue in this way: philosophy is a big crucible that heats itself up with the tinder of questioning. Questioning nourishes itself and explodes in a lively combustion of problems. Problems increase in heat and consistence until they separate from the crucible and from distinct furnaces. In the end, the originary crucible is completely emptied out. What remains are wisps of smoke, which only testify the death of questioning.

Philosophy is the originary will to science (the will to institute scientific knowledge). It completes itself in the figure of developed and autonomous sciences, so that there is no longer any fuel or tinder of questions to elaborate other philosophies. Properly, there is no longer reason to do so, since reason has completely transformed itself into scientific reason and its project of knowledge. Whatever the problem that bothers one may be, one should not go and ask the philosopher about it; one should go to a specialist. This mentality is so deeply rooted in the West that one looks for "specialists" even *in opposition* to science: specialists of orgasmic psychoanalysis, yoga practice, Zen meditation, alternative medicine, and so on. One looks for appropriate answers and techniques (which are naively uprooted from their originary context of life and meaning and are translated for European usage). Every question, even the simplest ("What am I doing? Have I gone crazy?"), is silent. All taste and attention are devoted to technical details and their external retinue (the style of hair and clothes, the nature of food, exercise in motion and at rest, reading, and so on).

In conclusion, the full unfolding of the autonomy of sciences and specialization "is in full swing today in all regions of beings. This development looks like the mere dissolution of philosophy, and is in truth its completion."[6]

19. *Information and domestication of souls.* The final feature of the fulfillment of philosophy into sciences assumes the figure of the "empirical science of the man,"[7] that is, of the humanities (psychology, sociology, anthropology, logistics, and so on). They recapitulate the "humanistic" intentionality that is at the very origin of philosophy, of the Socratic question (which separates human beings from the world of the gods, that is, from the world) and the Platonic "strategy of the soul." This intentionality realizes itself by projecting the human being "as an acting social being": that is, through a "planning and arrangement of human labor"[8] within which traditional natural sciences find their place and meaning too.

All particular sciences are thus led, ultimately, by cybernetics. It "transforms language into an exchange of news." Thus "the arts become regulated-regulating instruments of information."[9] This cybernetic character is nothing else than the fundamental feature of today's scientificity, that is, its "technical" or "technological" feature. It is the instrument thanks to which science "establishes [itself] in the world by *working* on it in the manifold modes of making and shaping."[10] Everywhere, then, "the scientific exploitation of the individual areas of beings" occurs.[11] This exploitation operates through instrumental hypotheses, the truth of which is measured in terms of their efficiency and effects. "The operational and model character of representational-calculative thinking becomes dominant."[12]

Not only questioning, but also the very question of technics has no longer a place or a way to unfold except in the naive form of the pretension to "humanize" technics: that is, to make it all the more practical and efficient. That is to say, to make it technologically increasingly more blind toward the genuine question of meaning that might concern it. "The end of philosophy proves to be the triumph of the manipulable arrangement of a scientific-technological world and of the social order proper to this world. The end of philosophy means: the beginning of the world civilization (*Weltzivilisation*) based upon Western European thinking."[13] *Zivilisation* [appears] as production and domestication (and not *Bildung*) of the souls. Work as hobby, hobby as work. [It is] the programmatic realization of the universal in human beings and in nature as information practice, as *computer science.*

20. *Whether a human being is a sign.* Today, nobody could fail to realize Heidegger's foresight. Nevertheless, there is some reason for a preliminary perplexity

regarding at least two issues. He claims that the categories of science derive from the "regional ontologies" of philosophy (nature, history, rights, art); although sciences technicize themselves, becoming merely performative and thus relinquishing any ontological claim, nevertheless the philosophical ideal of scientificity still speaks in them. The fact that they ignore philosophy does not mean that they can get rid of it. As a consequence, however, the more science shapes and rules the events of the world and the position human beings occupy within it, the less one feels the need to question technics.

In this way, science and technics configure themselves as blind instruments of the will to knowledge, of the "will to truth" of philosophy, as Nietzsche says. The more they specialize and informationalize [*informatizzano*] [14] themselves, the more they forget and obliterate the question from which they originated (that is, their connection to philosophy). Yet, precisely in this way philosophy "completes" itself into them and inevitably dominates them, whether from its silence or from its absence.

Things would truly be this way if the signs of the *logos* of philosophy alone were to speak in science. One knows very well that things are not this way, and once again one can appreciate the advantage of having asked the question not of truth but of the content of the form. Modern scientific rationality comes from philosophy on the one hand, but on the other it rests on its own revolution that makes use of signs and practices other than those of philosophy and ancient logic. As long as *this* revolution is not understood, any final evaluation of the meaning of scientific operations and destiny remains inadequate and thus superficial. Heidegger indeed occasionally says that the human being is a sign; but he has never truly thought it. This is the deep root of his going astray.

As far as "questioning" technics is concerned: is [technics] not the last, although unaware, consequence of metaphysical *questioning*? How can we, by questioning, relinquish it from the tenacious metaphysical servitude? Might it not be, on the contrary, that precisely in the exasperation of its "practice," that is, in its active inversion of the relations between theory and practice, there resides the "liberating appeal," though not understood, of which even Heidegger has once spoken?

21. *The unthought matter.* Having situated himself by himself in front of the insurmountableness of metaphysics, Heidegger wonders whether thinking (which would have nothing more to hope from sciences) might have the possibility of returning to the beginning of this whole "story," and find in it an alternative once neglected, then forgotten and concealed by the imposition of the philosophical form of thought. This would be a

> *first* possibility for thinking . . . a possibility from which the thinking of philosophy had to start out, but which as philosophy it could nevertheless not experience and adopt.[15] If this were the case, then a task would still have to be reserved for thinking in a concealed way in the history of

> philosophy from its beginning to its end, a task accessible neither to philosophy as metaphysics nor, and even less so, to the sciences stemming from philosophy.[16]

In all this contortion, what is most interesting is the fact that in this way Heidegger reaches the problem of the beginning, that is, of the origin of philosophy, while at the same time trying to keep philosophy and thinking separate. This can be instructive.

The hypothesis is that philosophy has not been up to the "matter of thinking," so that in it we should recognize (as Nietzsche has already done) the history of pure decadence. Yet what the "matter" or the question of thinking is, is really hard to recognize. The hypothesis is that it hides itself within, or behind, the matter itself of philosophy, "something which it is no longer the matter of philosophy to think."[17]

The intertwining of philosophy and thinking is therefore always on the verge of unraveling and reweaving itself. One should leave philosophy to itself to come finally across the matter of thinking. The latter is however hidden in the former, so that it is still to philosophy (to its entire "historiography" and still enigmatic "historicity") that we should turn. In order to recognize the matter of thinking, we must first ask what the matter of philosophy is. The answer is (from Plato to Hegel to Husserl): the thing itself, *to pragma auto*.

22. *Before light*. What is the matter that philosophy has brought to knowledge? In a general sense it is the "phenomenon" in the sense of the unfolding of a being into presence. It is not this or that phenomenon in its contingency, but rather the being of the phenomenon, its very aspect (its idea) as "the thing itself" of thinking (phenomeno-logy). Philosophy brings to knowledge the fundamental relation between being and thinking: the movement of the becoming present of the phenomenon in its being is the same as its thinkableness in knowledge.

Being can disclose itself, become phenomenon only thanks to a "brightness" that renders it manifest: the light of the good in Plato, the *analogon* of which is the sun, the *lumen naturale* of the intellect, and so on.[18] Light is the place where being comes to knowledge through a being, so that philosophy focuses on this light (the transcendental) and remains attached to it even when it denies the possibility of achieving it and speaking of it, as for example in Wittgenstein. It is in the light of thought that being appears, becomes phenomenon, is known; thus, this phenomenon achieves for example the sense of being "horse," and so on. But this is not all.

"Before" light, and so that light may enlighten something, the *openness* (*das Offene*), that is, the *Lichtung* (the clearing) must disclose itself: "all philosophical thinking which explicitly or inexplicitly follows the call 'to the thing itself' is already admitted to the free space of the opening (*Lichtung*) in its movement and with its method. But philosophy knows nothing of the opening (*Lichtung*). Philosophy . . . does not heed the opening (*Lichtung*) of being."[19]

We should, however, be heedful too. Heidegger is saying that a being stands there in front and is the "matter" of science (and of common sense). Underneath a being and so that a being may present itself, however, is the light of being, the transcendental; this is the "matter" of philosophy. Underneath the light of being and so that the light may occur, though, is the openness of the *Lichtung*, and this is the "matter" of thinking (which philosophy ignores). Is "thinking," however, not a typical "matter," even the essential *object* of philosophy? Is it not, once again, the philosophical imagination, the logical-defining practice, that speaks when one attributes the *Lichtung* to the matter of thinking? This genealogy, which would like to uproot the roots of metaphysics, remains still entangled in metaphysics.

23. *The* Lichtung *as* aletheia. The *Lichtung* is the clearing that opens up in the density (*Dickung*) of the forest. It is a *diexodos*: a path and countryside (*Gegend*) that opens up and liberates. As a center of lightened opening, the *Lichtung* (as is said in *Holzwege*) "is never a rigid stage with a permanently raised curtain on which the play of beings runs its course."[20] The *Lichtung* moves and, little by little, clears up the forest.

In this way, the *Lichtung*, which is not brightness [*luce*], nevertheless creates the clearing, in which brightness and darkness can play and present themselves. It is a movement that simultaneously opens and closes the horizon. In this horizon a being gives itself time after time thanks to the lighting that is peculiar to it. Yet, since the horizon is moveable (it is a "historical" destining), the light of the transcendental depends on it. Thus, being gives itself in figures of changing light: where it gives itself, it also hides itself.

Very skillfully Heidegger thus joins *Lichtung* and *aletheia*. *Aletheia* is the movement from concealment (*lethe*) to unconcealment (*aletheia*); at the same time, it is the further weakening, in concealment, of that which has made the manifestation of being occur, that is, the unconcealment. This is properly the "'epochal' *Lichtung* of being": being gives itself while also keeping itself in itself, suspending itself in *epoche*. More precisely, what bounces back and remains unattainable for thinking (for philosophical thinking) is the event (*Ereignis*) of the *Lichtung*. The event is the event of the world (of the "historical" world) as self-generation of *phusis*. This is "the rising-up of the clearing [*Lichtung*], and thus it is the hearth and place of light."[21]

What one has is confronted with here is a brief tour through typical and suggestive Heideggerian terminology. His images aim at freeing themselves from the "logical" terminology of metaphysical *logos*. Understanding whether and to what extent they succeed is not easy.

24. *The origin of the fire*. The *Lichtung* is certainly a grandiose invention. Linguistically, the term has nothing to do with *Licht*, light, and yet it recalls it. Moreover, in it there is, as Heidegger notices, an objective connection: precisely in the opening of the clearing, in the heart of the forest, light can appear and play

between brightness and obscurity. While not being light, nevertheless *Lichtung* recalls light, it is its premise, since "light never first creates openness. Rather, light presupposes openness.[22]

With these images Heidegger displays his understanding of the importance of light for metaphysics. The so-called metaphor of the light is not a simple metaphor. On the contrary, it is an essential invention for the birth of the metaphysical mind (mentality), as happens in the crucial pages of Plato's *Republic*. In the transference from the sun to the good, from the sensory sight to the intelligible vision, the fundamental notions of the soul and the reality in itself of things, image and concept, sensory and suprasensory originate—all the transcendental and empirical baggage of philosophy according to the double, opposite, and yet correlative conception proper to the children of the earth and the friends of the ideas. It is true that Heidegger does not walk far enough on this path;[23] yet, he sees it, opens it (thanks to Nietzsche), and shows it to all of us.

Heidegger's effort to think *beyond* light, going back to the event which is the condition of the possibility of light itself (the big Platonic fire, as Nietzsche says, from which we still get our brands): that is, his attempt at thinking the origin of philosophy and its epochal gesture by letting the unthought and the unsaid *of* metaphysical thought surface—all this is certainly worthy of the highest attention and greatest respect. Heidegger seeks its very taking place within and beyond the place of metaphysics.

25. *The voice of the clearing*. One should not overlook, however, a meaningful and typical embarrassment to which Heidegger falls prey. He speaks of light and *Lichtung*, of clearing and horizon, yet he knows very well that if he wants to recapture metaphysics and its truth, he must speak also about *logos*, about language. Therefore, he makes haste to add: "The clearing, the opening, is not only free for brightness and darkness, but also for resonance and echo, for sounding and diminishing of sound. The clearing is the open for everything that is present and absent."[24]

We take note, but we are not convinced. To say "not only . . . but also" is not sufficient to resolve the issue and show it in its "how." Heidegger claims that the unthought of the light of metaphysics is not only a *theorein*, a seeing; "more essentially," it is sound of silence, or of stillness. That is, it is something that has to do with *logos*, or with the hermeneutics of the meaning of being. It is "more essentially" because the place where the *Lichtung* brings *Dasein* to dwell is *essentially* language, the originary saying (*Sage*). *Die Sage* names and gathers into unity the free range of the *Lichtung* that is the scene of presence and absence.[25] This originary language is then "interpretation," *Erörterung*, which however also means "location" (*Ort*, which is also linked to *Ende*). Word and clearing belong to each other, Heidegger suggests. And with this last, thin remark he thinks that the matter is closed.

One should not, however, let oneself be enchanted. Heidegger has not closed anything at all. On the contrary, he has made a bit of confusion, albeit a genial and fruitful confusion.

26. *Matters in place.* In truth, Heidegger does not have the slightest idea of how voice and vision come to belong to each other within metaphysics (as it has actually occurred). Since he does not ask any question regarding the content of the logical form and the relevance of the event of the practice of alphabetic writing, he mistakes voices and visions, as happens to Derrida too, in the desperate attempt at opening himself a path toward *aletheia* and from here returning to join adjudicative *veritas*:hat is, in the desperate attempt at comprehending the origin of metaphysics and its destiny.

The light of the suprasensible vision does not have who knows what miraculous opening behind itself. Nor could it ever be gathered from the saying of the saga. Nor is the latter, in its nature of straight way (*methodos, diexodos*), truly an "originary saying." Nor can one attribute to it *sic et simpliciter*, as Heidegger sometimes does, the nature of hint, indication, or gesture as primordial revelatory sign. There is here a whole genealogy, a complexity of gestures and practices, of which Heidegger has no inkling.

Behind itself, the suprasensible vision has the purification of *logos* through defining and "elementary" writing. The opening is this very practice, and not the advent of imaginary clearings. Behind itself, this purified ("logical") *logos* does not have "language," but rather complex practices of voice, intertwined gestural expressions, of which *Erörterung* is an aspect among other aspects. "Language" is not at all the originary opening (assuming that, besides having ears, it also has eyes), although all other openings get translated into its opening. This happens not because of mysterious events and donations, but because of the peculiar nature of the vocal gesture,[26] of which Heidegger however knows almost nothing. This peculiarity of the vocal gesture should not be taken in abstract, metaphysically, but rather as an emerging through specific and concrete practices that change the meaning of what we call (metaphysically, logically) "voice," its gestural expression and its objects.

The metaphysical look that constitutes us does not listen, while contemplating, to any mysterious "voice of silence." It transcribes the soul of speech, that is, its definition, into the disembodied point of the line, thus making fictitiously visible its original inaudibility. It is a conventional re-embodiment of the voice, which had been previously desomatized. This gesture makes silence: not the primordial silence of the world flesh (as Merleau-Ponty would say), but rather the construed and constitutive silence of the voice of the soul. For this reason our reading (and writing) is essentially a looking at silence and seeing the suprasensible. All this is nothing else than *thinking*, which constitutes us as subjects of the logical mind, as subjects capable of the truth of judgment. Besides frequenting forests and clearings, Heidegger would have benefited from observing himself too—while reading.

27. *Naming without thinking.* In Heidegger, the thinking of the end [*la fine*] joins the thinking of the origin through the *Lichtung*. Since the *Lichtung* plastically names the movement of *aletheia*, Heidegger can say, albeit in a surprising

manner, that at the *origin* of philosophy one is actually speaking of *Lichtung*. This happens in Parmenides, where the belonging together of being and thinking (their being the "same thing," that is, "the matter itself") rests on truth as originary manifestation (*aletheia*). Here, *aletheia* still and essentially means *Lichtung*: opening, unconcealment, which Parmenides must have experienced to be able to name presence in terms of identity of being and thinking. Philosophy neglects the question of this opening, as it also neglects to ask on the ground of the necessity for what opening Plato *had to* name presence as idea, Aristotle as *energeia*, and so on. In truth, philosophy cannot even ask these questions. At least starting with Aristotle, metaphysics focuses on a being [*ente*] as such, that is, on the being present of presence, and inquires onto-theologically into its transcendental cause and ground of being. This does not occur because of a "defect" of philosophy. Rather, it occurs because of its "destiny": "The reference to what is unthought in philosophy is not a criticism of philosophy."[27]

At the origins, philosophy names the *Lichtung* with the word *aletheia*; it names it, but it does not at all think it as such. When saying *aletheia*, none of the Greeks, not even Homer, has ever thought anything else than *orthotes*, the correctness of representation and the precision of enunciation: that is, the truth of judgment. Here, Heidegger finds himself in front of the usual abyss which he does not know how to fill in. He reasserts that without *aletheia* (manifestation of a being [*ente*]) there is no *veritas* (correctness of judgment). The latter presupposes the former, since one cannot judge what is present without its very coming into presence; what "gives" is precisely the *Lichtung*, the opening. Thus, in the granting (*gewären*) of present unconcealment is the possibility itself of adjudicative truth (*Wahrheit*). The word play is ingenious, and it is like a rope thrown across the abyss. This, however, remains such. How, through what way, by what *methodos* one moves from the unconcealment of the *aspects* of what is present to the logical essence of the objects of judgment remains unthought and unthinkable in Heidegger because of the modalities of his attitude and questioning.

28. *The fury of reason*. The Greeks say *aletheia* and think *orthotes*. They say well (since their language is "philosophical" in and by itself), but they think badly. Yet, they are not alone. According to Heidegger, all human beings do the same (and without even saying it well) because they turn and focus themselves on the care and preservation of what is present, what is ready at hand and available, without asking too many questions about its provenance and its being in such a way. At most, they put forth *ad hoc* hypotheses of a mythical, theological, metaphysical, scientific kind, the more or less evident purpose of which is to grant humans the availability of presence: superstitiously, conceptually, or materially. I would say that the *event* of presence never gets to be thought.

One should not hold this against human beings, though, since all this does not occur because of a specific negligence in their thinking. Heidegger's hypothesis is that all this occurs because of the will of the *Lichtung* itself, which, as *aletheia*, loves *lethe*, and as *phusis*, loves to hide. Concealment is not added to unconcealment; it is rather the origin and the condition for it. While giving itself to being seen, while donating the horizon of presence in changeable guises, at the same time the *Lichtung* also runs to hide, preserving itself from inborn human rapacity. This rapacity is, however, willed by the *Lichtung* itself when lighting up human beings in such a manner that they are, at the same time and for that very reason, surrounded by a horizon of darkness.

All this has an odd "theological" flavor. Heidegger is especially careful to defend himself from the charge of irrationalism, and he does so in his own, unmistakable way. One can say that "to hide," "to preserve oneself," to give," and so on are a "ruinous irrationalism"[28] only if one can appropriately answer the question of what "*ratio*," "*nous*," "*noẹin*," "perceiving," "ground," "cause," and so on *properly* mean. It does not look as though there is anyone who can answer these questions (and this is the reason why I occupy myself here with the content of the form and with the tradition of thought). Speaking of irrationalism is therefore also without ground. Moreover, there is the legitimate suspicion that precisely the technical-scientific rationalization and the unstoppable spread of the uprooting fury of cybernetics are the extreme expression of the irrational.

29. *The task of thinking.* "To plunge one's sight deep" into the constitutive obscurity of the *Lichtung* creates quite a few difficulties. First of all, it induces one to wonder what *aletheia* (insofar as originarily *lethe*) has to do with truth, which is a question that for Heidegger can only remain unresolved: and then, whether *aletheia* is something less or something more than truth. This is the same as wondering whether it is truth or rather revelation that saves the world.

The question does not seem new, yet on his part Heidegger recognizes in it the "task of thinking." This occurs in the form of a question that goes like this: in general, can thought ask even one question of meaning on *aletheia* while remaining philosophical thought, that is, aiming at what is present only with reference to its presence (and not also to its concealing and withdrawing)? The question is clearly rhetorical, and rests on a tautological consideration. If, by inner necessity, philosophical thought means to thematize (that is, objectify) presence, then to think latency, or that which absences itself in presence, cannot be a matter for this kind of thought.

There are other questions that one should ask: are that to which the question alludes, the play of self-giving and self-withdrawing, presence and absence, truly something that remains outside, precedes, is other than philosophical thinking? Is it right to entrust "thinking" (be it as a task and as future thinking) with the thinkability of that which cannot be thought within philosophy? Which "thinking" is here invoked? How can the invocation escape philosophical conceptuality and hint at something truly different? If latency is latency *of* presence, is it not already thought within presence? Would thinking it as an in-itself not amount to the absurd claim of thinking it as presence? When one raises this difficulty, is one not mistaking a tautological impossibility (one cannot think that which by definition is a non-being) for an obscure and mysterious factual impossibility, for an enigmatic destiny? Moreover, if it is the *Lichtung* that wants human being to be unaware, and it decides and destines thus, why should one pose as a task that of exploring such an unawareness? Or would thinking here mean simply to become ready to accept? This is certainly not a small matter, but what does this have to do with thought and truth?

30. *Beyond disenchantment.* Beyond the abstract and ungrounded distinction between rational and irrational, Heidegger wishes for a thinking that is "more sober than scientific technology" and meanwhile "still more disenchanted."[29] That is, more disenchanted than the "disenchantment" of which Max Weber speaks. For example, if modern disenchantment prefers reason to myth and the profane to the sacred, disenchanted thought moves beyond these very distinctions.

More disenchanted also means "removed" and "without effect";[30] detached from beings [*ente*] and from the projectual fury that concerns them in techno-scientific (cybernetic) manipulation; empty of effective power and truth within the context of the unstoppable unfolding of *Weltzivilisation*. It is a marginal thinking that by itself banishes itself from the *universitas studiorum*, that is, from the specialization of research, the domination of informational devices and methodologies, the historical and historiographic passing of public truth, any archontic burden and claim of a political nature. "The direct or indirect effect of this thinking on the industrial age, formed by technology and science, is decisively less possible"[31] to this thinking than to current, merely epigonal philosophy.

While being disenchanted with respect to its ancient metaphysical function and its current technical completion (reduction of the meaning of all beings and events to the *social* category of work or cybernetic production), this thinking would however have its own peculiar necessity, rigor, and consistency. Naturally, it would not be the rigor of logic, that is, it would not be in the form of the simple presence-at-hand (of the "given") and the will to correctness and domination that belong to logic. Rather, it would be the rigor that is necessary to conform oneself to the opening and to the question that concerns such an opening, in the effort to derive the measure, rule, and discipline of one's own attitude from the opening itself.

31. *Exercise in circle.* Here one can see more clearly the "task of thinking." However, Heidegger claims that this task raises two paralyzing questions. The first concerns *this* very thinking: what kind of thinking is a thinking that can be neither metaphysics nor science?

The second question concerns the kind of education that is necessary for the *transformation* which is the very task of thinking. This task has a preparatory, not grounding character, and its goal is that of "awakening a readiness in man for a *possibility* whose contour remains obscure, whose coming remains uncertain."[32] This entails a coming to grips with the "philosophical tradition" (Heidegger uses exactly this expression).[33] To turn thinking and its task into a question is not an innocent gesture. It already contains in itself the burden of the tradition, its "critical" questioning, its way of educating to thinking. Yet we search for a different [thinking], one which is a new opening and is linked to the "opening" (of the philosophical tradition itself). "The task of thinking would then be the surrender of previous thinking to the determination of the matter of thinking."[34]

Are we (is Heidegger himself) clear, about "the thinking we have had so far"? What is it exactly? Is it the oblivion of *aletheia*, or is it rather the unawareness of the content of the form of truth? How does preparatory thinking "prepare"? With his exemplary acumen, Heidegger is the first to denounce the "circle." In the act of *deciding* for a new opening, we should already have *decided* and been reached by the evidence of the opening itself (of the "matter itself"). In this case, as one could add recalling Hegel, one would need no preparation.

If, on the contrary, preparation is necessary, how can we enact it if we do not know for what, and thus how to prepare? What is the nature of the "transformation" that is required? How does it still have to do with thinking? Has it perhaps already begun, and we have not realized it? Is it linked to our very questioning? Is it still far and obscure? Should we perhaps be content with immobility and arrest (which are themselves very difficult to reach)? Or, at the most, with a silent exercise practiced in the heart of the night?

CHAPTER 7

Practices

32. *The philosophizing self.* What is the tradition of philosophy? What is the tradition of thinking? What is, however, the starting point for these questions? The starting point is *one oneself* insofar as, by asking such questions, one already practices philosophy. Starting from this practice one asks and posits the question of *meaning* [senso], of the meaning of this practice.

Husserl, for example, asks the question of the "philosophizing self," that is, of the philosophical self in flesh and bones, considered in the concrete exercise of its philosophizing. Oddly, he has never been taken seriously, though. That which did *not* want to be a theory, but rather a practice, a "phenomenological exercise," has generally been brought back to theses of idealism, subjectivism, consciousness [*coscienzialismo*], and so on. Husserl surely has his own responsibility for that, and Heidegger has more than one reason for his objections to his master. The fact is that he has remained blind to the real question of the philosophizing self. For example, he has never applied it to himself. Professor Heidegger has questioned the meaning of metaphysics, and Rector Heidegger has questioned the meaning of history and the destiny of Germany and the West. Yet he never questioned the meaning of the concrete operations that he was exercising when lecturing and politically administrating the university. He exercised these practices as "obvious" and obviously important, even better, epochal.

We *are*, however, the practices that we exercise. While reflecting on the philosophizing self, I find myself already constituted by a complexity of practices and relations which come to me from the tradition. These practices define and determine my current status and, more or less obscurely, confer a meaning on it. This includes the meaning of the reflection on these very practices. The philosophizing self that I am, that one is, is never at first, and perhaps never at all, in self-transparency with respect to itself. The alleged starting point is in truth an arrival point. The two things are one. To come back to oneself is to discover oneself as other (other than oneself). The philosophizing self is a disquieting intertwining of what is own and what is alien. It is totally other than a solid ground. Rather, it is an indented and stratified abyss.

33. *Questions of style.* What is the meaning of the question of the philosophizing self? What does it truly ask? Ultimately, it asks whether one can continue to ignore those practices that one actively exercises, for example when one philosophizes and asks about the meaning of philosophy. Can we assume these practices as obvious, as meaningful, as void in themselves of their own stress and content, and therefore of specific consequences? Can we write, read, lecture, reflect on this and that, and never cast even a thought on this doing and the modalities that are characteristic and irremissible for such a doing?

Can we continue to act within these practices, which are completely neglected, and simply move on to ask, what do truth, being, being of a being, opening, event, and so on mean? Can we go on philosophizing in a naively direct way, maybe even asking ourselves what philosophy means, without ever considering the practice and game in which we are caught? To do so means to abandon oneself blindly to the public truth of the tradition. We can certainly inquire into it "critically," provoke its "destruction" or "deconstruction." Yet this only means that we believe that the tradition is made of meanings and concepts, doctrines and ideas (which we criticize) and not also and more deeply of the continuity–difference of practices (which we go on exercising without questions).

Can one really understand the historical, historical-destinal character of the tradition, if one neglects considering the practical and active modalities of its constitution, and asks instead the problem of the truth of being or the *Lichtung*? In the darkness of this negligence, how can one hope to truly clarify the nature of the "thought that we have had so far?" How can one operate its transformation, make it such that, as Husserl used to say, philosophy changes its style, if one does not wonder exactly in the place where this style constitutes itself and imposes its form? That is, if one does not wonder about the content of this form?

34. *The doing of the practice.* One says "practice," "to practice," "practices." But what does one mean by the word "practice"? We are constantly in *life practices* (Husserl and later Wittgenstein, each in his own way, say something about this), and we move within them. Every life practice is a [form of] "wisdom" *sui generis.* At the least, it is knowing how to do this and that (to stand, walk, grasp, and so on); then, it is a knowing how to say; and finally, it is a knowing how to write, in all the senses of this expression.

The general feature of doing is a relation, but not in the form "A does B," where A and B are already constituted as objects each in itself. Originally, doing is a relation that posits itself at its own extremes or posits its own terms. "A loves B" or "A runs" must be understood in this way: the active love relation situates A and B at its poles and makes them "lovers." The A that loves C (besides or after B) is not the same A; nor is it the A that runs. Thus, it is the action of running that puts A in relation with his or her legs, and makes them "runners." The action names a polarized involvement the consequences (and not the premises) of which are the subject and the object: points of solidification that are determined time after time.

It is within practices thus understood that we are given to ourselves (in connection with the others and in general with the world), and that we acquire eyes and hands, mouths and ears, and so on. We have eyes to see, hands to grasp, ears to hear, feet to walk: it is in this determined "to" that we have such things and the relative objects: colors, bodies, sounds, pavements, and so on. We do not have them separately and "before." One should not start from "abstract" elements (elements abstract from the practice) such as "eyes," "ears," and so on, and then join them *a posteriori*, thus creating an artificial image that has been over-intellectually construed by ourselves. If one does not grasp, one does not have hands, and depending on how one grasps, one has the hands one has (like a man, like a woman, like a woodman, like a goldsmith, and so on). Nothing is in presence, nothing discloses itself if not by virtue of a practice.

Practices are e-motions, which move and induce us to an answer. Thus, we are called into acting: from the world and in the world. Thus we are at-tracted into action. Therefore, we *are*: made by the action that calls.

35. *The intertwining of practices.* Every practice brings a universe of meaning to existence. Every practice delineates the world in a peculiar way. One should think of all that is entailed in practicing cattle-raising rather than farming, practicing navigation, casting metals, and so on, and then reading, writing, computing, and even simple walking (which at the origin was not easy at all, even if humankind has forgotten, and the adult forgets it). Meanwhile, each practice opens possibilities that go far beyond its beginning. In the opening of each life practice, potentialities are inscribed, the further development of which hands down an origin which is continuously reinterpreted and therefore transformed and relived within new horizons of meaning. Very different is, for example, the sense in which a Greek philosopher or a medieval monk practices philosophy, even though both of them are inscribed within the continuity of the philosophical practice, with its gestures and arguments, its concepts and logical methods.

In general, it is important to realize this: *there is no practice that can be taken as isolated in itself.* One should always keep in mind that each practice is linked to other practices and is an indefinite and nuanced set of many practices. Each practice assumes elements that have already been constituted and disclosed within other practices, and it makes them its own. That is, it transforms, adapts, subdues, specializes them, and thus it confers on them a new meaning.

—Yet, if no practice can be taken in isolation, how can one speak of "the practice of cattle-raising" rather than "the practice of farming," and so on?

—Through the practice of speech and writing that names and defines. This is not, however, a practice that can be isolated in itself; and it is a set of many practices. Like any other practice, it too can be defined not in itself, but rather in another practice.

36. *The example of the orchestra.* Imagine that one is in a big concert hall as someone in the audience. In front, on the stage, are the orchestra and its director.

They are playing a Haydn symphony. Now, think about this whole, exciting experience, and see how many practices it is made of. It is actually an impossible, because infinite, evaluation.

One sees the orchestra, its typical disposition (the strings, from highest to lowest: first and second violins, in the middle the violas, on the right the cellos and the basses; behind the strings, the woodwinds; behind the woodwinds, the horns; and still behind, the percussion, and so on). This disposition is the result of a century-old instrumental "profane" practice, which is rooted in the beginnings of music and which during the Middle Ages was expelled from churches and left to dancing festivals, markets, and tumblers. Little by little groups and families of instruments formed; their congregations and oppositions were created according to the needs of playing together (initially, "symphony" means nothing else than this), but also according to the desire to imitate human voice, and sacred and profane polyphony. Later, with the beginning of lyrical opera, the orchestra congregated, placed itself around the stage, and subdued itself to the director's baton, which was banged on the ground to keep the time. Little by little we arrive at Haydn, who is the father of modern symphony and establishes the basic pattern of orchestral timbres and colors, thus identifying the possibilities of each single instrument. Just at a first glance, one already has an immense and immeasurable quantity of practices.

Think about the single instruments. Each of them is the result of very ancient artisan practices, and then of productive techniques that progress together with the progression of building techniques. Consider just the violin's bow: what a complex story, from its curved shape in old viols, to the modern straight shape; and then, the evolution of its expressivity and technique, from Corelli to Paganini. All this must be considered also in relation to the practices of the human body: hands, fingers, chin and shoulder, lips, lungs, diaphragm, and so on. Think of what a refined exercise this is, which presupposes the practices of basic bodily gestural expressions (grasping, blowing, striking, and so on).

Now consider the scores that the orchestral players read. In them is sedimented the entire history of writing, and of musical writing from Guido of Arezzo on. In truth, modern music, its form, its language, would be inconceivable and impossible without writing. And one should not forget the paper itself as the product of complex practices, and also the music-stands, the chairs, the podium, the lights, the soundproofed room, the armchair on which one sits, the velvet on the doors, and so on.

If one then pays attention to what the orchestra plays, here one discovers an extremely high, complex, and refined result of musical thinking, in the evolution of its syntactical, dynamic, and expressive forms, to which centuries and centuries of researches within different and various contexts, practices, and sense have cooperated. The execution itself is a philological interpretation that is supported by interpretive practices by schools and epochs, traditions and innovations.

Lastly, the gestures of the director derive from very ancient hand gestural practices and their progressive transformation. They also contain the universal practice of expressivity through gestures, mimics, and looks, which is an essential part of communication. They are also a plastic show within the show, since any music lover knows that the pleasure of one of Haydn's symphonies comes not only from listening to the music but also from watching the orchestra perform it alive.

37. *The duplicity of practice.* A practice is *transcendental* with respect to its content of meaning. It is the *opening* of a meaning the content of which does not pre-exist, but rather is in function of the practice. At the same time, however, a practice is *empirical,* since it contains elements of other practices that have already evolved; it coordinates and organizes them, and thus confers on them a new opening of meaning. This duplicity (which would be scandalous or badly ambiguous [when considered] from the perspective of philosophical conceptuality) is typical of practice, and it must be constantly acknowledged and held onto.

A practice is measured by its end [*dal suo fine*]. It is the final cause, the *telos,* which organizes the elements and thus melts a multiplicity of practices into a synthesis. For example, a musical performance in a concert is the goal of the orchestra, and therefore also of the director's and instrumental players' movements, of the light disposition, of the chairs, of the room and its acoustic devices, of the microphones, and so on. Since the concert performance is a show and a social event, this is the end to which also the clothes of the musicians, the audience, and the ushers, the posters and the programs, the ticket counter and the sequence of seats, and so on subject and concur.

All these elements, which are in themselves empirical, since they have developed in other practices, subject themselves to a new meaning and acquire a new sense. The director lifts his or her arm to signal the beginning, but this is not equivalent to saying "Yo!" to catch the waitress's attention. Even coughing becomes subdued, not to disturb, and movements become calm and quiet. Next to this, as it always happens, float other practices, completely free, sufficiently hidden, and thus not interfering: casting a sidelong glance at the lady in the fourth row, checking whether we have buttoned the pocket that contains our wallet, tapping with one's fingers, thinking about one's own cases.

38. *Parmenides' meaning.* At this point, one should take a short detour and think about Parmenides composing and writing his poem (there were hours and days, presumably in Elea, when this undoubtedly happened and was happening). With his composing, Parmenides pursues an end [*un fine*] that gives meaning to his practice and is transcendental to its elements. Taken one by one, these elements are empirical; that is, they have already developed in other practices: the writing material, the language, the alphabet, the poetic measure, the mythical-religious images, the doctrines, the cults, the prospect of recitals or public readings, the

handing down to the school, and so on. Yet, all together they arrange themselves in a new universe of meaning, in a new opening, in a new *telos*.

What *meaning?* We could say that the end [*il fine*] of the poem is wisdom-oriented [*sapienziale*]: a mortal walks on the path of truth so as to become wise. In this sense, his practice inherits a complex tradition of wisdom-oriented practices which the historian will never be able to sound and resurrect in their depth. Yet the fact is that Parmenides renews such a tradition, giving to it a new meaning. But what meaning?

We could say it is a dialectical meaning. However, this would mean to consider the elements and the end [*il fine*] of the poem from the perspective of the re-elaboration and interpretation that belong to Zeno's practice. We could say it is a rhetorical meaning, and we would then assume the perspective of Gorgias' practice. Lastly, we could say it is a philosophical meaning, and then it is the interpretive viewpoint of Plato's practice that we endorse. This means that the meaning of the poem is neither simply wisdom-oriented, dialectical, rhetorical, nor philosophical (these are practices which, on their part, are in conflict among one another to establish the winning or dominating wisdom-oriented form, the "truth").

Whatever side one takes, one sinks into practices and their specific donations of meaning. The transcendental event of the poem, its opening of meaning, continuously escapes.

39. *The translation of the event.* As an opening of the world, each practice brings the event of the world to significance. It is thus essentially a taking place in the world by giving a place to its event; as such, it is an *ethos*, a dwelling and custom.

Being, for example, a musician, is not just a matter of technique and profession (as one likes to say today, according to the logic of specialization and "work"). Primarily, and more in depth, it is an ethical matter. Having been entrusted to the practice of musical tradition, through it the musician relives an originary event of meaning. One could call it the originary opening of the world in a sonorous, harmonic, musical semblance. This event is not given to the musician in its imaginary and ideal purity; rather, it is given through a chain of practices and signs, transformations and interpretations, which are nothing else than those potentialities inscribed in the originary event and continuously reinterpreted and relived according to new horizons of meaning. There is a big difference between vocally imitating bird songs and using the voice to retell the Passion according to Matthew.

The event, its active happening, its action are simultaneously something empirical and transcendental. It is always a sign: this sign that translates, expresses, interprets a distance (a provenance, a tradition, a destination). It is the concrete imitation of the nightingale with its specific opening of meaning. It is the chorale that begins with "O bleeding head." The event is always its interpretation, always "hermeneutic." Any attempt at grasping the originary event in itself, the *primum* (which, on its side, never "knows" of its being first), occurs within an interpretation, and presupposes an interpretation, with no break in continuity. The *primum* is always relocated further and further behind, or, which is the same, beforehand. The event gives itself in an infinite translation of codes and sign systems, one could say with Wittgenstein (substance can be understood only in its infinite attributes, one could say with Spinoza). Yet the event occurs only insofar as its interpretations and their transmutations of meaning occur. It is the transcendental surplus of happening in relation to its signified.

As a musician, one stands therefore in one's ancestral *ethos* as in the event that opens one's future and rules the emerging interpretation of one's practice as a musician, and all of one's practices as a human being. To be a musician in fact amounts for one to open oneself up to the world and life with the prevailing instrument of this specific language. Through this practice one "knows" mainly how to translate the world into meanings. For this reason, Beethoven (but also Nietzsche out of his philosophical *ethos*) bitterly regretted having one day ended up in a brothel.

40. *The play of the matter* [cosa]. A practice is opened by the revelation of a "matter." If Heidegger speaks of the "matter of thinking," I would like one to think of the "matter of practice." First of all, this means that to understand a practice one should not refer to subjects' intentionality. The latter is actually a consequence of the former. A subject's intentionality can be understood only starting from the practice in which the subject is situated, from its form and the content of its form.

The matter plays in two senses: as a *possibility* that calls for or claims action (properly, the matter is an *emotion*), and as an object insofar as it is a *telos* or ideal pole of operations. As possibility, the thing is truly an icon in Peirce's sense.[1] It is the image of *telos*, that is, the grasping of a sign relation, of a "possible resemblance": something can have the meaning of something else (that is, it can have a sense). In this way, possibility occurs as the emotion that directs toward a *telos*, toward the object-goal of the action. This opening shapes the physiognomy of the agent within itself, situates the agent on the way within its practice, within the disclosure of a world whose sign is the matter. The world that opens up occurs in an image, or in a resemblance, of the matter.

Thus the play of the matter, its circle that circles between image as possibility and object as *telos*, happens. Something announces itself by signaling (and indicating), and emotions [*emoziona*] presence, which enters in a tension (it intentions *telos*). The world announces itself to the agent as a "being for another." It finds in the other its own meaning and end.

41. *Before and after.* The disclosure of the matter does not occur in a void; rather, it happens within already activated practices. One should think of the Neolithic woman who *sees* in the seed the sign of the flower and the fruit. She is already the result of many practices (gathering, cleaning, cooking, and so on), within which she exercises the function of subject. It is from the re-elaboration of these

practices within the energy of a new meaning that she can open the practice of farming for a humankind still made of hunters and breeders.

How did the *first* practice constitute itself? Yet this very questioning is already a practice. Thinking about events according to a "before" and an "after" is due to the determination of a practice. Because we attend this practice unawarely, the question seems to us to be "natural." Before and after are the objects of a practice (that is, a set of practices). Yet we ignore this, and we take these objects as if they were realities in themselves, valid outside any practice. We think that their being before and after is in the nature of things, that this is their own form, and we do not ask about the content of this form, that is, about its connection to a practice (which temporalizes and "writes" time, thus letting it emerge).[2]

As a conclusion: one should also imagine that one can answer the question concerning a supposedly first practice. Yet this answer would not disclose at all the hypothetical beginning as thought in itself (as it would have been or could have been in itself). Rather, it would disclose the nature of the question and the sense of *its* practice. There are no beginnings in themselves, practices in themselves, "first" things and practices outside of any practice.

42. *The distance of the practice.* A practice requires distance, and therefore also a horizon. Distance is intrinsic to it because the event of a practice is essentially a distancing, a "taking place," a happening as *perspective* and *path*. The event is this very path that *situates* or places itself.

When one thinks the event, one should think neither of something objective in itself and absolute, nor of something simple (these are abstractions that are linked to an analytical practice of abstracting, for example by drawing Cartesian graphs or similar). The event of a practice has its meaning in a *digression* (Derrida would say in a differing), that is, in a distancing within itself. It spatializes and temporalizes itself (so to speak, but this is not well said because space and time are not properly objects of all practices) according to modalities that are intrinsic to the disclosive circle of the matter. The measure of this, or its form, is determined by the nature, that is, by the content, of the matter itself.

An event occurs only in this way. An event that had its meaning in itself, that is, an "absolute" (that is, unconnected, separate) event, would not be an event. Nothing absolute may happen. What happens is the relation, the being in a relation, the being here *for* a there. What occurs is the reference (the being at a distance), the image, the icon. From this, one can understand that *the event itself is a sign*, the event of a sign, something that has distance within itself and therefore "moves" (happens, moves, and falls). If one understands this, one understands what is most important.

The event of a practice is the event of the circularity of a matter, the event of the possibility of a matter as object of the practice according to a perspective and a discourse. The event connects in a circle every moment of this. At every moment there are the images of the opening and the object as *telos*. One *proceeds* within the circle; yet, because of its circular nature, the event itself has a *rhythmic* nature. It is a constant reinterpreting of the beginning in view of the end, and of the end in view of the beginning (thus, simple reference to time and space is inappropriate to express it).

Inappropriate is also the simple "thinking the event," as one might non-problematically believe we are doing. The issue is not *to think* the event (as Heidegger might induce us to think), but rather *to put it to work*. In what practice is the thought of the event as opening, as "transcendental" happening of the practice, put to work? *This* is the issue. Properly, it is the question, what are we doing?

43. *The symbolon*. Suppose that the "matter" is the disclosure of the practice of sexuality (of sexual emotion) in the by-now-grown-up puppies of some species. They move from a practice of playing to a practice of copulation. The gestures of courting, pursuing, grasping, and penetrating emerge within the circle of disclosure of the sexual "matter," and rhythmically come back into order (as a "series").

I call this rhythmic opening a *symbolon*: the broken part, or the fragment, of an ideal whole (one should think for example of a coin broken into two, and one has one half of it; this half is an image that "prefigures" the whole that one does not have, that is not there). By virtue of the opening, the animal's body becomes a *symbolon*, part of a whole. This part now discloses itself as "sexed" (which *is* its being sexed), that is, as a *sign* for something else toward which it hints or attracts (something else than playing, bouncing, eating, sleeping, and so on insofar as these are already consolidated practices, *symbola* already enacted and experienced).

As a sign, the body is the sign of a lack and a need, of a distance, which determines the direction and the path (the having to be of the *symbolon*). Analogously, one could say that the seed is a *symbolon* of the flower and the fruit.

One should think of the issue in this way: one half of the coin represents the body of a he-bunny [*coniglietto*]. It is a sign of his sexual tension, that is, of his being attracted from a distance by the image of a she-bunny [*coniglietta*]. This image is his possibility: that is, his object and *telos*. In the image (in the part that is missing from him, and that he represents in tension, that he intentions) the he-bunny finds the completion of himself insofar as he has been opened by sexual disclosure, and has fallen into the constitutive distance of sexuality. Now, one should reverse the example, and consider something similar for the body of the other half of the coin, which represents the body of the she-bunny, as she has fallen into the sexual relation. Coupling would be the reconstitution of the whole that has been disclosed by emotion: that is, the reunion of the two parts of the coin.

Between the two parts there remains, however, a fissure. One should not forget this.

44. *Completion as fading away of the matter*. In the completion of its *telos*, the whole to which the *symbolon* hints is not, properly, *realized*. There is no whole

either before or after. [The whole] is an image, an icon, a sign. Coupling itself is a sign of the whole but is not the whole. The fissure alludes precisely to this. In coupling, the object is reached in the sense that it is brought to the maximum, constitutive nearness that is possible. By this, however, it is also made further, kept distinct, and at a distance. The male rabbit has his sexual self in the other, in the female rabbit; and the female [has hers] in the male. Yet, in coupling, the male rabbit does not become the female, and they are not "one single thing."

At its maximum point the distance, which has been rhythmically filled, bounces back and breaks. The rhythm that has been opened by emotion closes up (the imaginative tension breaks, the two parts of the coin return to being simple, stranger fragments, erased potentialities). In completion, disclosure fades away. Fruition of the object closes up the circle of disclosure of the matter. In the completion of the emotion, its subject (insofar as it is an "eroticized" subject, which has emerged *in the* disclosure of the matter) disappears. With it, the object-*telos* disappears. The disclosure of the matter fades away. As an image, it disappears. The male and female rabbits become indifferent to each other. Or they resume the practice of playing like puppies. The now disappeared sexual emotion keeps itself in store, and prepares itself to a new opening and a new appearance of its stages.

From this, one can see how the subject experiences its own being sign, for example an image and appearance of sexual disclosure. The subject is a pure place (*oros* is the word that the Greeks would use), a field of potential disclosure of matters (*pragmata*), as Protagoras conceives of it, or a field of forces in perennial conflict, as Nietzsche sees it.[3]

45. *The horizon of practice.* Besides distance and perspective, one should consider now the *horizon.* The horizon of eros, for example, is the propelling, intentional center of the lover's *praxis.* The lover is, literally, a *to be in love* [in English in the text]: horizon of the world *sub* sexual *species.* Within this horizon a perspective gets determined, and possible paths emerge; that is, what needs to be done gets designed and scanned: the male rabbit furiously pursues the female, which runs away with the purpose of getting caught (or at least so some of us think, since, because of our being a male *symbolon,* femininity is constitutively at a distance from us in the figure of a great mystery, that is, as *our* mystery).

With copulation, the horizon closes up. The world, or being in the world, which has been brought to disclosure, fades. An image of the world (that is, a world), with its disclosive horizon thanks to which one has objects, emotions, paths, clever devices, tricks, tactics, and pretences, fades away with its baggage of practices and senses. Hopes that have been granted disappear, need dissolves.

Yet one has not pondered distance enough.

46. *The individual and distance.* Originary distance is the event itself of the sign: that is, the occurrence of something as opening, as *symbolon.* This happening means being situated at a distance by the disclosure of the matter, [disclosure

viewed] as possibility of reaching [the matter] in an image, that is, in the semblance of an object.

Opening up as horizon, originary distance distributes itself in the determined distances of the path in which practice articulates itself, practice which is motivated at each moment by the nature of its *telos* (running after the female rabbit, not to playfully make her flee, but to reach, subdue, and penetrate her). In this way, the initially disclosed possibility finds its completion.

In the object of completion or *telos*, that which is obliterated is not originary distance (that is, the event of the disclosure of the matter that posits the subject-*symbolon* in its constitutive emotioned distance in a tension toward the object-image). What is obliterated is the articulation of the originary distance in the path: that is, *that determined* practice of the disclosed horizon. Originary distance is rejected into indifference. The disclosive light of the path dies. What remains are the individuals in *their* distance, which is internal to the determined circle of another practice (to sleep, eat, play, and so on). As Hegel would put it, individuals cannot raise themselves to the "matter," they can only consume themselves. They can consume themselves as eroticized individuals, and fall back into another practice, in which they rhythmically consume themselves again, walking on that rhythm of rhythms that is their life until the final consumption.

In completion, that is, in the achievement of the object-*telos*, ever new particular events happen in particular distances: *this* copulation or, in the example of the seed, *this* little plant. From the individual comes the individual, says Aristotle. Originary distance is never obliterated. Eros as such remains unattained. It is a possibility in the sense of Peirce's *Firstness* [in English in the original] or Whitehead's eternal Object. As such, it is an ingredient of "reality" which can only occur in individuals (in facts). That is, [it can only occur] as *Secondness* (existence) in the horizon of *Thirdness* (of norm, of *telos*) [both in English in the original].

47. *Recapitulation*. One should try now to recapitulate some essential tenets with respect to practices. First of all, any practice is a practice made of many practices. Something comes from very far away, something else comes from much closer. Many worlds come together in one.

A practice comes from things' signaling. As signs, indications of *telos*, things open up *praxis*. Thus, every *praxis* opens up a world of meaning: an acted world much before a contemplated world. Practices are mainly centered on desire, on *eros*, on the obscure need for possession. Practices are, first of all, "economic" practices of life.

Practices run through individuals, through their bodies. Thus, the individual *has* a body shaped by practices. This occurs neither "before" nor in the abstract. Consequently, one should not conceive of the event of a practice as something individual. The *symbolon* is not properly and at first the single body active with its signs. The event is the happening of determined practices *through* individuals (the practice of cattle-raising, farming, writing, and alike).

By passing and developing in individuals, these practices determine that "intermonadic" corporality of which the individual is part. The individual is thus a concentration of practices, a knot of localized emotions. It is an image, (literally) a phantasm, a semblance of the "nature" of practices. It is a sign of the forces, of the emotions that traverse it. It is a field of forces in a (often antagonistic, as Nietzsche says) tension.

In every practice, individuals find themselves situated in a world horizon. In this horizon, something acquires this or that meaning. There is an enactment of gestures according to perspectives and paths defined and delimited by the practice.

If one now asks: how does the "consciousness" of practice occur? How does the event of being conscious and self-conscious happen for individuals? I will reply: This occurs within the practice of the vocal gesture, whose opening of meaning is such as to enable the assumption within itself of any other practice, and the translation of its meaning into the meaning of its own signs.[4]

48. *Exposing oneself to the text.* At this point, one may think one knows enough to return, once again, to Parmenides as the exemplary origin of the philosophical tradition and its practice. In what way does the event of Parmenides' wisdom-oriented gesture occur? In what way does the opening of his horizon of meaning occur, which designates perspectives and paths and measures its own symballic distance in its objects? How does the disclosive circle of the matter reveal itself in such event? (This is the matter that Heidegger generally and problematically understands as the "matter of thinking," which by necessity would have announced and subtracted itself in the "matter of philosophy").

To answer such questions, one can only expose oneself anew to the text of the poem (that is, ultimately, to a tradition constituted over the millennia. One cannot "see" Parmenides compose the poem; and had one been there to see him, one would have not asked *these* questions). But then, something becomes immediately evident precisely by virtue of these questions. That is, that one cannot expose oneself to the text if not moving from *one's own* practice, the practice that concretely assigns one to philosophy and its tradition. This is, essentially, the practice of the historiographic and philological look. One cannot expose oneself to the text as if one were a medieval monk or a fifteenth-century humanist (the awareness of these distinctions, of the differences in their practices is once again taught to us by the historiographic practice, as that through which the "matter" of philosophy simultaneously historicizes itself and hands itself down). One reads "mares," "cart," "paths," "the signs on the way," "the opinions of mortals," "double-headed human beings," and one wishes to be *informed*. What do all these things mean in that language? What could Parmenides mean? What could absolutely not belong to his "mental horizon," to his "epoch," to his language? One knows the limitations and paradoxes of the historiographic look when it is applied to philosophy. But not for this reason can one do without it.

Perhaps one can invent for oneself a new way of "exposing oneself" to the text? But the meaning of a practice is not invented by individuals. It first enacts itself obscurely, and then the individuals get "informed" by it. When one traces Indo-European roots or inquires hermeneutically into word etymologies, these refined practices actually presuppose the historic look, and avail themselves of it. Nor can one be so naive and expose oneself to the text with the purpose of saying anything that comes to mind (while perhaps invoking the example of Freud's free associations as a justification). These parrot-like practices proper to today's "culturalism" without culture are not even as original or strange as they think they are. If one takes a look at them, one finds that they are full of commonplaces, banalities, conformistic dogmas, misunderstood notions, aproblematic assertions, pure and simple nonsense. In them there are neither questions nor even problems.

49. *The historiographic look*. What does the historiographic look ultimately want? For example, it wants to give us back the truth of Parmenides' world *in itself*, the way such a world was *objectively*, which means independently from any external observer's interpretations. Perhaps to achieve this result, this ideally infinite research task, one does not neglect analyzing historically the empirical practices of that world: not only Parmenides' "text," which is read with philological sagacities, but also the economic, social, material, cultural, religious, political, and so forth life of that world.

The problem is that Parmenides' world *in itself* does not exist, and has never existed. There are no "events in themselves" and "practices in themselves." There are only dynamic intertwinings of practices that assume, absorb, and interpret other practices. One cannot place on the one side the event as it is in itself regardless of any other consideration, and on the other side the interpretive practices of the event (as Umberto Eco naively does in polemics with Derrida, for example), since the two things are always one single thing in continuous evolution. This holds true also for Parmenides, his world, and his "meaning." Not even for him is there the *poem* (and its *truth*); rather, there is a self-interpreting and re-interpreting at every moment of its apparition.[5]

To think the event, the meaning, or the truth of a world as they would be in themselves is not equivalent (as many naively believe) to thinking and seeking "reality." It simply amounts to pursuing the *object* (an imaginary object, as all objects) of a particular objectifying practice, such as the historiographic practice indeed is, whose assumption is the event of the historical look itself. Such a pursuit is the *putting to work* of the historical event itself: a practice that pursues the idea of a world in a historical-objective semblance.

50. *The secret of the historiographic look*. What is the secret of the historiographic look? It wants objective, "pure," that is, purified knowledge, unaffected by the subject's *interest*. In this way, historiographic look produces a peculiar *estrangement*. As affected by the historiographic practice, the subject estranges itself

from the unreflected living practices that come to it from the tradition. On these practices, it practices an estranging methodical reflection. The practices of the living tradition become "historico-objective" signs, until they touch the signs of the present and our innermost intimacy.

This is, however, only one side of the truth. In other ways, in fact, the subject that historiographically estranges itself from the living practices of the tradition actually attends a tradition unreflectively. Its practice of objective "disinterest" is still an "interest," a position of the subject in one of its peculiar figures (one could say, in the figure of the absolute subject or knowledge). The root of this methodical disinterest is the panoramic look that has been instituted by Greek metaphysics (and which has been brought to completion and to the foundation of the "historicity" of being by Hegel) and is the very *interest* of the philosophical practice. Interest in the figure of the truth as it has been instituted by philosophy (that is, the psycho-logical and psycho-historical truth) is the root of historiographic disinterest.[6] The estrangement that is peculiar to this look is possible therefore only on the grounds of an unreflected living involvement.

There are two secrets in the historiographic look. On the one hand, there is the objective and estranging practice, with its truth effect, with its "matter." On the other hand, there is the emotional opening of this very practice, with its peculiar and enigmatic "enchantment," that is, with its way of meeting the event of the world and making it happen.

51. *History and life.* Nietzsche claims that the historical look (reflection) kills life, the "enchantment" of experience. He, too, perfectly grasps one side of the truth. Yet there is another side: in its own way, the disenchanted and "nihilistic" look of historical consciousness and knowledge is also alive. It culminates in our time and pervades it, informing of itself the world of technics and (that is) information, that is, the cybernetically reduced world, Heidegger would say.

The question now becomes, what is the living meaning of this historiographic and cybernetic look? What is the *telos* of its practice? Within which enchantment and incantation does the disenchantment of the world move and proceed? Toward what does its perspective, the horizon of its path, gesture?

One should not forget the central difficulty of the historical look. Like any other, its truth is functional to its practice. We cannot rid ourselves of it simply by "relativizing" it, however: that is, by remarking that this truth is one among many, and nothing grants or will ever grant its absoluteness and unicity. To say this, we need another practice, which takes historical practice as its object and evaluates its meaning and truth function. What could this *other* practice ever be? It "relativizes" the historical and historiographic standpoint. Yet the one that relativizes (the one that "critically" reflects in an "objective" way on the truth of other practices) is still the same, that is, the historical practice. When thus framed, the question of the living meaning of the historical practice still attends this very living meaning; it does not comprehend it, but is rather comprehended by it.

52. *The strangeness of the past.* One should consider more closely the practice of estrangement that characterizes the historical look. The one who is part of this look in a completely unreflective way thinks that such a look regards the "past": the "past" is there, as an obvious thing, as a real entity among others, and the historical look has the virtue and merit of casting its own light on it. Nothing changes this conviction, not even the philosophical consideration, which is centuries old, that nothing is more contradictory and inconsistent than asserting the "reality" of the "past."[7]

There are no things outside practices, however, and the past is precisely the *object*, not the presupposition in itself, of historiographic practice. The institution of an estranged historical *ego* (through complex historiographic practices, first of all that of writing) produces, literally creates, the *alien*, the absolutely other from the present; that is, it creates *that* distance which is precisely called "historical."

Something thus *counts* for us as past and historical. It is something that we cannot be, or can no longer be, and that thus delineates our difference in relation to its extraneousness, that is, to its "strangeness": our being estranged from/by [*da*] its extraneousness.

53. *To participate and to criticize.* In directly interpretative living practices that are not affected by historical reflection, the subjects are *participating*, non-estranged subjects. Being defined by their very practices, these subjects do not know, cannot know, nor have any interest in knowing, that they are "historical." They practice the signs of tradition (within which they are situated and formed) in a living and, so to say, "actualizing" manner. Their notion of the past is not historical-objective. When they meet the "extraneous" (because they too meet it as that which is in all senses remote from their living practice), they "fabulize" it as the ancient, the ancestral, the grandiose, and so on. They imagine it on the ground of feelings, not on the ground of objective and disenchanted truths. While they place it at an unreachable and abysmal distance, at the same time and once again they actualize it in their imagination, like the medieval people who interpreted classical ruins in the guise of medieval castles and so on.

One should think of the extraordinary hermeneutic practice involving the Bible for centuries. This is the continuity of a living practice that continuously "errs" and modifies itself on the ground of the participatory and living need linking it to the tradition in light of a present community's present goals, and not in light of historiographic, universal truths.

The problem changes a great deal when Spinoza (and later Reimarus, Lessing, and so on) begins to approach the text (the "sacred" text) with a distancing critical attitude. Now the subject exposes itself to the tradition by estranging itself from it, and thereby by distancing [the tradition] into an alien place that has *its own objective* peculiarities. The long wave of historical comprehension and criticism will fall into this Spinozan bed.

The critical attitude grounding historiography has no longer the sense of a directly participatory practice in relation to the tradition. It does not pursue immediately operative and available finalities. On the contrary, it "suspends" action because it wants to be *objective*. In this way, it produces the so familiar figure of the historical truth, which is objective and in itself.

54. *The infinite object*. What is peculiar to the estranging historical practice is that, unlike participatory practices, it *does not consume the object*, insofar as it fades away in front of [the object] to open itself up rhythmically in front of its return according to a cycle of fruitions determined by the very nature of the "matter" (as in the case of "sexual matter," according to a previous example). The object of the historical practice is open to the infinite. It is marked by an infinite perfectibility, for example, according to the pattern of the infinite *telos* of reason that marks modern philosophy from the Enlightenment to Fichte, Hegel, and Husserl.

Philosophy still understands this *telos* as a living, "political" experience of historicity, whereas, in its aversion to "metaphysics," historiography translates and realizes it on a purely methodological level, turning historicity into a "technical" question. Philosophy then "completes" itself, as Hegel would say, in historiographism, insofar as it translates its own "will to truth" as *practice* of objective and controllable truth into historiographism.

The feature of this practice obviously depends on its opening, which consists in producing the estrangement of the absolutely other (the past as such). It is a practice that (ideally, that is, methodologically) suspends the *interest* in and toward all other practices. Precisely in such a way, it prepares itself to become interested *in* all other practices, pushing to the infinite its search for objective meaning. In principle, all other practices do or can translate into the peculiar character of historiographic practice. The translation consists in the crystallization of the researched paths and horizons. These are deprived of the mobile and changing unity of meaning that has little by little constituted and oriented them through its own self-interpretation backward and forward, and are instead reduced to *quanta* of pure occurrence, which are panoramically contemplated from the outside.

Historiographic practice is an occurrence that aims at the production of what has occurred; that is, it is an infinitely perfectible mosaic of events in and for themselves, according to the notion of a complete totality (completely removed in what has happened as "past"): that is, a totality of what has happened in and for itself, or in the way it would have appeared to God's imperturbable look. Indeed to the god of philosophers and historians, the god of onto-theology and European *ratio*, which is technologically put to work by the research "tools."

55. *Historiographic consenting*. One should not mistake the object of the historiographic practice (the pure past, eternally, that is, ideally fixed, in a microscopically and macroscopically infinite approximation) for its unreflected living

unfolding. The wholly other that is considered and produced by this practice is only relatively such. An absolute wholly other would in fact be unattainable and unthinkable: a pure "theological" idea.

In truth, like any other, even the historiographic practice refers to chains and stratifications of already enacted practices. For example: to assume the signs of Parmenides' poem as an estranged object of my historiographic interest, I must share practices of life and knowledge, language and writing, and so on with those signs. What we firstly have in common is the immense chain of Interpreters, the common wave of endless antiquity containing in itself the Alexandrian philologist, the amanuensis monk, up to our recent teachers, whose voice and human physiognomy we seem to be still perceiving in their being animated by the living practice of philosophizing.

We have this whole chain of practices insofar as it is assimilated into our own practice's interpreting distortion, which has value for us as the "tradition of philosophy." We posit it as the object of the historiographic practice of philosophizing, yet we inhabit it obscurely, drawing from it the mute body and the unperceived content of our own *praxis*.

Only because things are actually this way can one understand the intuitive relation with the past, with past practices and human beings; that is, [one can understand] the preliminary *Einfühlung* mentioned by Husserl, without which a purely objective and historiographic practice would be neither possible nor even conceivable.

56. *The object of physics*. One should now imagine the contemporary scientific practice. One should think, for example, of physics as an emblematic and paradigmatic scientific practice. An adequate discourse about this practice would require of course extremely complex analyses endowed with multiple senses that are still mainly undecided. Here one should limit oneself, however, to the exemplifying general function assumed by this general reference.

Is physics too, is its research not a process of estrangement that produces the absolutely other, that is, "nature," in the modern sense of the term? This process has its initial opening already in Descartes: [it is the] production of an operative scheme delineating the order of extended things, transcribing them, and reconstructing them in a scheme from which the thinking reality, the soul, is estranged by principles. Nature as the infinitely other that can be calculated by the ego, and the ego as the infinitely other that cannot be calculated by nature: this is a connection of such importance, and loaded with so many consequences for us that one could not exhaust its meaning no matter how long one were to devote oneself to thinking and comprehending it.[8]

Even the wholly other of physics, however, is relative, insofar as it is produced in subtly specialized and currently highly technological practices, which nevertheless are rooted in a multiplicity of other originarily producing practices of meaning, starting with the bodily practices of the senses and common sense, writing, logic, and so on. That is, they are rooted in that entire precategorical world of *doxa* that Husserl correctly vindicates when showing it already at work in any categorical scientific practice.

One should add, however, that the claim to make such a pre-categorical world thematic within the transcendental descriptions of phenomenology discloses irresolvable paradoxes and misunderstandings: last illusion of the traditional philosophical practice, ultimately still Platonic and Cartesian, toward which scientists remain indifferent, since they are busy *producing* their meaning as sense of the wholly other (other than the soul and of the soul), into which the "proper" of philosophy has long since disappeared.

57. *The methodic unity of science and history.* One should consider the analogy between historiographic and scientific methods in these terms: they both estrange the subject and produce the absolutely other. The first does so through the chronological distancing into the past (historical time, up to the point of touching our present in statistics—as Kant already intuits—in data banks, in live recordings on videos, and so on); the second through a distancing into the future (cosmic time, and forecasting character of physics and its technical planning).

We could then say (following the however tenuous and general thread of this analogy, functionally paradigmatic of what we want to say): historiography works as historicization of any past practice; physics as physicization of any future practice. With their practices, they both produce the suspension of the participatory *charm* of all practices (of the unreflected living tradition). That is, they produce a *disinterested practice*: disenchanted, disinterested, objective observation of all enchantments (one should not cry, should not laugh, should rather understand).

What occurs in fact is the integral unity of historic and scientific methods (the "psycho-historical strategy"); only in appearance or on the surface has [such unity] given birth to the so-called two cultures (the humanistic and the scientific). In depth, the speculative unity of the sciences of nature and the sciences of spirit has been guaranteed ever since the Platonic origins.[9] Today, it reveals and fulfills itself in a technological key.

58. *The calculable future and the undecidable future.* The predictive-objectifying practice of science is made possible by the modern opening accomplished by mathematical writing and thus by the mathematization of logical signs (from metaphysical *logos* to the techniques of mathematical logic).

Like historiography, science also suspends common interpretive practices. Its path, however, is not a regressive path toward the objectification of the "historical" openings of all living practices. Rather, it is a progressive methodic path: translation of the objects of all practices into mathematical signs (allow me this generic expression), that is, into the exact calculability of "facts." As such, they are made available to living *praxis*, to the actuality of common sense and its needs, so that it may *decide* which facts it desires.

This, however, is only an illusion. Progressively estranged from its practices, made to conform to the technological production of facts, common sense has no grounds from which to decide (the only ground being the living tradition, from which it is continuously distanced and estranged). Confronted with questions that *demand* a choice for its own good, it cannot imagine anything else than what "one already does:" that is, a super-science capable of "objectively" establishing the (legitimate, augured) sense and limit of science—for example, bioethics. Thus, common sense mistakes the antidote for the problem. It says what it knows (the prejudices and the superstitions that have informed it, its naive belief in reality and objective truths in themselves), but it does not know what it says.

59. *The physical objects.* One could thus define the manner in which science translates the objects of all practices into its own technological practice: translation of everything into a *quantum* of disinterested observation. To realize such observation, at first absolute coordinates (space and time) were needed; then, science relativized them too. Today the "informative," that is, the informationally computerized [*informatico*] or cybernetic character of science is completely evident. The use of particle accelerators to discover the "bricks of matter" needs increasingly more powerful computers, capable of hundreds of thousands of operations per second. This elaboration of data, this unimaginable calculating power, is not a consequence of, or a mere operational support to the experiment; rather it guides the experiment, makes it possible, gives it sense and logic. It is its condition of possibility. The computer and its technical language are the content of the logical form of the experiment.

All this goes beyond any logic of common sense. Observation, calculated through technical instruments (not through senses), inscribes its findings on the plane of a future predictability that is not opened by the event of the world in the body and language within which common sense has little by little formed itself (within the so-called natural history). Cybernetic opening is a new event (which recapitulates and reinscribes previous events within itself) that one day may appear as "the natural history of information."

What results is that the language and thought of common sense cannot "say" the world of physics, which is a construct of the calculating computerized operation according to the mode of its distancing. From here come all paradoxes of microcosm and macrocosm within contemporary physics, and the inexpressibility of physical "objects."

60. *The method of estrangement.* Scientific knowledge is *sui generis*. It is not the knowledge proper to average know-how-to-do and know-how-to-say. These are characterized by their belonging to a kind of practice whose circle of disclosure of the matter closes upon itself; the object is rhythmically consumed, and thus pathically inhabited under the sign of an originarily giving enchantment. On the contrary, as estranging practice of disenchantment, physical practice

does not participate but rather *produces* its infinite object, whose observational possibilities (that is, its cybernetic translatability and calculability) it continuously stimulates.

Scientific practice has its roots in metaphysical practice as representation of a being which is thought in its being and truth (that is, in its ground of being and in its cause). Through the institution of a logical *logos*, which exploits the universality implicit in the practice of the voice and the explicit universality of the transcription of the voice into the practice of alphabetic writing (two practices philosophy has always exercised), philosophy "produces" the theoretical, estranged, absolute subject, the pan-oramic, universal ego. Inheriting such practices, science participates in the "rational" tradition of philosophy. Yet such practices produce the progressive estrangement of the operative subject from all participatory practices.

Science transforms this estrangement into its own very method. It pursues a total technical transcription, in which voice and alphabetic writing have no longer a "reason to be." The search for the ("natural") cause turns into the production of the (calculable) effect.

61. *The truth of practices.* Each practice culminates in some form of knowledge, that is, in a know-how-to-do that is determined by its opening. Each practice has meaning, truth, and success within its limits, that is, within its own disclosive circle. Thus the practice of walking, as a putting to work of limbs, legs, and feet, has the meaning of the walkability of the earth, which, in that disclosive circle, has its truth in its being flat. This truth is however indifferent for the life practices of vegetables, or for the observational practice of an astronaut.

The success of science in terms of its putting-to-work is directly proportional to the status of the methodically estranged subject and the figure of its truth (the universe from *its* distancing-calculating perspective). Scientific truths, which on the contrary we superstitiously assume as absolutely true in themselves, that is, rescinded from all practices and from their own practice, make sense in relation to this subject. It is in relation to this subject that scientific objects have reality. One should get accustomed to thinking (which is difficult, since it greatly clashes with our prejudices) that a tree is burning wood only functionally to the work of the hatchet, and human beings have a brain only functionally to the work of the lancet. "In themselves," human beings have no brain, and the brain is not an object "real" in itself, outside of surgical practices.

Putting to work the estranged subject of science means, for example, asking what happens at a certain point of space-time when one abstracts from the particular "concrete" subjectivity of the scientist, from the public and historical universality of scientific humankind, and from the research practices that science employs. From this abstracting ultimately derive the paradoxes of relativity and the principle of indetermination, which physicists have discussed for long with extreme difficulty, that is, without knowing how to render and how to interpret them. On the one hand, these paradoxes challenge their naive objectivistic naturalism. On the other hand, they stimulate mystical escapes and images, the "Tao of physics," and other conceptual and verbal cheap stuff that only creates confusion.

62. *The binding erring of science.* Like all practices, science produces *a* truth linked to *its* own practice. And yet it produces it as *the* truth. This entails a peculiar way of "being in error," and thus of "erring";[10] that is, [it entails] situating itself within its own horizon, tracking its own path, that culminates in an object whose sense is infinite (infinitely perfectible search for *the* "truth").

One might say: is it not fair, or right, to acknowledge that science however possesses *more truth* than other practices? That it *knows* things better and more? To express a banality: the scientist "knows" why it rains, whereas the rain wizard and the magician do not.

I would answer that the scientist knows insofar as his or her matters are *put to work* from the perspective of the anonymous and estranged subject, the universal and absolute panoramic subject. This kind of knowledge is in itself indifferent with respect to the truth and sense of other practices. For example, the truths pertaining to physiology, anatomy, or genetics are incongruous to the enchantment determining the opening and horizon of the love experience and sexual practice of a man and woman who are in love. Scientific truths are indifferent with respect to determined and concrete emotions manifesting and producing themselves in such a relationship.

There is also another aspect of no small importance, however; namely, that scientific practice can promote or impede pregnancies, modify malformations, heal disease, and so on. This fact is indeed not a matter of indifference to, or without influence on, the amorous practice itself.

63. *The particularity of the universal.* The truth of the scientific practice has the character of a *universal* (or ideally, the methodically universal) *practice.* The particularity, the specialty of this practice is *to produce the universal.* It is *a* practice, as alphabetic writing is. This singularity, however, consists of making *universal* events and objects occur, as alphabetic writing makes the universal reader and its peculiar truth occur.

The feature of the universality of such practice consists in this. It intervenes in all practices, twisting and transforming their forms of knowledge. This is exactly like the logical voice and writing, which can translate every specific knowledge of the hand and the eye, the tongue and the ear, and so on into their own "general" truth. It is a universal translation, whose content of the form does not leave unchanged the content and the form of the practices that have been translated. Under the domination of scientific practice, even the amorous practice and the practice of making children are not and cannot be any longer the same practices, have the same meaning, the same particular and general paths they had once.

This fact is not peculiar only to science,.but to all practices, insofar as they always entail and influence others. In the practice of hunting human beings, sexual relations and figures are not the same as those of human beings devoted to agriculture, and so on. The enchantments of experience always change meaning, and so do the figures of the world and of the subjects' being in the world.

This, however, should not make one forget that the assimilation operated by scientific practice, the universality of its particular manner of self-production, is a translation *sui generis*, whose sense and specificity must be understood.

64. *Sense and nonsense*. As absolute universal practice, science produces and reproduces itself not as *a* practice, but as the practice that tends to regulate and subject all other practices to its own meaning [*senso*]. In itself, it twists all forms of knowledge of all practices, and thus it actually modifies their enchantment and opening.

This modification of meaning actually assumes the figure of *nonsense*. Meaning is in fact determined by the participatory character in relation to the horizon and path determining the disclosive circle of the matter, which is consumed through the image of the object. On the contrary, in the scientific practice participation is suspended. What returns in it is not the rhythmic image of the emotion for the matter, but rather the practice itself, methodically exercised. This practice has some matter only as infinitely arranged in the image of a scientific object, that is, as posited and arranged in the image of an infinite object (whose "fruition" is by principle impossible).

One could think of a man and a woman engaged in the sexual practice of having a child. They cannot start and then start again when they want; they can only do so by participating in the rhythm of their emotional openings. The doctor instead practices artificial insemination outside of any personal emotion and disposition, in a multiplicity of cases arranged by the temporality of technological devices and professional practice, aiming at "pregnancy in general" and "the child in general," according to an infinite perfectibility (whereas the natural practice has a sense and an intentionality that are already perfect in themselves, fully completed in the very act of their completion).

In scientific practice, what is infinitely reproduced is *distantiation* as universal and absolute opening and enchantment of the practice itself. The "meaning" [*senso*] is "postponed." This means that by principle it is not lived. What is immediately lived is the nonsense.

65. *The insurmountable look*. Here one can easily find again the analogy with history. The historical look assumes the absolutely other as "historicity of the past." That is, it assumes the other only insofar as it distances and temporalizes it in its strangeness, confining it to its own peculiar "historical chronicity." The other is thus assumed and seen in its historical *relativity*.

The historical look itself, however, as universal act of estrangement, *cannot change into something other than itself*. That is, it cannot *have* history, it can only *do* history (or better, historiography). "Historical" are "the others," those who have been distanced in historical chronology, and who are unaware of being in it "methodically." Their existence is grasped in function of the historical look. It is a being *for* the historical look. It is a living interpretation of the tradition while ignoring one's "doing" history, which means first of all having it in itself *for* us (the historical observers).

As universal practice of the absolutely other than all other practices, the physicist's look cannot exit, escape from itself, and move to a further practice (it can only reproduce itself technologically, methodologically, according to an infinitely perfectible ideal). Analogously, the historical look infinitely reproduces itself methodically, according to sophisticatedly perfectible techniques which ideally never quit perfecting themselves and immensely enriching the data bank of the past. They are exactly like the pictures of an immense telescope aimed at perceiving billions of past, present, and future (or supposedly so) signals from the universe. These are data for whose classification one will have to program unimaginably powerful computers in "real time," as one is accustomed to say.

66. *Technological erring*. Science and historiography cannot produce participatory truths. Their opening, the event of their enchantment are in fact characterized by the estrangement of being a subject *for* an object. Thus, the horizon of scientific and historiographic practice can only produce *the* estranged truth. (One should notice that this is not a value judgment, but simply a mere phenomenological remark.)

The estranged truth is *a* truth relative to a practice, which however posits itself as *the* nontranscendable, universal practice of *the* truth. Since the experience of truth is nothing else than the experience of its constitutive *being in error*, that is, sign and distance,[11] *this* figure of truth assumes the experience of being in error in its radical and full form (one should not overlook the importance of this move). *Erring* (which is a consequence of being in error) thus becomes for it a methodic nontranscendable necessity: a perpetual becoming that is centered on the same constitutive distance (eternal return of the same as the essence of technics).

Participatory practices experience being in error insofar as they objectify the event of the circle of the matter and their own opening into an image of the object: that is, into a sign that escapes ultimate possession, vanishes, and is consumed in fruition and in the closure of distance. This is their way of *living* the truth (by erring *in* it and rhythmically disappearing outside its circle). Conversely, scientific practice does not live but rather infinitely *researches* [*ricerca*] the truth in an object: [the object] can never be consumed (participated), but rather is infinitely produced and re-produced in ever new, that is, technologically perfectible and replaceable forms (the newest replaces the newest, says Heidegger).

One should add that this infinite productive quest is accompanied by (rather, is part of) the production of need, which is fictitiously solicited for its fictitious objects.

67. *Weak nihilism*. In court, Socrates asserts that a life without *examination* [*ricerca*] is not worth living, thus delineating the profile of the "theoretical man."

In turn, as Nietzsche recalls, Lessing, "the most sincere of theoretical spirits," declares that he prefers the *search* [*ricerca*] for truth to truth itself. This originary opening of philosophy produces the metaphysical searching subject, which is structurally and methodically estranged, "ironical." Such gesture founds the advent of the "scientific spirit."

This is accompanied by what Nietzsche names "nihilism": estrangement determined by the will to power of technics, which dominates on a planetary scale in the figure of *Weltzivilisation*. In substance, this has to do with the conflict that arises between the participatory truths of traditional practices and the truth of science and historiography, which appropriate all enchantment and "taking place," that is, any *ethos*, and twist their meaning.

What results from this is the human being of "weak nihilism" (as Nietzsche puts it): uprooted, without "home," superficially "pitiful" (a bit "socialist," a bit "Christian"), rhetorically "democratic" and friend to "people," intimately restless, utilitarian, rough, rascally, and selfish, and finally dogmatic and violent (precisely the one who conversely boasts of his or her "relativism" and "tolerance") as soon as his or her technological comforts are threatened.

68. *The uprooted subject*. "People" in general do not consider science from the perspective of its nihilistic component. They admire its power in a conformist way, and share its naive naturalism in a "science-fictional" manner. The common attitude spontaneously turns to participatory sensory practices and the consummation of objects endowed with meaning. Science and technics are thus experienced as mere instruments capable of favoring and multiplying the availability of objects and their consummation.

"People" do not understand the tremendous power of the "neutral" (that is, neutralizing) attitude of science, the transforming and devastating grandiosity of its programmatic and methodic "objectivism." When confronted with technological degenerations, "people" rather appeal, in an absurd and silly manner, to science itself. What nobody wants to see is the unavoidable necessity for an "ethical" transformation that science imposes on the subject: that is, the necessity to elevate nihilism from method (*methodos*) to path (*odos*) rather than deluding oneself into thinking that one can withstand [nihilism] through the appeal to "values," "human being," "reason," and so on. As Nietzsche understands, there is no longer any ground behind.

Analogously, "people" do not understand the intimate power and necessity that belong to the "neutrality" of the historiographic look. They even use historical truth ideologically, so as to justify their own operative passions and interests. They do not realize that, once it has entered the light cone of historicity, the subject cannot avoid historicizing itself too.

69. *The end of history*. Science and historiography produce pure technological practices. What follows is that to do historiography amounts to canceling oneself as a "historical" subject. The "end of history" thus prospects itself (end of

history that in fact "opened" as a consequence of the institution of the "logical mind," which was made possible by the practice of alphabetic writing).

For centuries philosophy has been a practice that wished *to make history*. Its deepest intentionality is therefore "political," from Plato to Hegel to Marx, continuing in the Husserlian dream of phenomenology as a theoretical *praxis* that regenerates the European ideal of reason, or finally in the ontological-existential decisionism of the first Heidegger (who then changes his mind within the turmoil of Nazism, to which he opposes his interpretation of Nietzsche as the opening of the question of the essence of technics).

Exactly insofar as it is a neutral technological practice, historiography is incongruous with the meaning and truth of the philosophical practice, whose intentionality is to produce historical events that have been pathically lived. Plato wants to make a revolution, he does not want to write its objective history. In truth, both projects are under the power of the practice of writing, which, in accordance with its technical destination, wants neither one nor the other; rather, it wants still another thing, that is, our present disquieting and exciting opening, our disenchanted enchantment. Philosophical historiography is (marks) the *end of philosophy*. Analogously, the advent of modern physics marks the end of all metaphysical cosmology, as Kant perfectly realizes.[12]

After the historiographic end of philosophy, the practice of thinking can no longer be situated within the traditional philosophical *ethos*. The end of history and the end of philosophy are the same. And, in fact, philosophy fights against itself starting with Bacon, Locke, Hume, and Kant, up to the Neopositivists, Wittgenstein, Heidegger, and Derrida.

70. *The end of politics*. In the revelatory circle of the matter that is marked by the opening of technics, public happenings and events are no longer determined by the historical spirit and politics. No one can any longer practice a historical-destinal thought and action. One can "imagine" doing so, for example when one destroys a wall in Berlin or overthrows statues in the Red Square. These events are determined, however, by technological practice, projections, and usage, insofar as "people's" conscience, requests, and actions conform to them.

The technological practice and planning produce objects and representations of objects, turn fragments of a wall into living room decorations and tourist souvenirs, transform a trip into a travel agency program. Everything is subjected to this technological projection, including the "psychology" of those who should be making the "choices." The psyche has been opportunely "informed" and explored through statistical analyses to the task of better "orienting" it.

Political thought ("democracy"), with its very ancient metaphysical grounds, no longer has "effectuality"; that is, it no longer has any power over reality. It is only a ceremonial allocution, ritually tranquilizing, good to fill the photographic sections of magazines, together with other "mundanities." Parties and institutions lose their traditional dialectical-ideological connotations, and are assimilated and made similar to one another in the bureaucratic technical administration of the existent. The real match is elsewhere: an enigma that worries the public and regularly escapes the reiterated invocations for "democratic transparency." The fact is that the world of technics is not at all transparent to itself yet.

71. *Question without answer.* A practice of reason that becomes practice of historic (historiographic) reason inevitably relativizes its own practice. One may ask, what is the tradition of philosophy in relation to the tradition of thought? Heidegger asks, what is Parmenides' "matter," as matter of thinking that escapes philosophy? Before these questions, which are exacting and epochal, there is another question that imposes itself and is apparently more modest, but in the end is not the least problematic. One could phrase it in this way: why can these questions have *for us* no other meaning than an infinite historiographic one?

As subjects of *our* practices, when we ask about Parmenides we cannot avoid taking into account historiography as well as the "scientific (inconclusive, infinite) character" of the historiographic method.

Even when realizing the incongruous character of historiographic practice in comparison to practices that hand down philosophy as a living practice, we still owe the possibility of such observation to historiographic consciousness. We cannot exit the historiographic practice. We cannot avoid noticing its incongruousness and relativity. What else can we do?

72. *The production of the archaic.* We should not forget, however, what we already know: that is, that our historiographic practice does not have the meaning of telling *the* truth in itself of Parmenides. It "believes" that it is telling [such truth], or that it must tell it in an infinite methodical approximation, insofar as it is characterized by the prejudice of the "truth in itself" of things (the metaphysical prejudice turned into "technical" methodology). In a certain way, this belief is even *correct*, since researching *the* truth is precisely the way of proceeding of *its* practice. Such correctness, however, is also its paradox and nonsense, since in truth it is *a* practice (among many) that clashes against the vicious circle of pursuing itself as *the* practice of *the* truth.

Analogous is the behavior of contemporary scientific cosmology, which, in an infinite approximation, claims to tell *the* truth of the universe. This belief is as much naive as it is disproportioned; yet, since it is the very opening of its methodic project, it cannot be relinquished. What other attitude could one assume toward the universe? A "poetic" attitude? And why should such a latter practice (itself *one* among many) be better or more reliable than the former?

One should stick, however, to what we have found out—namely, that the deep meaning of the historiographic practice is not the one that [such practice] believes. Rather, [its meaning is] that of *distancing* Parmenides, situating him inflexibly in the past, and thus rendering him stranger to our truth by "historicizing" him. Nevertheless, is it not already Plato who opens this path? He declares that he can no longer understand Parmenides' "saying": it is too "archaic."

73. *The relativization of the relative.* If contemporary cosmology distances the world by "physicizing" it, that is, by pursuing the flight of galaxies technologically, historiography distances the world by "historicizing" it. It rescinds the hermeneutic efficacity of the past as it occurs in living interpretations. That is, it marks the end of the tradition of philosophy, thought, and all traditions. It is the end of the influence of the past precisely insofar as it is "made past." When preserved in the historical memory as *the* past, the past dies.

This fact ends up casting a problematic light on our historiographic activity itself. Committed to historicize everything and everyone with contrite scientific probity, we cannot avoid looking at ourselves, in the end, with the same historicizing and relativizing eyes. In our historic time we discover how many, and in how many ways, human forms of wisdom are and have been. Philosophy is no exception. It is a form of wisdom among infinite others. The tradition of its practices is not void of connections with other wisdom-oriented forms; in its specificity, there is no ground for an absolute preference.

One could say the same, and actually cannot avoid saying it, with reference to the historiographic practice that reaches such conclusions. How much such a practice owes to the tradition of philosophy should not escape us either. The historic look cannot ultimately ignore its being a child of the "history of being." And this, in turn, is nothing more than a history among many other histories—so one says foolishly as a good nihilist. But then one corrects oneself: the very image of "many histories" is nothing else than a product of the history of being: something *radically* relative, not in a horizontal (many histories that follow and overlap one another) but in a vertical sense (historical understanding is only *one* way of understanding). When such evidence grasps us, our historiographic practice too enters the whirlpool of the "hermeneutic circle."

74. *The return of the removed* [il rimosso]. The past that has been historicized and distanced by the historiographic practice *returns* at the moment in which, by relativizing itself, this practice discovers itself to be child and consequence of the event (the philosophical intentionality) that it would like to reduce to a historiographic object. The past returns not as problem (a historiographic problem), but as *question*, to which one cannot give an answer.

What one can now see clearly is that the past (that one historicizes) contains in itself the gesture (the "historical mind") that has made the very historicization possible. Such gesture is the pre-comprehension of one's historical comprehension. This is what the historical comprehension has *removed* exactly at the moment when it has cast it into the figure of a historical event (which by itself it could not be). The removed [*il rimosso*] comes back as the event of the opening of our disenchanted and estranged practice. It is an in-stant event, in whose circle our whole historical chronology unfolds. Therefore, it is an event without time, without chronology, and without history.

In this figure, Parmenides comes back to haunt our thinking. It is not as if we could reconnect again with him by interpreting him in a living way as, for example, Gorgias, Plato, or Hegel do. This is only the recurring temptation of reactionary archaism, the dream of resurrecting the past *against* the present, which is ridden with *Angst* and meaningless. Except that the dream itself is a meaningless nightmare of the present, with which one does not have the strength to fully confront oneself (*therefore* the reactionary continuously shows his or her muscles, and idolizes strength).

Parmenides remains for us "past," distanced, and consigned to historiographic erudition. What returns is the removed [*il rimosso*] of his look, insofar as it is an event of our own look and destiny (that which cannot be looked at by our look and which nevertheless lets us see, including letting us see this very impossibility). This is the destiny of our being without a living tradition. In the light of sunset one discovers one's roots, Nietzsche writes: they are the roots of our nihilistic uprooting.

75. *The illusion of the life-world.* To understand one must have pre-understood, according to the hermeneutic circle. One should think of it in this manner: a practice cannot establish itself by itself. It must always insert itself in a previous practice, it must already be *comprehended* in a previous practice. This becomes the empirical basis of its transcendental horizon, and of the meaning of its path.

Thus, the event of a practice is never absolute. Its transcendentality is at the same time empirical. What in it is empirical, inherited from other practices, is interpreted in the light of its transcendental opening of meaning. One should think, as an example, of the use of myth in Parmenides and Plato. Parmenides assumes myth into his *logos*, and this is not without consequences for the way in which Plato employs myth in his turn. We (that is, our way of thinking and interpreting depend on those gestures) are already comprehended or pre-comprehended in them, and there is no hope that we can look at them from the outside. We can only re-interpret them finally asking ourselves about their meaning, without hiding from us their aporeticity.

In this perspective, one may well see what the goal of Husserl's *Lebenswelt* is: to find the foundation of the originary practices, the life-world common to all human beings from which all interpretive and categorical practices emerge. Yet there are no such originary or purely pre-categorical practices. Insofar as it is taken in isolation, thematized and abstracted from its context, by this very fact every practice, and every element of a practice, is already inserted and interpreted, that is, mediated within another practice and *its* opening of meaning. The phenomenological look that aims at the *Lebenswelt* is not at all "pure"; rather, it is the estranged philosophical and scientific subject itself, the result of *this* practice, put to work through the metaphysical practice of the Socratic "doubt."

76. *The blind spot of the look.* As an event of philosophy, Parmenides' look accompanies and hiddenly founds every scientific and historiographic practice of ours. However, this "hiddenness" has now come to light. But this does not suffice to

free us from its enchantment, since the light in which we see it is still that of its practice (that is, of the tradition that derives from it). To distance it historiographically is still to have it close; to distance this very distancing, however (since we see that historiography, like philosophy, is *a* practice, not *the* truth), does not let us exit the paradox, that is, the figure of the distancing practice.

In virtue of *this* paradox, when asking what "the matter of thinking" is, Heidegger still finds in his hands the "matter of philosophy" in the form of an unthinkable and even unformulatable question. The unthinkability of the "opening" of philosophy does not depend on a mysterious self-subtracting of *aletheia* in *lethe*. It depends on the fact that the philosophical practice is a practice which, by causing a crisis in all specific wisdom-oriented practices (by "suspending" them), determines the very crisis of knowing. Philosophy embodies such a crisis in itself, and carries it with itself.

The "end of philosophy" thus configures itself as the end of a practice (the end of a "tradition"), since by configuring itself ever since its beginning as criticism and suspension of the tradition (that is, of any other practice), in the end this practice suspends also itself.

Seeing itself ultimately as itself *a* practice, philosophy denies all privileges (all "truth") to itself, and relocates itself among other practices. This "historiographic" gesture, however, ambiguously recoils upon itself. It still embodies a claim to a methodically absolute truth, whose opening is still and again the "suspension" of living practices and traditions.

77. *The paradox of the practical suspension.* How does the suspension of the philosophical practice occur in our time? It occurs "practically," that is, as a historiographic "know-how to do" that does not ask questions; it is a historiographic-technological practice of truth that nihilistically relativizes all knowing (all values) and thus actively promotes the end of philosophy as living tradition of historical-destinal ("political") knowing.

The historiographic practice can neither speak nor write of such "practical" suspension because it still thinks of it metaphysically as *the* truth in itself. It does not pause to think that *the* truth is precisely a truth-result of its practice and is opened by the very event of philosophy as "science of truth" (as Aristotle says). Historiography is not capable of thinking the paradox of the *relative* character (relative to a practice) of the *absolute* truth. It is not capable of thinking *beyond* truth, as Nietzsche, Heidegger, and Wittgenstein start to do.

The "practical" suspension of historiography is the practice of (philosophical) *questioning* that has been translated into a historiographic *problem*. It multiplies problems methodically and technologically; yet in this manner it does not come one inch closer to grasping the question, which is the opening of its very event. Focused on the consequences of the Socratic question, historiography *does not know* it should question the question itself (at most, it turns [the question] into a problem). Thus, it does not notice the paradox that is intrinsic to it; neither does current hermeneutics (fatally "epigonal," as Heidegger claims), in its belief that everything has been said once one stresses the horizontal infinity of interpretations and "cultural" horizons, thereby remaining however blind to the vertical "abysmality" of the problem; that is, [it remains blind] to the fact that this very saying is under question, paradoxical and inconsistent; it is not an "alternative truth" (as some somewhat foolishly say), but rather the nonsense of truth.

Historiography does not expose itself to the paradox that is intrinsic to it: the question of the question is still a questioning practice that, because of its very intentionality and nature, one cannot avoid subjecting to question.

78. *The circle of subjectivity.* Born from Socratic questioning, the estranged "critical" subject is at the origin of the event of suspension that is philosophy: that is, a suspension of all participatory, non-"critical" practices. The world of technics suspends such a subject "practically," that is, without knowing it, without raising its own doing to a question for thinking. Suspending such a subject, it actually consumes its transcendental space, since it produces and reproduces the subject "technically" through cybernetics, computers, automata, information, and, on another side, through historiography and "the humanities."

The last consequence of this event is its very vicious circularity. In the end, we cannot avoid suspending and distancing the practical doing of the world of technics itself as a necessity inscribed in its very logic, in its aim. Its very operations and the nonsense that they structurally produce move us toward such *telos*.

Insofar as we are circularly centered on the metaphysical-scientific-technical practice, we cannot go back to the beginning; that is, we cannot avoid practicing the question of the question and expose ourselves to its paradox.

79. *The enchantment of the question.* To practice the question of the question means to *insist* on the question. That is, to practice the opening of philosophy. Was Parmenides' opening really a questioning? Certainly it was a suspension: of the sensory evidences of eyes, mouth, and ears, of mythical cosmogonies and Dionysian cults. It determined the difference between the "pure" subject, characterized by pure thinking (*noein*), and the pathic subject of the tradition.

Parmenides is still at the threshold of philosophy, however, neither on this side nor on the other (or at least, so it appears to us). It is only with Socrates that philosophy consciously opens with the question, or practicing the question.

The philosopher is the *spokes-person* [*porta-voce*, literally voice-bearer] for a question. To insist on this means to understand that what really matters, in the question, is the *enchantment* of the question. To insist on a question is to understand this difficult notion: that one must *inhabit* the question, its peculiar enchantment, without overcoming or wanting to overcome it in the answer.

80. *The shock of the question.* What really matters in the philosopher's question is not the *determination* of the question, or its possible *answer.* The philosopher

asks this and that (What is *arche?* What is *aitia?* What is *truth?* and so on). However, what he or she asks hides the great *opening* of the question within itself—that is, [it hides] the event of the practice of questioning, the questioning habit (*ethos*) or attitude, the questioning *vis* [power].

The philosopher answers this and that. What the philosopher answers tends toward a cancellation of the question and a leading astray of the philosopher from his or her originary location. Thus the practice of philosophizing specifies itself as a particular discipline ("philosophy"). It begins to turn into the "history" of this discipline itself.

Dwelling upon the question, that is, in-dwelling, is not easy. In general, we are always already projected onto the answers of the practices we practice, which aim at their objects according to different modalities of the disclosive circle of the matter. We are always already in a world that has occurred, with its horizons and its paths. Even the practice of philosophical questioning is, in its own way, the answer to an appeal or to a disclosure of a world. By questioning, philosophy answers an event or an enchantment of the world; for example, it answers the torpedo-fish enchantment that, according to Plato, issues from Socrates.

The philosopher asks so that a particular enchantment of the world may be disclosed by the gesture of such practice. The question invites one to inhabit the enchantment, and not simply to answer. This is so also because the particularity or peculiarity of such question is that it is "universal." By desiring its own difference, it erases all differences, and thus the sense of all answers. It does not proceed; rather, it recedes and suspends.

81. *The philosophical* ethos. The one who does not inhabit and is not inhabited by the question does not exercise the practice of philosophy, even if that person knows its historiography by heart. One may encounter, therefore, great scholars of philosophy and refined technicians of its historiography, who nevertheless are not at all philosophers, have no real inclination for philosophy, and do not properly know what philosophy is about. It is astonishing how often this happens.

To be inhabited by the question is a *status*, a pre-comprehension, an involuntary habit, something which has nothing to do with "professionalism" or academic titles (which are always superficial facts). It is true, however, that these "professionals" of philosophy, these "professors" and scholars have provided not an indifferent, [but] actually an non-renounceable contribution to the constituting and enduring of the tradition of philosophy. They are like the "performers" of musical practice as opposed to the creators (today "criticism," with its superficial and relativistic "culturalism," has a nihilistic tendency to deny this distinction). The performer must have a great, rare, sometimes very high sensibility to be able to understand creative thinking and reproduce it, handing it down historically. The opening of the world by Haydn, Mozart, or Beethoven, however, is something different.

One cannot acquire the habit of questioning by *making an effort* to question or to raise questions within oneself (questions that one does not already have and that already urge even when one does not want them and tries to avoid or restrain them). As Plato asserts in the *Seventh Letter,* ours is a particular science, which cannot be acquired through notions or school *curricula.* It is a disposition that lights up by itself in the soul of those young ones who, being so predisposed and encountering a teacher, share the enchantment with him or her. This must of course be understood in a substantial sense, that is, far away from all rhetoric.

One should notice also that the insistent dwelling on the question comes from the tradition (that is, from the tradition of philosophy); and yet, at the same time, overcomes [the tradition] because of the very nature of the question, from which the tradition cannot escape.

82. *The enchantment of philosophy.* If the question sums up in itself the meaning of the philosophical tradition, then all philosophies are not important as "answers," but only insofar as, by answering, all of them *practice and interpret the question.* Studying philosophy, becoming competent in it, have no other purpose than that of *making one proximate to the question.*

For this reason one may do authentic and high philosophy even when one knows very few, or even only one philosophy (as it has often occurred in the past, and with the Greeks themselves, who invented philosophy; and today one should think of the emblematic case of Wittgenstein) as long as, from the philosophy or philosophies one knows, one has learned the question, or has learned to give voice to the pre-comprehension of the question that one has within oneself. But how can one *have* it within oneself? Obviously it is from the form and the content of the form of the practices that constitute us as "European" subjects.

Philosophy is much different from what one normally understands as culture or erudition. As such, the philosopher is not an individual of culture. He or she can be such in addition [to being a philosopher] (one should think of the exemplary figure of Socrates as he is described by Plato). This is so not so much because of a mystic or archaic trait (which might very well be there) in the philosopher's wisdom and its exercise. Rather, it is so because the philosopher is the *event* of "culture," which is object and consequence of the practice of alphabetic writing, and to each event there belongs a peculiar *enchantment of experience* that precedes all signs of the intellect.

83. *The idea of philosophy.* We understand the answers of philosophy only if we know how to bring them back to the question. Therefore, historiography is insufficient, and even "kills" philosophy. It does not aim at re-living the question in a participatory manner; rather, it objectifies it by distancing it "historically" in the answers.

As answers, philosophies bring us back not to *the* question, but to its translation into correlative *determined questions* (What is a being? What is substance? What is *Geist?* and so on). Thus, we never find *the* question. The question, actually, is not *a* question. Rather, it is the transcendental side of the empirical practice of questioning that is philosophy (practice of voice, of writing, of panoramic-universal locations, hence the peculiar character of philosophical questioning, which is not questioning in the common sense of the term, and so on).

For this reason, philosophy never reaches the completion of its idea. The tradition of philosophy is constituted by the reiterated question of what philosophy is. Every great thinker reinvents philosophy from the beginning in order to answer the question. Philosophy is a plurimillenary effort to arrive *at* philosophy. It is a tradition of efforts moved by an ideal that is never reached in its purity; nor is it attainable, because of its transcendental character.

If philosophy is the "science of truth," as one loves to say, the fact that there are many philosophies is a scandal, a nonsense, an evident defeat. This judgment, however, is superficial. It looks at the object of philosophy and it neglects the event of its practice (from which the object comes to it). This event is such that both the transcendental unity of philosophy (its "idea" or question) and the empirical multiplicity of its expressions (its determined questions and answers as putting-to-work of the idea) necessarily derive from it.

The transcendental character of the question is an *ethos*, a place and a custom. It is something that precedes and simultaneously grounds the philosophical linguistic practice of questioning and answering. Focusing on the answers and on *the* philosophy, philosophers mistake the transcendental for the empirical, the intentional event of practice for the image of its object (that is, *the* truth).

84. *The impropriety of the question.* As one can see, the question of philosophy is not of such a nature as to require or be exhausted in an answer. It is a transcendental opening, not an empirical question. In depth, it is not a matter of particular questions and relative answers. The question of philosophy is in force in its being a question itself.

The being in itself of the philosophical question, which is not even a determined and particular question, is not *properly* a question and a questioning. Rather, it is a habit, an *ethos*, a "practical" self-location in a world and with regard to a world, a particular self-situating of the subject and as subject. Since it cannot be formulated as an answer or even as a question (insofar as it is a transcendental question), no "theory" is ultimately congruous with the question of philosophy. What is more congruous is the opening of an ethics, a practice, an exercise (the *ability* to question, of which Socrates' and perhaps even Zeno's dialectics speak).

The specific questions proper to various philosophies interpret and translate *the* question. Precisely thus do they give it an answer. Precisely by doing so, they lose the dimension and the location of questioning.

85. *Utopia as power.* If one understands this, one understands how, coming from the tradition of philosophy, we find ourselves thrown out of it at the moment when we see the inanity of the efforts of philosophy—that is, when we see the pretense of giving an answer to the question by formulating it properly. In fact,

all *good* formulations are translations into specific questions with the respective specific answers, from which *the* question escapes and which it evades.

What is created is thus a tradition of answers and their respective habits, from which other determined questions and answers are generated. This is nothing else than the description of a philosophical "school" (the Eleatics, the Platonics, the Peripatetics, the Cartesians, the Hegelians, and so on).

The determined habits that philosophers historically embody (marking thus "history" and its epochs) give birth to paths whose horizon is empty, without objects, since the true object of philosophy is a transcendental place, a spiritual Athens and a *Jerusalem caeleste*. Hence comes the "utopian" character of philosophy. This character does not prevent [philosophy] from inspiring concrete historical actions, and the Western will to truth as "rational" will to power.

86. *The cipher of the end*. As one can see, there is no need to suppose "mysteries of being" in order to understand why in the tradition of philosophy something essential, and even originary, by necessity evades the thought that is inscribed in this very tradition. This depends on the habit of philosophical questioning and on the content of the form of its word and writing, which are institutive of the place of the ideal, panoramic, ultrasensory and distanced ("suspended") subject.

How does the matter stand for us today? The determined questions of philosophy and their correlative answers have given birth to scientific questions and answers, and these in the end to the problems of technological practices that have completely annulled all space for questions ([they have annulled] all habit as *Bildung* in favor of *Weltzivilisation*).

The possibility of inhabiting the question has become unusual, anachronistic. The genuine exercise of thinking is, as a matter of fact, expelled from the organization of knowledge. "Thought" has entirely turned into a psychological or neurological object (any other meaning is not "serious," is not "concrete"; it has no worth, no right to be inscribed in any "research" budget). Reason is only a bankrupt metaphysical residue. It has meaning only in a "methodological" (that is, "technical," instrumental) sense.

One can very well understand why today we are spectators of this great, epigonal comeback of "Kantianism," which is the true *koiné* of contemporary philosophy, from Neopositivism to epistemology to hermeneutics. It is an eloquent sign of the complete surrender of thought to the world of ideology and technics. It is the cipher of its end.

87. *The system and the question*. The issue is this: the matter is neither that of comprehending the *content* of the philosophical question (which is always ideological and historically relative) nor of being comprehended by it. It is a matter of its opening, its possibility, and condition; that is, it is a matter of the *status* of the question.

This already amounts to thinking the tradition "beyond" mere historiography (although not "without" it). In this way, one employs the tradition; one practices it to practice the question. Is this not exactly the practice that we have been practicing ever since the beginning, with our questions about the tradition of thinking?

To practice philosophy in this manner would mean to return every philosophical "system" to its *status* as interpretation of the question. This would be the "unthought-of" in thought, which is exactly that which is no longer thought *within* the determined question of any determined system.

One thus retrieves the question, that is, the event of philosophy, *behind* and *through* the system. The system is then exhibited as the place in which the habit of questioning manifests and hides, unveils and loses itself. Our philosophical exercise would then be to *employ* the system so as to practice the question.

88. *The knot of theory and praxis.* One should ask oneself again, what does it mean to *insist* [stay on] on the question? In the impossibility of asking particular questions (in the current impossibility of practicing philosophy "systematically," since any particular question and problem are delegated to science), this insisting is at the same time paradoxical and in conformity with the experience of the "end of philosophy."

Questioning the question produces an infinite *praxis* (as we have seen exemplified in the case of "Parmenides' "matter"). In appearance, [such *praxis*] addresses *the* truth in itself of the object (the event of philosophy, and so on). This object is increasingly "objectified," distanced, made empirical, that is, turned into a historiographic "fact" (the philological, social, material, cultural aspects in Parmenides' poem). If one looks deeply, though, this way of practicing the question leads to the complete consumption of its transcendental character.

With the emergence of the theme of practices (for which historiography itself gives an opening), the transcendental achieves its last figure and foundation. It becomes clear that all meanings of the historical world are functions of determined practices, beginning with the philosophical practice itself. It is on the basis of practice that they have to be understood and explained. This disclosive event is on its way at least starting with the theme of *praxis* in Hegel and Marx (but perhaps seen still earlier in Bruno) to reach its climax in Peirce, Nietzsche, Husserl, and Heidegger, and continues in Wittgenstein's linguistic games or Foucault's discursive practices.

The reflection that takes practices as its object is in turn itself a practice and not a "theory of practices," since it cannot apply to itself its own measure. Philosophical *theorein* and its participatory and living tradition then fade away. To speak of the transcendental character of *praxis* does not amount, in fact, to access a new transcendental figure, a new theoretical foundation of the "truth of the world" (nor to access its simply nihilistic and instrumental relativization). This speaking no longer says *the* truth, in any way. It says and *does* otherwise.

In this way, one experiences first of all the paradox or the hermeneutic circle of practices (one cannot speak of the transcendentality of practice if not within another practice, and already referring every meaning to practices is only the interpretation proper to *a* practice, that is, to the one we are exercising). Moreover, what is at stake in this experience is the traditional knot between theory and practice. It finally relinquishes and disposes itself for a new figure.

89. *The false problem of thought.* It is thus that the *tradition of philosophy* disappears as living participatory hermeneutics of determined, transcendentally foundational questions and answers. In this way we experience the "end of philosophy" (a vivacious, far from funereal event); however, in this way, the *tradition of thinking* also disappears. We are now, in fact, in the condition of realizing that this problem ("the tradition of thinking") and the correlative Heideggerian question of the "matter of thinking" are only a *false problem.*

The questions we were pondering at the beginning—Is the tradition of philosophy within the tradition of thinking, or *vice versa?* And how are these thresholds characterized?—are problems that do not get solved, but rather disappear. That which raises the question of the tradition of thinking is in fact still the voice of philosophy. It is only within the "logical" and conceptual tradition of philosophy that expressions such as "thinking" or "thinking in general" can occur and have meaning. Once this has been understood, then the double circle of the initial questioning (whether philosophy can be represented as a circle inscribed in thinking or *vice versa*) breaks up and annuls itself.

A thinking that is wider and thus comprehensive of philosophical thinking is a misleading and illusory image. It is only philosophy, and starting from philosophy that one can give meaning to notions such as *thinking.* It is philosophy that names and enucleates them, starting with Parmenides' *noos* and Heraclitus' *logos* and culminating with Plato's great conceptual and ontological systematization.[13] To ask about "thought" before and outside philosophy amounts to putting into action, backward and from the outside, a typical, maybe the most typical object and concept that is put to work by the typical philosophical logico-defining practice.

90. *The tradition of civilization.* Should we then think that human beings did not "think" *before* philosophy? How will one answer this question? But the question itself is a paralyzing philosophical trap.

One should start by considering that, as far as we know, there have always been multiple wisdom-oriented practices, interpretive and formative activities that can be more or less translated into our word "thought." We approach them from the historical distance that has been instituted by our thinking look.

These translating, approaching, and distancing practices presuppose a tradition and a common continuity of practices: a general interpreting of the world, signaling and designing it, understanding it in an intelligent way according to multiple intertwined practices, among which linguistic practices stand out. This intelligent transmission is what, starting from the specific event of philosophical wisdom, starting from its conceptuality and language, *we* call the "tradition of thought." Yet, this continuity of transmission should not make us believe that there is something such as *thought*, a universal faculty, an unmoved substance underlying all intelligent practices. Our metaphysical expression "thought" names the continuous intertwining and handing down of intelligent practices, each of which has its own practical specificity, its own form, and its own content of the form.

Such are the practices that splinter stone, engrave rocks and caves, make weapons and tools, build dwellings, elaborate linguistic habits, invent writing systems, and so on: in a word, the whole of what *we* call civilization or culture, with its intelligent and meaningful practices. It is within this vast sea that the icy stream of the wisdom-oriented philosophical practice stands out, with its specific difference that is precisely *thought*.

It is out of and within this practice that we retrace and interpret the whole tradition: that is, starting from a particular interpretation and putting-to-work of intelligence and the "logical mind," or of the "history of civilization" (which is exactly what Aristotle starts doing at the beginning of *Metaphysics*).

91. *Future assimilations and habits.* On the basis of our logical practice of thinking and its transcendental gesture we reconsider and re-elaborate the empirical elements of multiple other practices (elements which, in their event of opening, are in turn and in their own way "transcendental gestures"). In our eyes, speaking and writing, clay molding and animal taming, hunting and fishing, street building and navigating, and so on, become material testimonies of "human thought." The whole is assimilated in the interpretation by our practice, skipping the infinite events of meaning with their peculiar circles of disclosure of the matter and the related enchantments as well as the peculiar self-interpretations.

One can very well see how the Heideggerian question "what is called thinking" reveals all its ambiguity and inappropriateness. It leaves us problematically on the ground of metaphysics (or, more in general, of philosophy) while having taken up the posture of wanting to overcome it.

What results is that the Heideggerian "task of thinking" cannot be said as such or in these terms, since its terms and perhaps also its purpose are still configured in a completely metaphysical manner. One cannot say or think it because of the intrinsic contradictoriness that is connected to the expression "thinking," not because of some mystery of *Lichtung* or some donation that enigmatically withholds and preserves itself in being. One should beware such murky conjectures. This is already a first task for *our* thinking.

If one wants to talk of a "task of thinking," one should realize that [such a task] will be more likely to configure itself as a practice (as an "ethics"), whose presuppositions are in the practice of philosophy that has reached the "end" in the time of domination by the practice of historiography and science: that is, in the time which, with a generically philosophical expression, we call "the world of technics."

CHAPTER 8

The Ethics of Thinking

92. *The fact.* In the iterative paradoxical character of the question on the question, which is here being raised, the traditional thinking of philosophy changes style and sense. It declines as "foundational" transcendental knowledge exhibiting a *theory* of truth, a theory of the first cause or principle of beings.

If one calls "transcendental" the event of a practice insofar as its opening of meaning always implicates within itself empirical elements that are drawn from previous practices (and this is always true of every practice, no matter how far back or deep one goes), then before any practice as a transcendental event one should admit the existence of an empirical *fact* that is irreducible to any practice.

This "fact" should not be thought of as a "determined fact" because any determined fact is *as such*, that is, as determined, always internal to a practice and recognizable only within it, that is, starting from its event. That *fact*, then, is nothing else than the event as such, its having always and already occurred and unfolded. It expresses the opening of the *symbolon*.

One should not claim that this opening *cannot* be thought. It does not require being thought, and it should not be thought. The claim to think it is a nonsense that does not know what it says: it does not realize that thinking is always a determined practice with *its* internal objects, and the event is not an object. Rather, the opening asks to be inhabited and practiced. Its nature is "ethical": it is the already being *made* that is proper to any habit, including the habit of thinking.

93. *The ethics of the question.* In which practice is the event of thinking as opening put to work? This practice is precisely the one that begins delineating itself on the thread of the question of the question.

This practice no longer thinks the metaphysical ground. To think of grounds is the result of a practice of questioning whose event makes the panoramic look of an absolute universal subject (a "pure" subject) occur. It asks, What is a being as such? and thus it distances the subject by estranging it into an ideally universal site. In their more and more predominantly technical value, scientific and historiographic practices unfold starting from this very site, which, questioning, determines itself in particular problems (what is gold? the philosopher asks. Locke however counters: Is it not better if the goldsmith and the chemist, with their practices, ask such a question?).[1] One overcomes the question ("what is a being?"), however, when one asks about the question itself.

This ultimately means that the question of the question cannot have the meaning of asking for the ground or cause *of the question*. It can only have the meaning of an *ethics*.

94. *The conclusion of the path*. The question of the question asks in order not "to know" but rather "to be able to do" (knowledge). Understanding what is here said, its explicit and implicit meaning, opens the place for the conclusion of the path that has led us so far and started with the opening of the horizon that ever since the beginning governs [such a place] with its event.

What approaches is the conclusion of the circle of disclosure of the "matter," which opened through questioning the tradition of thinking and the tradition of philosophy in the time of the "end" marked by the world of technics. To approach the conclusion is already to come out of it, to dispose oneself for a new location with the disclosure of its event and the opening of its horizon of possibilities.

95. *The gallery of figures*. The question of the question is in turn still a question. This is definitely the first thing that one should notice. By its nature, then, it concerns that *pure*, estranged *knowing* that belongs to the "purified" and "suspended" subject, that is, the metaphysical subject. It is still within the practice of this subject that the question of the question takes shape.

Even if all of one's practices still occur within [the metaphysical] circle of light, one is no longer the metaphysical subject of the origins, which raised itself to *logos* and saw the ideas. Behind one's shoulders is the long thread of the tradition in which the originary philosophical question turns into a "theory" of questions and answers determined according to the historical-factual circumstances of the questioning.

The putting to work of metaphysical knowledge produces awareness of the "historical" character of such knowledge. The tradition of philosophy that lies behind one's shoulders and pervades one is the movement of "absolute knowledge" that generates the deepening within itself of the philosophical *subjectum* in the gallery of its historical figures. This opens the way to the historiographism that characterizes us with the rigor of a scientificity increasingly estranged from the living tradition of philosophizing and marking the time of the "end of philosophy."

The historiographic practice, which has taught us what kind of interlacement of practices (the Alexandrinian philologist, the monk, the humanist, and so on) substantiates the tradition of philosophy, and how it itself is simply one among many, and in the end can only historicize itself also, and see itself as *one* among the many practices and infinite forms of human wisdoms that put to work truth in the manner of their own disclosive circle.

The historiographic practice aims at universal truth, and even produces it, by cooperating with the technological, cybernetic production of estranged universal human beings, bureaucrats and officials of *Weltzivilisation* who are conformed (and conforming) to their objectified knowledge and know-how in which all philosophical sense and intentionality have disappeared. At the same time, however, the historiographic practice clashes with the deep sense of its vicious circle, and cannot avoid opening the need for a genealogical rethinking of itself and a self-exposure to the paradoxes of beginning and end. And this is, ultimately, us.

96. *The practice of the event.* By raising the question of the question, one shows the being in act of the historiographic subject's exposition to the event. The historiographic practice characterizing one's way of referring to the philosophical tradition no longer explicates itself as simple putting-to-work of a disclosive event, that is, as unaware participation in an event to which we are already assigned. To question the question is *to practice the event itself as opening.* If one understands this, one has already attained the conclusion of the path in which the horizon closes to open itself to a new meaning.

It has already been said: The question (of Parmenides' or Socrates' "matter") bounces back upon itself and becomes the question of the question. It has been claimed that it is still, and always, a question. Yet [the question] can no longer retain the sense of a giving way, or giving origin, to an answer, as [it occurs] in all practices that are practiced in the unawareness of the opening [of such a question]. This question rather asks [us] to dwell on and attend to the question: [it asks] to show itself as question in its evenemential dislocation.

The question of the question is thus a practice of the event, not of the question. This question does not assume the traditional figure of "knowing not to know." Rather, it takes up the figure (difficult to understand) of "not knowing to know."

97. *To know and not to know.* The insistence upon the question, that is, the question as practice of the event, is a practice of thinking *sui generis.* It has its peculiarity in this: it does not turn the question into the premise of a saying; that is, it does not ask *in order to know.* Neither does it turn the question, however, into the premise of a keeping silent, as if it were a discovery place [for the facts] of *not knowing* and not being able to know.

These are "ideological" conclusions that, in the end, demand "absolute knowing" (whether they attain it or are pleased by or despair in the show of its unattainability). That is, they turn knowledge into an absolute matter, whereas it is always a relative practice linked to knowing how to do, how to say, how to write in determined and circumscribed ways.

The question of the question leads neither to *logos* nor to the boundaries of *logos* nor to its turning into something not clearly identified. These are the traps through which contemporary hermeneutic questioning weakens and shipwrecks.

98. *The interested suspension.* To practice the event via the question of the question means to assume a *suspension* that is *interested* in the intertwining of practices characterizing all events, that is, all openings of a practice. This is what one has done (not knowing that one was doing it: that is, without truly practicing the question of the question) when one showed to oneself the plurality of practices making up the event of philosophy and its tradition.

Why "interested suspension," though? Insofar as one practices the question, one factually finds oneself in the practice of suspension of the subject and its participatory and "living" practices (the question of the question is, in the end, still a question). This question that bounces back upon itself, however, does not produce "disinterestedness," that is, the typical figure of a scientific, "objectively" posed subject. It rather produces an *interest*, which is nevertheless *sui generis*.

This practice is not *interested in the object*, as happens in all unreflective, participatory, and direct practices, which are completely caught up in the circle of disclosure of the matter, and are captured by *praxis* and the paths of putting it to work and attaining it. Neither is it *disinterested in the object*, considered through a distancing and objectifying technique so as to produce its truth and manifestation methodically according to logical-operational criteria (as in the case of artificial insemination). This practice is *interested in the event*.

99. *The known and not known knowledge.* If one suspends "critical" suspension (which characterizes the metaphysical, and then historiographic, subject), if one questions the question, this means neither to throw oneself into an acritical practice, nor simply to rivet criticism to a "criticism of criticism."

In the first instance, it would be the case of a doing that simply puts to work the opening of the event ignoring it as such (the so-called "common doing," which can in itself be very refined and highly shrewd, or specialized and technicized). Properly, this doing is a *not knowing to know*; that is, it ignores the knowing how to do that characterizes it, and which it causes to occur and puts to work. In the second instance, it would still be the case of a critical and questioning knowledge that doubts everything and suspends everything except itself. It claims to *know not to know*; yet it does not put into question this very gesture (or its genealogical possibility, the content of its form). It does not know the problematicity of its critical opening.

In this sense, the Socratic knowing not to know changes now into a peculiar not knowing to know (into an *ethos* of peculiar knowing). It has its peculiarity in this: that it is a *known not knowing to know* [a *not knowing to know* which is itself *known*].

100. *The theme of the event.* What does one mean by these abstruse expressions? What is this "not knowing" (to know) that is, at the same time, known? In which sense does it overcome, or encompass, the Socratic and generally philosophical knowing not to know?

What is here "known" is the event as opening, *symbolon* or *symballic* moment of all practices (that is, of all paths and horizons of signs). This opening becomes, so to speak, "thematic," not as object of an objectified knowledge, but rather as practical circle and paradox.

One should keep well in mind that the thematicity of the event emerges precisely by virtue of the objectifying historiographic and scientific practice. This practice in fact aims at translating and assimilating all practices into itself, into its absolute and definitive truth. In this way, it produces the estrangement of the subjects who iterate the gesture of knowing not to know when they dispose themselves to knowing the matter critically, that is, according to a "disinterested" distancing from the object. The distancing is first "theoretical," in its metaphysical practice and version. Then, it becomes techno-methodological: the object is produced "theoretically" (mathematically) and hence realized technically.

The subject enters the domain of transparency of *praxis* and the comprehension of its ultimate transcendentality: there is no thing that is not functional to an enacted *praxis* (this starts with the subject itself, who is always originality subjected *to* a practice before possibly becoming subject *of* the practice). This means, however, that the subject never *knows* the opening, the event of [the subject's] own doing. The subject puts [the event] to work as an active knowledge in which it itself is already inscribed and of which [the subject] does not know anything (in this sense, its knowledge is a not knowing to know).

What we have said ultimately turns necessarily upon itself. Also, the knowing not to know that critically (historiographically, scientifically) scans all forms of knowledge and practices in order to objectify their meaning and reduce it to its own truth, is a doing that "does not know," a practice that ignores its own event of meaning. It is an acted but unknown doing (a not knowing to know), since this belongs to any event that opens a practice, including its own. It is thus that the question of the event finally becomes "thematic."

101. *The drift.* In this way, one comes to know about the event. The issue is, however, that "to know the event" is not a "knowing." In the known not knowing to know, what is *known* does not have the form of a knowing. It is rather a situating oneself *in the drift of the event.*

Human beings once understood themselves in the drift of God. In general, this occurred to them in two ways. [It occurred] in the form of *not knowing to know,* that is, in the pathic self-abandonment to the event of the sacred. This means in the directly lived practice of the nomination of God, his cult, and his rite. This sacred, wisdom-oriented practice proceeds unaware of its disclosive circle and event. It limits itself to frequenting them in a lived celebration of the ultimate meaning of existence and the inscrutable drift ruling it. Later, the drift took up the form of *knowing not to know*, as a critical suspension of the gods and what would be "dear" to them (as seen in Xenophanes and later with Socrates). This gave rise to the "scientific" knowing of theology (of onto-theology), whose apparently opposed, but congruent and mirroring (and thus *equal*) extremes are rational faith in the existence of God and atheism.

It is in the drift of both these events that human beings of technics start to see themselves located. That is, in the drift of all events and practices. This possibility started to open up as early as with Spinoza; it was then Nietzsche who uttered it openly and experienced it painfully in his person. His catastrophe (which is ambiguous and in conformity with the smallness of the "last man," in whose figure we all still are) is the price that has been paid for us so that we could live its consequences without our own breaking, as it occurred to Socrates and Jesus in other periods and according to rather different standards. One should remain faithful to one's "smallness," though: one should neither get carried away nor be ashamed because of it. Hence, one should take distance also from these considerations which are too "historical" and too "theological."

All of one's courage and dignity are consigned to this: that one *insist*, through questioning, on confronting the drift, on locating oneself in its inexhaustible non-sense, being mistrustful of all meanings, even the highest, that claim to buy up for themselves the truth of the earth while hiding the concrete practice of their event, the content of their form. And one should ultimately insist on mistrusting also this very mistrust, since it must itself be known.

102. *The ethical question*. The insistence on the question is not properly a questioning. It is the drift that demands [*domanda*][2] to be practiced. In practicing the practice we are practicing, this is precisely what has happened to us ever since the beginning. It started to come into the open when, questioning, we asked: in what practice is the thinking of the event as opening put to work? It was then that the drift openly started to demand [*domandare*].

If insisting on the question is properly not a questioning, but a being demanded [*domandati*] (that is, a being called and provoked to an answer understood as *exposure* to the provocation itself), then this insistence can be called *ethical question/demand*. Ultimately, it is a provocation to find a place in the non-place of technics, to inhabit its drift while conforming to it.

To inhabit the ethical question/demand is a self-opening to the awareness that every opening is always a "sending" [*invio*], a being inscribed without properly knowing it in a form of wisdom, in a determined doing, which is the production itself of the event of the opening. This holds true also for questioning (that form of wisdom unknown in its opening—in the content of its form—that characterizes philosophy and culminates in technics). The fact that now, by inhabiting the ethical question/demand, that is, by addressing the drift itself of the opening and the event, one can finally "know" the not knowing the knowing that the opening makes possible—this fact does not imply that it becomes the "object" of a knowing. This would amount to falling back into the circle that rules technical production. That is, it would amount to duplicating it.

The "known" is such only insofar as it is inhabited. That is, insofar as one consciously exposes oneself to the sending [*invio*] by one's own not knowing that produces and acts.

103. *The undecidable.* In the frenetic activity of the productive world of technics, according to the progressive figure of *Weltzivilisation*, all subjects are provoked to respond and cor-respond according to objectifying and self-objectifying paths. The ethical question/demand asks that one *dwells* in the provocation itself.

To dwell means to dispose oneself to a comprehending habit. But comprehending what? That the provocation of technics embodies a "truth" (as it says), or better an "enchantment" and an opening (as we say) that are *undecidable*. This is so first of all because, exposing oneself to the drift, confronting and inhabiting it, one now *knows* that the drift is ungrounded and ungroundable in a "knowing." It grounds the forms of knowings, including those that ascribe the truth to themselves, so that the truth cannot be inscribed or grounded with truth. Secondly, because every provocation is always something that has already been decided, has already "occurred." One, and everyone, has already been decided by it; one cannot take possession of the event that has already decided of one, since the case is rather that one belongs to it. One can only welcome its (one's) undecidability as an already decided decision to which one has entrusted oneself.

The claim to *decide* through the question (the critical suspension), that is, the claim to reduce meaning and "values" to a "matter for consciousness," is nothing else than that figure that Nietzsche calls "will to truth," and whose resolution into "will to power" he shows. To question starting with knowing not to know implies within itself the destiny of the will to knowing. This is a grandiose destiny, so that Nietzsche is correct also in this, when he points to Socrates, the man who affirms that "only conscious values have value," as to the turning point of "universal history."

Since one now takes place in the undecidability of this and all decisions, also the possibility to judge according to "turning points" and "universal histories" disappears. If truth disappears, also any "public truth" and any "history of the world" sink to an even greater extent.

104. *Facts and values.* The opening to the undecidable truth of being provoked in the mode of technics does not require a "historical" corresponding, since it produces the elision of the historical subject and historicity (as one has seen). Nor does it require a pure and simple "technical" corresponding, since the meaninglessness that has become method, which wraps itself up in chatters about "values" (the values of *Weltzivilisation*), progressively loses credit ("political legitimacy") and discloses itself for what it is: exactly chatter, functional to the practices of "information" of the souls, which are produced and tamed.

This chatter often takes up the aspect of the contrast between *facts* and *values*. There is no way to have morality and science agree up to the strange idea of inventing a *science of values* (a *bioethics*). That is only a verbal contradiction: if it is a science, it can deal only with facts and not with values, of which there can be no "methodic" competency; if it addresses values, it cannot be a science, as Wittgenstein already understands very clearly.

The fact is that the very opposition facts–values is only an appearance. The world is subjectively reduced to objective "facts" and, conversely, values are brought back to the subject because of an identical will to metaphysical truth and power. It is *for* the same subject that the world is a set of external objective facts and that values are internal facts of subjectivity. The radical undecidability of the event of this very subjectivity, the extreme figure of its technological nihilism, make it such that there is no possibility of warranting that facts produce values (as *Weltzivilisation*, with its methodic and conformist propaganda, claims to believe), or that values become facts so that all humans finally become good, democratic, peaceful, rich, tolerant, and happy. This should occur in both the "public" and the "private life," where the two sexes will finally make peace: understanding, mature, responsible, reciprocal, unselfish, fulfilled; only slightly restless because of the incomprehensible hostility of their children. Technics and "scientific" pedagogy will take care of this too.

105. *Time and nihilism*. The undecidable character of the opening asks that the *doing* of thinking assume the figure of an *ethics of thinking*: a taking place (*ethos*) in the provocation itself of the technological drift and its apparent nihilism—apparent in the sense that it manifests itself and is striking. There is no real reason for a "judgment," however, at the moment when one has opened oneself to its undecidability, which also means to its "enchantment" and its unforeseeable possibilities. Nihilism is such on the ground of the meaning of traditional participatory practices. Yet the horizon that in itself unfolds prepares mute names and other appellations.

One should beware, therefore, of imagining the possibility of one's taking place elsewhere than in this drift itself (what one is and what one is to become), for example, by going on cultivating the imaginary objective *public time* of historiography and science. This ideological image of the object in the time of technics hides its content behind the form. That is, it distracts one from the practice and the event of the practice that puts to work and produces public time, historical time. The event itself that lets itself be seen in this perspective, though, is neither public nor historical, and not even temporal. With their radical a-historicity and anonymity, the very products of technics already allude to this.

One should also not cultivate imaginary *eschatological times* that still take their measure from the illusion of history, which they want to "save" and to which they want to "confer meaning" while remaining blind to their own operations, the traditional practices they embody and their undecidable openings (and how can one save, or give meaning to, an imaginary object?).

These two illusions plunge their roots in the same soil: that of "public truth," of "the truth in itself of the world"; this soil has been instituted by metaphysics and has been put to work technologically by *Weltzivilisation*. These two illusions resist the paradox of the finitude of all practices, and to the consequent decline of truth (be it "public" or "eschatological"). They think they escape nihilism; in truth, they reassert it, and they themselves are nihilistic, insofar as they express not at all the "destiny" of nihilism, but rather its ideological and imaginary covering up. What is in fact more nihilistic that the notion of "time in itself"? The whole of Western nihilism, from Plato to Heidegger, has focused on it.

106. *The habit*. To take place in the drift of technics does not mean to ask about its meaning. This, as should be clear, would still be a metaphysical asking about the meaning of the event of being, without even realizing that precisely this distancing and critical asking originates nihilistic meaninglessness and the rebounding question of meaning.

To take place instead means to turn *not knowing* into *the meaning* of its impossibility to be reduced to a "knowing" because of the constitutive undecidability of the event; [it means to turn *not knowing*] not into the object of a would-be "new knowledge" (or "new thinking"), but rather into a habit (*hexis*).

All ideological thinking fades away, and thinking keeps in itself as practice: that is, as *ethics of speech and writing*. This practice has inserted itself on the line of the question addressing the meaning of the tradition of philosophy and the tradition of thinking. It still grounds itself *on* that tradition, and does not forget how much it owes to the grandiose courage of [the tradition's] "ethics of truth."[3] Precisely because it grounds itself on it, it questions it and questions itself starting from it, turning to its event insofar as such event is also its own: it inhabits its signs and words once again, on the verge of overcoming the meridian of truth.

107. *Doing and not doing*. This ethics of thinking, this ethics of speech and writing, has the meaning neither of having something done, nor of critically suspending doing and knowing. This is difficult. In the same way, it is difficult really to abandon the claim to truth, which is connatural to all our discourses and *praxis*. How not to feel disoriented by this? How to understand that the event is richer and deeper than the claim to truth, even the one that it itself initiates? How to inhabit this . . ."truth"?

How to embody a practice that is neither a doing nor a not doing, since it situates itself beyond the traditional opposition between theory and *praxis*? Being urged by the "actuality" and ambiguity of its active imposition, how can one avoid both voluntary exile, which is sterile and resented, and prone acquiescence, which is stupid and alienated? This new habit, to be balanced as if on a knife blade, is largely still alien to us, and therefore is threatened, uncertain, ungraspable.

One should understand very well how one can no longer wish that the practice of thinking should turn into "political actions" and make "historical facts" happen; it no longer has a "historical" meaning, and this way is fine. On this issue, and having had a tragic and personal experience, Heidegger sees correctly. Today, an authentic (and not epigonal) thinking can only be detached from *actuality* and *effectuality*. These, however, have themselves become ghosts [under the form of] the actuality of magazines, and the effectuality of the cultural industry of information. One cannot wish, either, for the suspension of doing that is pure historiographic erudition, in which all philosophical intentionality has died out. This is, in the end, functional to data banks and computers' memory programs. It is at the boundaries of these two possibilities that the ethics of thinking sets in.

108. *The cure of the subject*. The ethics of thinking, its practice of speech and writing, suspends both the "critical" question and the "technical" answer. This suspension does not "prepare" a "truer" thinking; it rather makes one ready for the event. It prepares one for one's self-location in the event as testand as ethical exercise.

In this sense, one could also say (recalling Wittgenstein) that it "cures" the subject. [It cures] both the technical subject, which is alienated in its objectivistic productive *praxis*, and the metaphysical and pre-metaphysical subject, since they both still inhabit us. Their ancient and ancestral practices belong to the complex stratifications of our own practices; even if they have been translated and altered in their horizons of meaning, nevertheless they still fill us up materially with their dogmatisms and their superstitions. Thinking can still distance itself from all this, and produce itself in a new figure of subjectivity, if it does not become itself a dogma and a superstition.

As it cures the subject and its ideologies, at the same time (but in truth *now* it is the *same* thing) the ethics of thinking cures *praxis*. The cure even consists totally in a *praxis*, in the Husserlian sense of suspension as "exercise" of suspension. The exercise however does not aim at achieving "pure consciousness" and the transcendental standpoint. We are already aware of the *content* of such a purity (the content of its form): the transcendental standpoint is nothing else than the estranging and totalizing distancing of the old metaphysical subject and its not "known" practice. In truth, the exercise suffices to itself, just as life does. It does not take up the form of the phenomenological exercise, but rather that of the *phenomenographic* exercise, in which the content of the form is "known," that is, exhibited and inhabited—*exposed* as the place of its own event.

109. *The transcription*. In the genealogy of the logical mind and its form, the content of writing configured itself for us as an "epochal event" in the forms of both the writings of the world and prealphabetic, alphabetic, and lastly mathematical writings. This depends on the very fact of our own self-location within writing, which turns [writing] into the eminent place of "knowing" (of knowing how to do, how to say, how to write: the world, the body, the voice).

The ethical exercise can very well be configured as a deepening (and an exhibition) *within* the event of writing. For example, as a "transcription" (into its own evenemential writing exposed to the event) of the writing of other practices, in the disclosive way of their distances, that is, of their paths and horizons; this is the transcription of the complex and meanwhile simple event that characterizes them, rules their path, institutes and puts to work the meaning which remains unknown to them. An exemplifying instance of these possible transcriptions was already (though very vaguely) alluded to in the example of the practice of the symphonic orchestra.

This exercise of transcription can be also applied to the "technical" practices that most directly characterize us in our doing and not knowing, or, better said, in our not-known [kinds of] knowing. Here, to transcribe them (one should remember this) does not mean "to raise them to knowing," or to a higher knowing: this would still inscribe itself into an edge of not knowing; that is, this would also configure itself as a not-known doing and knowing. The exercise of transcription is only a locating of oneself there where one is.

110. *The game of the way.* The ethical exercise of the transcription of practices does not mean to "tell the truth" of practices, or tell a higher truth. In the ethics of thinking, the figure of truth (as well as that of the distinction between theory and *praxis*) has vanished as far as its superior and absolute form is concerned. The truth is now a *finite* figure of the practice, that is, of determined practices; analogously, the distinction between theory and *praxis* is a *finite* object of a determined practice.

Transcription is like an exercise that renders our body and the inhabitation of our body differently available. It in fact *alters our location in the practices that we exercise and that are exercised through us.* Unlike athletic exercise, which is instrumental and has its goal outside itself, ethical exercise has its goal in itself. In other words, it is a wisdom-oriented [*sapienziale*] practice, an "initiation" of the subject. Through the writing of philosophy and the exhibition of its methodical event (of its *methodos*), also the wisdom-oriented *odos,* which has been transcribed into it and has since then always been more or less obscurely preserved and handed down, is retrieved *in act.*

How does such a location change? The general answer is easy enough: it changes because in the transcription one considers practices, and one's own practice, *starting from the event,* not from the object. In some way, one withholds the answer while answering. One changes direction to one's interest (as Husserl claims); one follows the path step by step, bringing each step back to its opening; one subverts the imaginative abstract temporal *proceeding* and every time one inserts it into the rhythm of the circle of disclosure of the matter, one trains at the rhythm of one's own *ek-sisting* as subject: there where all things appear and disappear, are given and taken away in image. The dear, good things, as Nietzsche claims, their game surrounding us as a "round dance of stars."

111. *Particular exercises.* In general, one can answer in this manner, and this can be fine for "us philosophers." In particular, though, one must not answer at all.

To say *how* the ethical exercise should be configured in order to change the location in the practices is no longer a task that philosophy should attribute to itself. By locating itself ethically in the finitude of its practice, [philosophy] dismisses the archontic-truth related [*veritativo*] habit. Its practice is not in possession of any hegemonic knowing to which other practices should conform. Why should it *say* what the ethical exercise is? Why should it *define* the practice of speech and writing once and for all and for everyone? It no longer believes in a superior or inferior *doing* and even less in a general theory.

In this sense, staying within itself [*stare a se stessa*] is enough for it; that is, it is enough to ask itself in which various forms (why should there ever be only one?) it can go on situating itself within its own tradition and transcribing it once philosophy has disappeared, "ended," as "science of truth." [This applies] also to the philosophical exercise: one has to practice it every time by oneself, that is, one has to invent it individually, inscribing one's erring within the constitutive event of being in error which constitutes us, insofar as we have always been inscribed within the claim to truth and its drift. One *experiences* this location insofar as one opens oneself up to the possible, and not to the pre-established, modes of its exercise.

Why should the others not do the same? The way to alter *their* location in *their* practices is entrusted to them, to *their* knowing how to do, say, and write. They are the only ones who can and must invent it by experiencing it.

112. *The mime.* The encyclopedia of sciences is over. We can say farewell to Aristotle and Hegel (although they always come back, in the expository transcription of our being in error—which, first of all, is theirs and *therefore* it is also ours). The philosophical way, its exercise, is only the salt, the ferment of knowing: *a* (*finite*) example of knowing how to do, say, and write. Thus, the philosopher goes back to being what Plato once intuited: a *mime*, who exhibits in his or her behavior, his or her habit (his or her *ethos*) the experience of the question of truth.

This is not, however, a "moral" mime. Nietzsche cures the mime of this nihilistic claim, exposing him or her rather as a clown, an actor, a square and street preacher, who cries and laughs and sets the farce of truth on stage. That is, as one who is one and the same with his or her cousin, the sophist, who like the former loves to be disguised as a "politician." The dog and the wolf have the same event.

113. *The event of the subject.* The ethics of thinking, its exercise, rewrites the subject (as an example for everyone's dwelling). By subtracting it from the unconscious exercise of living practices, from its not known forms of knowing, the experience of technics reconsigns [the subject] as naked for a further possibility. Because the subject that one is, that we all are, is and has always been nothing else than is: a being subject *to*, that is, subjected to the intertwining of its own practices that conform and shape it as their object. We thus ignore what being subject *of*, that is, subjects of our practices in the aware presencing to their event,

means or may mean. As [William] James says, all our forms of knowing and convictions are always grounded on someone else's faith, and the same is true for [the subject].

The ethics of thinking is a possible initiation to [being] subject; it is a path of meaning that has always belonged to all formative forms of knowing within which human beings have come to themselves and have discovered themselves; it is a legacy that constitutes the core also of the philosophical (Socratic) revolution, which in turn welcomed and reinterpreted even more ancient legacies in its own way, and by handing itself down handed them down as far as us.

One should now take up this path of meaning by installing oneself in one's own "practice" (in *one's* practice) with a vigilant eye for the content of the form. And one should discern the possibility for the institution of a subject of an unheard-of figure. One should not stop at that being made subject which means being subjected to practices and their paths of meaning (be they the highest and noblest) because, thanks to the exercise that has been done here, one now discerns one's distance from *this* subject, and sees its *alienness*. One nevertheless accepts it because one is nothing else and is made of nothing else than such an alienness. The subject is always the "Other," the other that one is; this acceptance is precisely the result (the "superject," as Whitehead would say) that finally turns one into a subject on the verge and at the point of the event: [the subject is] its place and horizon of meaning.

One can accept that in the present time the ancient city of human beings, its signs and its symbols, its monuments and its customs, its arts and its forms of knowledge collapse into what superficially shows only the aspect of nonsense, devastation, and nihilistic anarchy. The "practical" possibility of an ethics of the subject, which perhaps opens up and in the end results from it, can pay the price for it and be worthwhile.

Notes

1. THE QUESTION

1. See Carlo Sini, "Wittgenstein e l'immagine," in *I segni dell'anima* (Bari: Laterza, 1989), 213–63.

2. On the timeliness and relevance of the question of normative sciences as it has been developed by Charles S. Peirce, see Carlo Sini, *Semiotica e filosofia* (Bologna: Il Mulino, 1978).

3. See Martin Heidegger, *Basic Questions of Philosophy: Selected "Problems" of "Logic,"* trans. André Schuwer and Richard Rojcewicz (Bloomington: Indiana University Press, 1994), 8–9.

4. Ibid., 10.

5. The universes are not as numerous as blackberries so that one can submit them to induction, said Peirce. See Charles S. Peirce, "The Probability of Induction," in *The Writings of Charles S. Peirce: A Chronological Edition, 1872–1878* (Bloomington, IN: Indiana University Press, 1986), 300. On the cosmological question here referred to, see Carlo Sini, "Confini del mondo e ubiquità della mente," in *Il silenzio e la parola* (Genoa: Marietti, 1989), 153–59.

6. Heidegger, *Basic Questions of Philosophy*, 13.

7. Ibid.

8. This issue is central to understanding the meaning of metaphysics and logic. It is structurally bound to the question of the image, which is the secret, or fundamental knot, of the entire European *episteme* (this is the thesis developed in Sini, *I segni dell'anima*). The essential issue is not, then, as Heidegger claims, the preliminary self-giving of being, its manifestation (*aletheia*), but rather that very modality of self-giving that is the idea. It is only because of it that something can emerge as "being" and "a being." It is not being that gives itself to be seen as idea, rather it is the idea that, by looking in the peculiar, that is, ultrasensible, way of its looking, lets being be seen.

9. For the meaning and the unfolding of my expression "strategy of the soul," see Carlo Sini, *Passare il segno. Semiotica, cosmologia, tecnica* (Milan: Il Saggiatore, 1981), Part III; Carlo Sini, *Images of Truth: From Sign to Symbol*, trans. Massimo Verdicchio (Atlantic Highlands, NJ: Humanities Press, 1993), Part II, and the already mentioned Sini, *I segni dell'anima*, where the question finds its conclusive treatment. The

first part of this present work, being centered on the themes of logic and writing, could show, as it were, the genealogical foundation thereof.

10. On this issue, see "The Task of Thinking," in Part II of the present book, where the Heideggerian theme of *Lichtung* is addressed.

11. See Carlo Sini, *Il simbolo e l'uomo* (Milan: Egea, 1991). On the birth of the concept of the soul, besides the classical study by Bruno Snell, *The Discovery of the Mind*, trans. T. G. Rosenmeyer (Cambridge, MA: Harvard University Press, 1953), see Eric Havelock, *The Greek Concept of Justice from Its Shadow in Homer to Its Substance in Plato* (Cambridge, MA: Harvard University Press, 1978); and, especially, Mario Vegetti, "Anima e corpo," in Mario Vegetti, ed., *Il sapere degli antichi* (Turin: Boringhieri, 1985), whose arguments, I think, especially resonate with my "strategy of the soul."

12. On the attribution of the invention of the alphabet also to Heracles, and on the importance of such a myth, which I will mention later, see Sini, "Eracle al bivio," in *Semiotica e filosofia*, 277–99.

13. Strangely, Saussure also, when talking of the signifier, uses the examples of the clothes and the way. See the first part in Sini, *Passare il segno*. For an in-depth analysis of Creuzer's thesis, see Sini, *Il simbolo e l'uomo*.

14. See the Appendix in Sini, *I segni dell'anima*, 213–63.

15. On the originarily dynamic character, linked to action and practice, of Chinese ideograms, see Ernest Fenellosa and Ezra Pound, *The Chinese Written Characters as a Medium for Poetry* (New York: City Lights Publishers, 1968).

16. This is the thesis grounding the study by Alfred Kallir, *Sign and Design: The Psychogenetic Source of the Alphabet* (Plymouth, MA: Latimer, Trend & Co., 1961).

17. In this sense, Plato combats art to have science (*episteme*) triumph. Since he looked at the issue from the perspective of writing, Havelock was consistently the first to understand the profound meaning of the Platonic condemnation of art; see Eric Havelock, *Preface to Plato* (Cambridge, MA: Belknap Press of Harvard University Press, 1963). In his own way, Nietzsche had already arrived at this; by destroying the truth, he reverted to the Dionysian and anti-Platonic world of art.

18. For a study of this myth, see Sini, "Eracle al bivio," In *Semiotica e filosofia*. On the move from *odos* to *methodos*, see Carlo Sini, *Metodo e filosofia* (Milan: Unicopli, 1986).

19. On the meanings of the tree of life, see Snell, "Il simbolo della vita," in *La cultura greca e le origini del pensiero europeo*, trans. Vera Degli Alberti and Anna Marietti (Turin: Einaudi, 2002); and Mario Untersteiner, *I Sofisti*, vol. 1 (Milan: Lampugnani Nigri, 1967), 27–8.

20. For a detailed criticism of this Heideggerian passage, see Carlo Sini, "Il problema della verità in Heidegger," *Segni e comprensione* 4, no. 9 (1990); and also, more in general, Carlo Sini, "La fenomenologia e la questione del pensiero," in *Filosofia '88*, ed. Gianni Vattimo (Bari: Laterza, 1989).

21. On "stylization," see Kallir, *Sign and Design*.

2. WRITING

1. Eric Havelock, *The Muse Learns to Write: Reflections on Orality and Literacy from Antiquity to the Present* (New Haven: Yale University Press, 1986), 39.

2. Ibid., 1.

3. Ibid.

4. Ibid., 3.

5. Ibid., 5.

6. That is, with the "strategy of the soul" and the construction of the psycho-logical concept of image. In the present work, see chapter 1, "The Question," notes 9 and 11.

7. Havelock, *The Muse Learns to Write*, 8.

8. Ibid., 4.

9. Walter Ong, *Orality and Literacy* (London and New York: Methuen, 1982), 51. See Alexander Luria, *Cognitive Development: Its Cultural and Social Foundations*, ed. Michael Cole, trans. Martin Lopez-Morillas and Lynn Solotaroff (Cambridge, MA: Harvard University Press, 1976).

10. Havelock, *The Muse Learns to Write*, 94.

11. Ibid., 96.

12. Ibid.

13 Ibid., 41.

14. Havelock denounces once, although without dwelling on it, this paradox of the logical mind that wishes to understand itself. See Ibid., 122.

15. Martin Heidegger, *Introduction to Metaphysics*, trans. Ralph Manheim (New Haven: Yale University Press, 1959), 92.

16. Havelock, *The Muse Learns to Write*, 105.

17. Ibid., 106. Havelock refers to Bruno Snell, "Die Ausdrücke für den Begriff des Wissens in der Vorplatonischen Philosophie," *Philologische Untersuchungen* 29 (1924): 20–119.

18. Havelock, *The Muse Learns to Write*, 105.

19. Ibid., 77.

20. See Marcel Detienne, *The Creation of Greek Mythology*, trans. Margaret Cook (Chicago: University of Chicago Press, 1986).

21. Havelock, *The Muse Learns to Write*, 110.

22. Ibid.

23. Ibid.

24. Ibid., 111.

25. Ibid., 113–14.

26. Ibid., 120.

27. Eric Havelock, *Origins of Western Literacy* (Toronto: Ontario Institute for Studies in Education, 1976), 2.

28. Ibid., 6.

29. Ibid., 44.

30. Ibid., 24.

31. Ibid., 31.

32. Ibid., 29.

33. Ibid., 28.

34. Havelock, *The Muse Learns to Write*, 60.

35. Havelock, *Origins of Western Literacy*, 43.

36. Havelock, *The Muse Learns to Write*, 60.

37. See Enrico Montanari, *Il mito dell'autoctonia. Linee di una dinamica mitico-politica ateniese* (Rome: Agra, 1979). Montanari also underlines the parallelism between letters and atoms.

38. Havelock, *Origins of Western Literacy*, 42.

39. Havelock, *The Muse Learns to Write*, 80.

40. Ibid., 100.

41. Ibid., 112.

42. See the analysis of corporeal graphemes and especially the vocal gesture in Sini, *Il silenzio e la parola* and, more analytically, in Sini, *Il simbolo e l'uomo*.

43. Havelock, *Origins of Western Literacy*, 34.

44. Ibid., 35, 37.

45. See Sini, *Il simbolo e l'uomo*.

46. Havelock, *Origins of Western Literacy*, 36.

47. Trans. Note: In Italian, *coscienza* indicates both conscience and consciousness.

48. Havelock, *Origins of Western Literacy*, 44.

49. Ibid., 46.

50. Ibid., 46.

51. On the removal of the sacred as a "removal of the animal" and the birth of Galilean science, see Sini, *Passare il segno*, Part III.

52. Havelock, *Origins of Western Literacy*, 49.

53. Ibid.

54. The connection between alphabetic writing and birth of scientific spirit is currently universally admitted and begins to inspire specific inquiries. For an introductory view, see Giorgio R. Cardona, *Antropologia della scrittura* (Turin: Loescher, 1981).

55. Havelock, *Origins of Western Literacy*, 50.

56. Ibid., 8.

3. ARCHEWRITING

1. See Jacques Derrida, *Of Grammatology*, trans. Gayatri Spivak (Baltimore: John Hopkins University Press, 1974). Quotations are from this work with minor emendations.

2. Ibid., 3.

3. Thus one should read the beginning of Heidegger's *Sein und Zeit* with reference to the theory of judgment in Plato's *Sophist*: metaphysics does not ask what the meaning of the copulative "is," of that "being" is. It is true, however, that only rarely and hastily has Heidegger understood clearly the terms of this issue.

4. Derrida, *Of Grammatology*, 4. Trans. Note: The word "today," on which the author dwells, does not appear in the English translation.

5. Ibid., 3.

6. Ibid.

7. Trans. Note: The author is playing with the double meaning of the term "*senso*," which in Italian means both direction and meaning/sense.

8. Derrida, *Of Grammatology*, 3.

9. Ibid., 4.

10. Ibid.

11. Ibid., 5.

12. On the coincidence between experience of truth and being in error, see Sini, *Images of Truth*, Part II.

13. Derrida, *Of Grammatology*, 6.

14. Ibid., 7.

15. Ibid., 8.

16. Ibid.

17. Ibid., 7.

18. See Jacques Derrida, *Speech and Phenomena*, trans. David Allison (Evanston, IL: Northwestern University Press, 1973). See also chapter 2, "Writing," note 52 in the present work.

19. Derrida, *Of Grammatology*, 8.

20. Ibid.

21. Ibid., 11.

22. On the logical issue of resemblance in Peirce and Wittgenstein, see Sini, *I segni dell'anima*, 213–63.

23. Such is what Nietzsche claims on the ground of his "perspectivism" and the theme of infinite interpretation as unfolded in his later writings. See for example Friedrich Nietzsche, *The Will to Power*, trans. Walter Kaufmann and R. J. Hollingdale (New York: Random House, 1967). There are no "things," although maybe there are saws, hatchets and trees whose look is difficult to define.

24. Derrida, *Of Grammatology*, 12.

25. In the same way, he ignores the path opened in this direction by George H. Mead, *Mind, Self, and Society* (Chicago: University of Chicago Press, 1934). For a critical assessment of Mead's position, see, beside Sini, *Il silenzio e la parola* and *Il simbolo e l'uomo*, the lecture notes Carlo Sini, *La fenomenologia e la filosofia dell'esperienza* (Milan: Unicopli, 1987).

26. For a criticism of the "term phenomenology" different from Derrida's, see Sini, *La fenomenologia e la filosofia dell'esperienza*, 236–37.

27. Derrida, *Of Grammatology*, 13.

28. Ibid., 14.

29. The ultimate clarification of such a "panoramic look," which is addressed in Sini, *Images of Truth* and Sini, *Il silenzio e la parola*, is here genealogically based on the theme of the content of the logical form and the theme of practices, which are discussed in the second part of the current volume.

30. Trans. Note: Again, the author is playing with a double meaning present in the word "*senso*," which in this case means both judgment and meaning.

31. Derrida, *Of Grammatology*, 19.

32. Ibid., 19 n. 9.

33. Ibid., 22.

34. Ibid.

35. Ibid., 23.

36. On the identity of determined being and nothingness, see the conclusion to Sini, *Images of Truth*.

37. Derrida, *Of Grammatology*, 23.

38. Ibid.

39. Ibid.

40. Ibid., 47.

41. Ibid.

42. Ibid.

43. Ibid., 50.

44. Ibid., 51.

45. Ibid., 56–7.

46. Ibid., 57.

47. Ibid., 60.

48. Ibid., 61.

49. Ibid., 62.

50. On the experience of the origin as rhythm, see Sini, *Il silenzio e la parola*, and the lecture notes published as Carlo Sini, *Il tempo e l'esperienza* (Milan: Unicopli, 1985). In the pages from Derrida's *Of Grammatology* I have here analyzed, the question of time emerges in connection with writing and the trace. This would require a precise analysis and commentary. The conclusion, however, would be the same: Derrida thinks *against* time, but he does not find the path of an ultra-temporality (such as rhythm, in my terms and perspective).

51. Derrida, *Of Grammatology*, 61.

52. Ibid., 62.

53. Ibid., 63.

54. Ibid.

55. Ibid., 66.

56. For a criticism of these positions of Saussure, see Sini, *Passare il segno*, Part I.

4. THE CONTENT OF THE FORM

1. See Maurice Merleau-Ponty, *The Prose of the World*, trans. John O'Neill (Evanston, IL: Northwestern University Press, 1973).

2. On the constitution of the object as image of the world, see the conclusions of Sini, *I segni dell'anima*. The "irregular" character of corporeal gestural acts is analyzed in Sini, *La fenomenologia e la filosofia dell'esperienza*.

3. Trans. Note: Once again, the author is playing with the double meaning of the Italian word "*senso*," which means both meaning and direction (it also means "sense" as faculty of sensory perception such as sight, touch, hearing, and so on).

4. On the move from *odos* to *methodos* in Parmenides, see the lecture notes in Sini, *Metodo e filosofia*.

5. Trans. Note: The author is playing with the double meaning of the word "termine," which in Italian means both "term" and "end."

6. See Kallir, *Sign and Design*.

7. For this criticism, see Sini, *Il silenzio e la parola*.

8. Trans. Note: As usual, the author is playing with the double meaning of the term "*senso*," which indicates both meaning and direction.

9. For a criticism of proper and literal sense, see Anna Cazzullo, *La verità della parola. Ricerca sui fondamenti filosofici della metafora in Aristotele e nei contemporanei* (Milan: Jaca Book, 1987).

10. See the subtle analyses by Mario Vegetti, *Il coltello e lo stilo* (Milan: Il Saggiatore, 1979).

11 See Havelock, *Origins of Western Literacy*, 79–80

12. See Giulio Giorello, *Lo spettro e il libertino* (Milan: Mondadori, 1985).

5. THE TRADITION OF PHILOSOPHY

1. On the character of philosophical speech, see Sini, *Il silenzio e la parola*.

2. On the forming of the foundations of the historical look already in Greek metaphysics, see Sini, *Passare il segno*, Part III.

6. THE TASK OF THINKING

1. Trans. Note: The inconsequentiality in the numbering of this section is repeated from the original.

2. See Martin Heidegger, "The End of Philosophy and the Task of Thinking," in *On Time and Being*, trans. Joan Stambaugh (New York: Harper and Row, 1972), 55–73.

3. Ibid., 55.

4. Ibid.

5. For an agreement on the evaluation of Platonism as the essence of metaphysics, but for a different understanding of the reasons for that, see Sini, *Passare il segno* and Sini, *I segni dell'anima*.

6. Heidegger, "The End of Philosophy and the Task of Thinking," 57.

7. Ibid.

8. Ibid., 58.

9. Ibid.

10. Ibid., 57.

11. Ibid. Trans. Note: Stambaugh's translation has "discovery," which has been modified to "exploitation" to follow the Italian more closely.

12. Ibid., 59.

13. Ibid.

14. Trans. Note: the neologism *informatizzarsi*, here translated as informationaliz[ing], refers to the pervasive adoption of informational technology in all fields of life.

15. Ibid., 59; translation amended.

16. Ibid.

17. Ibid., 64.

18. This light is the origin of the mental image or concept; see Sini, *I segni dell'anima*. On the theme of *lumen naturale* in Peirce, see "Abduzione e cosmologia" in Sini, *Semiotica e filosofia*.

19. Heidegger, "The End of Philosophy and the Task of Thinking," 66.

20. Martin Heidegger, "The Origin of the Work of Art," in *Poetry, Language, Thought*, trans. Albert Hofstadter (New York: Harper and Row, 1971), 54.

21. Martin Heidegger, *Elucidations of Hölderlin's Poetry*, trans. Keith Hoeller (Amherst, NY: Humanity Books, 2000), 79.

22. Heidegger, "The End of Philosophy and the Task of Thinking," 65.

23. On the children of the earth and the friends of the ideas, see Sini, *I segni dell'anima*.

24. Heidegger, "The End of Philosophy and the Task of Thinking," 65.

25. See Martin Heidegger, "The Nature of Language," in *On the Way to Language*, trans. Peter D. Hertz (New York: Harper and Row, 1982), 107–108.

26. On the issue of the voice in Heidegger, see Sini, *Semiotica e filosofia*.

27. Heidegger, "The End of Philosophy and the Task of Thinking," 69.

28. Ibid., 71.

29. Ibid., 72, translation amended.

30. Ibid.

31. Ibid., 60.

32. Ibid.

33. Ibid., 72.
34. Ibid., 73.

7. PRACTICES

1. On iconism in Peirce, see Rossella Fabbrichesi Leo, *Sulle trace del segno. Semiotica, faneroscopia e cosmologia nel pensiero di C. S. Peirce* (Florence: La Nuova Italia, 1986), Chapter 1. See also chapter 3, "Archewriting," note 22 in the present work.

2. On time as "tempography," see the conclusion of Sini, *Il tempo e l'esperienza*.

3. On Protagoras, see Sini, "Eracle al bivio," in *Semiotica e filosofia*. On the topic of the body in Nietzsche, see Carlo Sini, "Simbolicità e storicità del corpo," in *Corpo e cosmo nell'esperienza morale*, ed. Romeo Crippa (Brescia: Paideia, 1988), 99–117. See also Leonardo Casini, *La riscoperta del corpo. Schopenhauer, Feuerbach, Nietzsche* (Rome: Studium, 1990).

4. On the universality of assumption of the vocal gesture, see Sini, *Il silenzio e la parola*; Sini, *La fenomenologia e la filosofia dell'esperienza*, and also Sini, *Il simbolo e l'uomo*.

5. See my essay "La verità iscritta e circoscritta" in Sini, *Il silenzio e la parola*, 123–40.

6. On pan-oramic look, see in the present work chapter 3, "Archewriting," note 29. On psycho-historical truth, see Sini, *Passare il segno*, Part III.

7. See my essay "Che ne è del passato?" in Sini, *Il silenzio e la parola*, 62–72; also, Sini, *Il tempo e l'esperienza*.

8. See Francesca Bonicalzi, *L'ordine della certezza. Scientificità e persuasione in Descartes* (Genoa: Marietti, 1990).

9. On the speculative unity of the sciences of nature and the sciences of spirit, see Sini, *Passare il segno*, Part II, and Sini, *I segni dell'anima*.

10. On the meaning of the overturning of the Heideggerian relation between "erring" and "being in error" see Sini, *Images of Truth*.

11. See, ibid., Part II, note 189.

12. See Sini, *Passare il segno*, Part II.

13. See Sini, *I segni dell'anima*.

8. THE ETHICS OF THINKING

1. See John Locke, *An Essay Concerning Human Understanding*, ed. Roger Woolhouse (New York: Penguin, 1998), in which the example of the definition of gold appears repeatedly.

2. Trans. Note: The author is playing on the double meaning of the terms "*domanda*" and "*domandare*," which in Italian indicate both question/questioning and demand/demanding.

3. Nietzsche, for example, writes: "To walk alone along a lonely street is part of the philosopher's nature. His gift is the rarest gift of all, the most unnatural one in a certain sense, exclusive and hostile even toward others with similar gifts. The wall of his self-sufficiency must be built of diamonds if it is not to be destroyed and broken into, for everything and everyone is in league against him. His journey toward immortality is more difficult and burdensome than that of other men. And yet no one can believe more firmly than the philosopher that his journeying will lead to the

goal, for where could he stand but on the widespread pinions of all time. A lack of consideration for what is here and now lies at the very core of the great philosophical nature. He has hold of truth: let the wheel of time roll where it will, it can never escape truth. It is important to find out from such people that they once existed. Never, for example, could one imagine such pride as that of Heraclitus, simply as an idle possibility. Looked at from a general point of view, all striving for insight seems, by its very nature, forever dissatisfied and unsatisfactory. No one will believe, therefore, in such regal self-esteem and calm conviction that he is the only rewarded wooer of truth, except by the instruction of history that such a man did once exist. Such men live inside their own solar system; only there can we look for them" (Friedrich Nietzsche, *Philosophy in the Tragic Age of the Greeks*, trans. Marianne Cowan [Washington, DC: Regnery, 1962], 660).

Bibliography

Agamben, Giorgio. *The Coming Community*, trans. Michael Hardt. Minneapolis: University of Minnesota Press, 1993.

———. *Infancy and History: The Destruction of Experience*, trans. Liz Heron. London: Verso, 1993. Amoroso, Leonardo. "La *Lichtung* di Heidegger come *Lucus (a non lucendo)*." In Gianni Vattimo and Pieraldo Rovatti, eds. *Il pensiero debole*. Milan: Feltrinelli, 1988.

Aristotle, *Metaphysics*, trans. Hugh Tredennick. Cambridge, MA: Harvard University Press, 1968–69.

———. *Physics*, trans. P. H. Wicksteed and F. M. Cornford. Cambridge, MA: Harvard University Press, 1963.

———. *Politics*, trans. H. Rackham. Cambridge, MA: Harvard University Press, 1977.

Berti, Enrico. *Le vie della ragione*. Bologna: Il Mulino, 1987.

Bianco, Francesco. *Giudizi di valore e riabilitazione della filosofia pratica*. Naples: Guida, 1991.

———. *Pensare l'interpretazione. Temi e figure dell'ermeneutica contemporanea*. Rome: Editori Riuniti, 1991.

Bodei, Remo. *Geometria delle passioni. Paura, speranza, felicità: filosofia e uso politico*. Milan: Feltrinelli, 1991.

———. *Ordo Amoris. Conflitti terreni e felicità celeste*. Bologna: Il Mulino, 1991.

Bonicalzi, Francesca. *L'ordine della certezza. Scientificità e persuasione in Descartes*. Genoa: Marietti, 1990.

Cacciari, Massimo. *Dell'inizio*. Milan: Adelphi, 1990.

———. *Icone della legge*. Milan: Adelphi, 1985.

Cardona, Giorgio R. *Antropologia della scrittura*. Turin: Loescher, 1981.

———. *I sei lati del mondo. Linguaggio ed esperienza*. Bari: Laterza, 1985.

Casini, Leonardo. *La riscoperta del corpo. Schopenhauer, Feuerbach, Nietzsche*. Rome: Studium, 1990.

Cazzullo, Anna. *Il concetto e l'esperienza. Aristotele, Cassirer, Heidegger, Ricoeur*. Milan: Jaca Book, 1988.

———. *La verità della parola. Ricerca sui fondamenti filosofici della metafora in Aristotele e nei contemporanei*. Milan: Jaca Book, 1987.

Creuzer, Friedrich. *Simbolica e mitologia*. Rome: Editori Riuniti, 2004.

D'Alessandro, Paolo. *Darstellung e soggettività. Saggio su Althusser*. Florence: La Nuova Italia, 1980.

———. *Il gioco inconscio della storia*. Milan: Angeli, 1990.

———. *Linguaggio e comprensione*. Naples: Guida, 1982.

Dalmasso, Gianfranco. "*Consulere veritatem*. Soggetto del discorso e soggetto dell'etica in Agostino." In *Di-segno. La giustizia nel discorso*. Milan: Jaca Book, 1984.

Degérando, Joseph-Marie. *I segni e l'arte di pensare*. Milan: Spirali, 1991.

Deleuze, Gilles. *Difference and Repetition*, trans. Paul Patton. New York: Columbia University Press, 1995.

———. *The Logic of Sense*, trans. Mark Lester and Charles Stivale. New York: Columbia University Press, 1990.

Derrida, Jacques. *Of Grammatology*, trans. Gayatri Spivak. Baltimore: Johns Hopkins University Press, 1974.

———. *Speech and Phenomena*, trans. David Allison. Evanston, IL: Northwestern University Press, 1973.

De Saussure, Ferdinand. *Course in General Linguistics*, trans. Roy Harris. La Salle, IL: Open Court, 1983.

Detienne, Marcel. *The Creation of Greek Mythology*, trans. Margaret Cook. Chicago: University of Chicago Press, 1986.

———. *The Masters of Truth in Archaic Greece*, trans. Janet Lloyd. Cambridge, MA: Zone Books, 1999. . Fabbrichesi Leo, Rossella. *Sulle trace del segno. Semiotica, faneroscopia e cosmologia nel pensiero di C. S. Peirce*. Florence: La Nuova Italia, 1986.

Fenellosa, Ernest and Ezra Pound. *The Chinese Written Characters as a Medium for Poetry*. New York: City Lights Publishers, 1968.

Foucault, Michel. *The Archeology of Knowledge*. New York: Routledge, 1973.

———. "The Order of Discourse," trans. Rupert Swyer. In *Social Science Information* 10, 2 (1971): 7–30.

Giorello, Giulio. *Lo spettro e il libertino*. Milan: Mondadori, 1985.

Givone, Sergio. *Ermeneutica e Romanticismo*. Milan: Mursia, 1983.

Guzzi, Marco. *La svolta. La fine della storia e la via del ritorno*. Milan: Jaca Book, 1987.

Havelock, Eric. *The Greek Concept of Justice from Its Shadow in Homer to Its Substance in Plato*. Cambridge, MA: Harvard University Press, 1978.

———. *The Muse Learns to Write: Reflections on Orality and Literacy from Antiquity to the Present*. New Haven: Yale University Press, 1986.

———. *Origins of Western Literacy*. Toronto: Ontario Institute for Studies in Education, 1976.

———. *Preface to Plato*. Cambridge, MA: Belknap Press of Harvard University Press, 1963.

Hegel, Georg Wilhelm Friedrich. *Phenomenology of Spirit*, trans. A. V. Miller. New York: Oxford University Press, 1979.

———. *Science of Logic*, trans. A. V. Miller. London: Allen and Unwin, 1969.

Heidegger, Martin. *Basic Questions of Philosophy: Selected "Problems" of "Logic,"* trans. André Schuwer and Richard Rojcewicz. Bloomington: Indiana University Press, 1994.

———. *Being and Time*, trans. Joan Stambaugh. Albany: State University of New York Press, 1996.

———. *Elucidations of Hölderlin's Poetry*, trans. Keith Hoeller. Amherst, NY: Humanity Books, 2000.

———. "The End of Philosophy and the Task of Thinking." In *On Time and Being*, trans. Joan Stambaugh. New York: Harper and Row, 1972.

———. *Introduction to Metaphysics*, trans. Ralph Manheim. New Haven: Yale University Press, 1959.

———. "On the Essence of Truth." In *Pathmarks*, ed. William McNeill. Cambridge: Cambridge University Press, 1998.

———. *On the Way to Language*, trans. Peter D. Hertz. New York: Harper and Row, 1982.

———. "The Origin of the Work of Art." In *Poetry, Language, Thought*, trans. Albert Hofstadter. New York: Harper and Row, 1971.

Herder, Johann Gottfried. *Another Philosophy of History and Selected Political Writings*, trans. Ioannis D. Evrigenis and Daniel Pellerin. Indianapolis: Hackett, 2004.

Husserl, Edmund. *Cartesian Meditations*, trans. Dorion Cairns. Dordrecht: Kluwer, 1988.

———. *Crisis of the European Sciences and Transcendental Phenomenology*, trans. David Carr. Evanston, IL: Northwestern University Press, 1970.

———. *Ideas Pertaining to a Pure Phenomenology and to a Phenomenological Philosophy, Third Book. Phenomenology and the Foundation of the Sciences*. Vol. 1, trans. Ted Klein and William Pohl. Dordrecht: Kluwer, 1980.

———. *Ideas Pertaining to a Pure Phenomenology and to a Phenomenological Philosophy, First Book. General Introduction to a Pure Phenomenology*. Vol. 2, trans. Fred Kersten. Dordrecht: Kluwer, 1982.

———. *Ideas Pertaining to a Pure Phenomenology and to a Phenomenological Philosophy, Second Book. Studies in the Phenomenology of Constitution*. Vol. 3, trans. Richard Rojcewicz and André Schuwer. Dordrecht: Kluwer, 1989.

Jäger, Werner. *Paideia*, trans. Gilbert Highet. New York: Oxford University Press, 1986.

Kallir, Alfred. *Sign and Design: The Psychogenetic Source of the Alphabet*. Plymouth: Latimer, Trend & Co., 1961.

Kant, Immanuel. *Critique of Pure Reason*, trans. Lewis White Beck. New York: Bobbs and Merrill, 1956.

Leroi-Gourhan, André. *Gesture and Speech*, trans. Anna Bostock Berger. Cambridge, MA: MIT Press, 1993.

Lessing, Gotthold Ephraim. "The Education of the Human Race." In *Lessing's Theological Writings*, trans. Henry Chadwick. Stanford, CA: Stanford University Press, 1957.

Luria, Alexander. *Cognitive Development: Its Cultural and Social Foundations*, trans. Martin Lopez-Morillas and Lynn Solotaroff. Cambridge, MA: Harvard University Press, 1976.

Marramao, Giacomo. *L'ordine disincantato*. Rome: Editori Riuniti, 1985.

Marx, Karl. *Capital*, trans. Ben Fowkes. New York: Penguin, 1990.

Mead, George Herbert. *Mind, Self, and Society*. Chicago: University of Chicago Press, 1934.

Melchiorre, Virgilio. *Corpo e persona*. Genoa: Marietti, 1987.

Merleau-Ponty, Maurice. *Phenomenology of Perception*, trans. Colin Smith. London: Routledge, 1962.

———. *The Prose of the World*, trans. John O'Neill. Evanston, IL: Northwestern University Press, 1973.

Montanari, Enrico. *Il mito dell'autoctonia. Linee di una dinamica mitico-politica ateniese.* Rome: Agra, 1979.

Moravia, Sergio. *Enigma della mente. Il* mind-body *problem nel pensiero contemporaneo.* Bari: Laterza, 1988.

———. *Il ragazzo selvaggio dell'Aveyron*. Bari: Adriatica, 1984.

Moretti, Giampiero. *Heidelberg romantica. Romanticismo tedesco e nichilismo europeo.* Lanciano: Itinerari, 1984.

Natoli, Salvatore. *Teatro filosofico. Gli scenari del sapere tra linguaggio e storia*. Milan: Feltrinelli, 1991.

Nietzsche, Friedrich. *The Birth of Tragedy*, trans. Walter Kaufmann. New York: Vintage Books, 1967.

———. "On Truth and Lie in an Extra-Moral Sense." In *The Portable Nietzsche*, trans. Walter Kaufmann. New York: Penguin, 1976.

———. *Philosophy in the Tragic Age of the Greeks*, trans. Marianne Cowan. Washington, DC: Regnery, 1962.

———. *The Will to Power*, trans. Walter Kaufmann and R. J. Hollingdale. New York: Random House, 1967.

Ong, Walter. *Orality and Literacy*. London and New York: Methuen, 1982.

Peirce, Charles Sanders. *Collected Papers*. Cambridge, MA: Harvard University Press, 1931–1960.

———. *Writings: A Chronological Edition*, Vols. 1–6, ed. Peirce Edition Project Staff. Bloomington: Indiana University Press, 2000.

Plato, *Works*. Cambridge, MA: Harvard University Press, 1998.

Ronchi, Rocco. *Bataille, Levinas, Blanchot. Un sapere passionale*. Milan: Spirali, 1985.

———. *Bergson filosofo dell'interpretazione*. Genoa: Marietti, 1990.

Rossi-Landi, Ferruccio. *Semiotica e ideologia. Applicazioni della teoria del linguaggio come lavoro e come mercato. Indagini sulla alienazione linguistica*. Milan: Bompiani, 1972.

Rovatti, Pieraldo. *La posta in gioco. Heidegger, Husserl, il soggetto*. Milan: Bompiani, 1987.

Ruggenini, Mario. "Linguaggio e differenza." In *Heidegger e la metafisica*. Genoa: Marietti, 1991.

———."La tecnica, il soggetto e la ragione in Marx"; "Marx e la tecnica. Dialettica della liberazione come dialettica della produzione." In *La tecnica e il destino della ragione*. Padua: Marsilio, 1979.

Sini, Carlo. *Images of Truth: From Sign to Symbol*, trans. Massimo Verdicchio. Atlantic Highlands, NJ: Humanities Press, 1993.

———. "Simbolicità e storicità del corpo." In *Corpo e cosmo nell' esperienza morale*, ed. Romeo Crippa. Brescia: Paideia, 1988.

———. *La fenomenologia e la filosofia dell'esperienza*. Milan: Unicopli, 1987.

———. "La fenomenologia e la questione del pensiero." In *Filosofia '88*, ed. Gianni Vattimo. Bari: Laterza, 1989.

———. *Metodo e filosofia*. Milan: Unicopli, 1986.

———. *Passare il segno. Semiotica, cosmologia, tecnica*. Milan: Il Saggiatore, 1981.

———. "Il problema della verità in Heidegger." *Segni e comprensione* 4, no. 9 (1990).

———. *I segni dell'anima. Saggio sull'immagine*. Bari: Laterza, 1989.

———. *Semiotica e filosofia. Segno e linguaggio in Peirce, Nietzsche, Heidegger e Foucault*. Bologna: Il Mulino, 1978.

———. *Il silenzio e la parola. Luoghi e confini del sapere per un uomo planetario*. Genoa: Marietti, 1989.

———. *Il simbolo e l'uomo*. Milan: Egea, 1991.

———. *Il tempo e l'esperienza*. Milan: Unicopli, 1985.

Snell, Bruno. *The Discovery of the Mind*, trans. T. G. Rosenmeyer. Cambridge, MA: Harvard University Press, 1953.

———. "Die Ausdrücke für den Begriff des Wissens in der Vorplatonischen Philosophie." *Philologische Untersuchungen* 29 (1924): 20–119.

———. "Il simbolo della vita," in *La cultura greca e le origini del pensiero europeo*, trans. Vera Degli Alberti and Anna Marietti. Turin: Einaudi, 2002.

Spinoza, Baruch. *Theological-Political Treatise*, trans. Samuel Shirley. Indianapolis: Hackett, 2001.

Untersteiner, Mario. *I Sofisti*. Milan: Lampugnani Nigri, 1967.

Vegetti, Mario. "Anima e corpo." In *Il sapere degli antichi*, ed Mario Vegetti. Turin: Boringhieri, 1985.

———. *Il coltello e lo stilo*. Milan: Il Saggiatore, 1979.

Verra, Valerio. "L'ermeneutica di Gadamer in Italia." In *aut aut*, marzo-aprile (1991): 49–60.

———. "Esistenzialismo, fenomenologia, ermeneutica, nichilismo." In *La filosofia italiana dal dopoguerra a oggi*, ed. Valerio Verra. Bari: Laterza, 1985.

Vico, Giambattista. *The New Science*, trans. Thomas G. Bergin and Max H. Fisch. Ithaca: Cornell University Press, 1968.

Vitiello, Vincenzo. *La palabra hendida*. Barcelona: Ediciones del Serbal, 1990.

———. *Utopia del nichilismo. Tra Nietzsche e Heidegger*. Naples: Guida, 1983.

Volpi, Franco. *Heidegger e Aristotele*. Padua: Daphne, 1984.

———. "La riabilitazione della filosofia pratica e il suo senso nella crisi della modernità." *Il Mulino* 35: 6 (1986): 928–49.

Whitehead, Alfred North. *Process and Reality*. New York: Free Press, 1978.

Wittgenstein, Ludwig. *Notebooks 1914–1916*, trans. G. E. M. Anscombe. Chicago: University of Chicago Press, 1984.

———. *Tractatus Logicus-Philosophicus*, trans. David Pears and Brian McGuinness. New York: Routledge, 2001.

Index